KU-178-463

JIMMY THE WEED

P. 95. LES SIMMS — PUB?

JIMMY THE WEED

INSIDE THE QUALITY STREET GANG

My Life in the Manchester Underworld

JIMMY DONNELLY

MILO BOOKS LTD

First published in hardback in November 2011

This paperback edition published in November 2012 by Milo Books

Copyright © 2011 James Donnelly

The moral right of the author has been asserted.

All rights reserved. No part of this publication may be
reproduced in any form or by any means without
permission in writing from the publisher, nor be otherwise
circulated in any form of binding or cover other than that in
which it is published and without a similar condition being
imposed on the subsequent purchaser.

ISBN 978-1-908479-19-8

Typeset by e-type

Printed in Great Britain by
CPI Group (UK) Ltd, Croydon, CR0 4YY

MILO BOOKS LTD
www.milobooks.com

'Jimmy the Weed won't use no muscle,
That cat's so sly, slick and subtle.'

Thin Lizzy, 'Johnny the Fox Meets Jimmy the Weed'
© Universal Music Publishing Group

WHO ARE THE QUALITY STREET GANG?

'There never was any such gang, but several Manchester characters had styled themselves that way as a joke, in commemoration of a Quality Street TV advertisement of the 1960s, depicting rather suave, debonair crooks. In fact, they worked hard almost every day on their car sales pitches, in all weathers, which is hardly to be expected if they were indeed criminals. None had any serious convictions, though it was an obsession of certain senior officers within the Greater Manchester Police force to try to tie them in with serious organized crime ... The official argument was that they were guilty but had avoided prosecution. It was more likely that they were a convenient peg on which to hang unsolved crimes.'

Kevin Taylor, *The Poisoned Tree*

'I don't like the title. It is misleading. It gives the impression of an organised gang which, from my information, didn't exist on the same scale as other gangs. There was no hierarchical structure. I have no direct information of a gang of that type, comparable with other street gangs and gangs within the Manchester area that presently exist and have existed for the last ten years.'

Supt Bill Kerr, former head of Manchester drugs squad

'The QSG were hugely respected in Manchester, and in some ways, they were greater celebrities than the rock stars and footballers they knew and partied with. But they never hurt anyone too badly, and were never arrested for anything major; so I could never understand why they ended up with such a big reputation. However, they were legendary characters, and remain so even to this day. Maybe they did something that nobody else knew about ...'

Stan Bowles, *The Autobiography*

'It depends on one's outlook whether by the 1960s Manchester crime was free of protection or was firmly controlled by the so-called Quality Street Gang which included the redoubtable ex-boxer Jimmy Swords. The police view is that they were a group of minders and enforcers who, as the years passed and they grew older, had moved into the more respectable lines of club and restaurant owning.'

James Morton, *Gangland Volume 2*

'From the late sixties to the mid-eighties, the QSG and their crowd were 'faces' in the city, men you didn't mess with. Notoriety gave them glamour – heads turned when they walked into a club – and they rubbed shoulders with entertainers and the more flamboyant footballers of the day.'

Peter Walsh, *Gang War*

'The QSG might have been the hard men of Manchester but amongst their number were some of the most genuine, moral and decent people you could ever wish to meet.'

Malcolm Wagner, *George Best & Me*

'The gang gained, and still enjoys, a notoriety among the public and police in Manchester, and many an unsolved crime has been laid at its door. Like many criminal fraternities, however, its precise membership is impossible to discover. Many friends and associates of the principal figures would not be involved in crime. For the police, looking in from the outside, it would have been easy to mistake a social friendship for a criminal conspiracy.'

Peter Taylor, *Stalker: The Search for the Truth*

'Jimmy [Donnelly] was a member of the Quality Street Gang, a group of men accused by the press of being behind most of Manchester's major crime. The press are very careful not to mention them by name as they are largely businessmen – men of some substance. They are also very tough boys but I never saw any of them take a liberty.'

Eric Mason, *The Brutal Truth*

'I don't want it to be thought I'm accepting there was a Quality Street Gang. Since his retirement, a very senior detective has said they were a myth and if they had existed they would have been put behind bars many years ago. He would have been the man who would have done it.'

Former Deputy Chief Constable John Stalker,
Liverpool High Court, 1995

CONTENTS

To the memory of my beautiful wife, Rita. Rest in peace.

To my sons, Tony, Dominic and Raefe, and my grandchildren, James, Josh, Rory, Tira and Nathan. I hope you will never have to follow the path I took.

To my brothers and sisters.

To Valerie, Jason and Sharon, thank you for all the years of friendship and help.

To my friends in Thailand, especially Nancy, who inspired me to write this book.

Lastly, to the wardens where I now live, who look after me – especially Donna. Thanks.

PREFACE

I TELL THIS story to reveal some truths and explode some myths. My life and the lives of my friends and associates, known collectively as the Quality Street Gang, have been the subject of more speculation, innuendo and rumour than those of any similar group of men I know. We have been labelled a crime mob, and dismissed as a myth. We have been described in police reports, books and newspapers, with varying degrees of inaccuracy. Some of us have even been called organisers of major crime in Manchester, our home city. I sometimes think there are more exaggerations about us than there are about the SAS.

For forty years, the stories have gone unchecked. So I want to set the record straight. I was, for much of my adult life, one of the so-called QSG. I was, in fact, one of the seven or eight close friends at the core of the group, although as I will explain, we were not the 'gang' of popular perception. Many of my circle were simply rough-and-ready lads. We grew up together. Some picked up convictions in their youth, for fighting or other relatively minor offences. Many went into business as they grew older, and made a good job of it. Others went into crime. But we all continued to associate together because we were pals. That never meant we were some kind of conspiracy. It just meant we were loyal.

For my part, I *was* a villain; a successful one at that. I have handled stolen gems, illegal firearms and piles of cash. I have hurt people, though never someone who did not deserve it, and have survived attempts on my own life. I have had friends who were killers and others who have been killed. I have been investigated by various police forces, Her Majesty's Customs and Excise and the Special Branch, and have been accused or suspected of just about every crime on the statute book. I have been arrested more times than I can remember, and have seen the inside of numerous lock-ups. Yet through it all, I have served no more than a few months in prison, most of them on remand. I have endured nearly a dozen court trials and have walked free at the end of every one.

I also made my way in the straight world. I have been a publican, a ticket scalper, a boxing promoter, a bookie, a scrap dealer, a car salesman, a market trader, a club owner and hotelier. I have socialised with famous actors and actresses, singers and musicians, footballers and fighters, many of whom became close pals. Many of my friends are legitimately wealthy and have been for many years, while I have walked the line between straight and crooked, sometimes on one side, sometimes on the other. It was all the same to me.

Despite all that my closest friends and I have seen and done, this is the first time one of us has put down his memories on paper. I had mixed feelings about doing so. So why do it? One reason is that, for many years, I have heard and read that London is the only place that has a serious 'gangland'. Many men, including some that I know, have written books about the capital's underworld, and to read them you would think that all the top villains and gangsters originate there. Well, there are many who live north of Watford Gap who are just as tough, men who have never been heard of or written about. Don't get me wrong, I am not knocking anybody. I have some very good friends, and have done a lot of business, in

London. I have met all the top faces and respect them. Most of them know the score and are close with people in the north. But there are some who think we have two heads and are basically not as sharp as them. We call it the Watford Gap Syndrome.

In Manchester, we have had our own tearaways, our safeblowers and blaggers, our hardmen and gangsters over the years, and I want people to know who they were. Old-school characters like Bobby Critchley, Stan Ritchie, Les Simms and Ronnie Camilleri may not be household names, and if you went into the East End of London and mentioned them, no-one would know who you were talking about. But they were in many ways my city's own 'mafia', and their stories deserve to be told. At least now someone may say, 'Oh yeah, I heard of him, he came from Manchester.' I am a proud man and I want people to know a little bit more about us Mancunians, about how we think and operate.

I also want to show people that you can get out of deprived areas by hook or by crook. Most of my friends came from very humble beginnings, some surviving approved schools, borstals and remand homes, where they were beaten daily, brutalised and treated like dogs. It is not vanity to say that we went on to achieve something resembling iconic status in our city, feted and befriended wherever we went. That takes some doing.

Finally I hope this book will put to bed some of the lies, and above all, answer some of the questions. Who is Jimmy the Weed? Who were the Quality Street Gang? Did they do all, or some, or even any of the things attributed to them? What became of them and their contemporaries? I have tried to be honest in my answers to those questions. And if I offend anyone, it is not intentional.

The last thing to say is that we haven't gone away; not most of us, anyway. So if you are ever find yourself in the Ancoats area of my city, and you see a small group of well-dressed, elderly gents talking over coffee in a corner cafe, they may be the Quality Street Gang. They will be quiet, respectful, low-key. But believe me, they will all have some stories to tell.

This is just one of them.

Jimmy 'the Weed' Donnelly

1

BORN THIEF

I WAS BARELY one month old when Adolf Hitler took his best shot. Having lost a straightener with the RAF in the Battle of Britain, Der Fuhrer instead unleashed his vast fleet of bombers on our major cities. First they blitzed London, then they ranged north, sending ports and industrial centres such as Birmingham, Coventry and Liverpool up in flames. It was only a matter of time before they attacked Manchester.

I was born James Anthony Donnelly on 25 November 1940. Four weeks later, the Luftwaffe launched a massive series of raids on my home city. They dropped incendiaries to start fires, then high explosives to blast the place to pieces. Flames swept through the shopping and commercial centre and the docks and factory districts of Salford and Stretford, killing nearly 1,000 people and injuring thousands more. Landmark buildings such as the Free Trade Hall, the Royal Exchange, the Corn Exchange, Manchester Cathedral and Smithfield Market all took hits.

But even then I was a slippery character. My good fortune was to live on the new Wythenshawe housing estate, about seven miles south of the centre. We and our neighbours avoided the inferno, although I am told the glow of the blaze could be seen for many miles against the black sky. There was little industry where we lived and nothing other than houses and fields to target, so apart from the odd stray shell or crash landing, we were pretty safe. We would continue to escape the worst of it over the next five years.

My father, James, saw his brothers go off to war to serve with the famous Chindits in the Far East, but was himself turned down by the army because of his trade as a master bricklayer. Of Irish descent, he had moved north from Shrewsbury to help build the Wythenshawe estate, a new concept in public housing often referred to as the largest council estate in Europe. Designed by an architect called Barry Parker as a 'garden city', it covered a huge area, with wide, tree-lined roads and spacious parkland, a world away from the slums and back-to-backs from which many residents moved.

My dad was a typical working man of the time, with a trowel always stuck down his belt in case of work at short notice. His evening pleasure was a few pints and his Woodbines. My mother, Helen, was a silver service waitress at the Royal Oak pub on Barlow Moor Road when she met him. They married in the mid-thirties, as the country struggled to recover from the Depression, and were offered one of the new Wythenshawe houses, so we were among the first tenants. I was the third of their seven children: first two girls, Louise and Anne, then three boys, me, Arthur and John, then two more girls, Marie and Clare. We were never well off but we had a decent life compared to many others during the War, and we wanted for little. Our house not only had three bedrooms but also that great rarity, an inside toilet.

The Blitz eventually tailed off, though on occasions we could still peek through our bedroom blinds to see Manchester lit up like a bonfire. When the drone overhead grew loud, my mum would push us under the dining table; I don't know what good it would have done if we had taken a direct hit. Sometimes we ran out to the Anderson shelter in the back garden, though I don't think that would have helped much either. There was great excitement one night when a burning plane came down on the playing fields of Sharston School, facing our house. All us kids were desperate to see it but were not allowed near, though we could hear machine gun bullets rattling in the fire as they exploded.

VE Day is a hazy memory: running around at five years old, a big street party, balloons and bunting. It meant that we could now enjoy normal childhood pursuits. All around Wythenshawe were green fields and places to play and explore. The Anderson shelter became our den, especially in the rain, and we held little tea parties inside. We could also celebrate Bonfire Night for the first time, and soon found a way to make money out of it. Rationing meant shortages of everything, including fireworks, so we bought as many as we could, stored them in a little hidey hole in the Anderson shelter and sold them when the shops ran out, putting a few pence on top. We would raid other gangs and steal their wood for the bonfires, hide it in people's backyards and then swap it for more fireworks. It was my first lesson in making money.

We were also given gifts by German prisoners of war, who were still being held at the Dunham Massey camp in Altrincham years after the armistice, waiting to be repatriated. They would come by truck to an area called 'the allotments' to grow cabbages and cauliflowers or to repair the roads with picks and shovels, guarded by US soldiers from the giant Burtonwood base. They were allowed to fraternize and gave us kids American playing cards, gum and chocolate. I also saw English POWs arrive home. They were offloaded at the railway station at Northenden and marched to the Sharston Hotel where, on the car park, they were put in designated groups and then marched on to Ringway Airport, where they were billeted before going home. They looked tired and emaciated, and we watched them in awe.

My mum was deeply religious and trooped the family to church every Sunday. She would think nothing of going to Mass three times in a day and two of my sisters would later enter as novice nuns, though they did not stick it. Who would have thought her sons would turn out villains? Our neighbours in Lyndene Road used to say that the Donnelly boys would never amount to anything. Years later, my brothers and I would give them something to talk about when we turned up to visit my mother driving three Rolls-Royces.

My pleasant little life turned upside down when I was eight years old. Dad was working away in Belfast and my mum was left at home, pregnant again and with five children already. She could not cope, so one day I was packed off with Arthur and little John. We thought we were going on holiday, but instead we were taken to St Joseph's, a home for orphans and children under the age of twelve whose parents couldn't look after them. It was more common in those days to put children in large homes than to place them with foster parents. Arthur was seven years old and John was just three.

St Joseph's was in Patricroft, in the Eccles area of Salford. It was only about eight miles from Wythenshawe but might as well have been on another planet. Owned by the Catholic Protection and Rescue Society and run by Franciscan nuns, it was infamous. We spent three or four horrific months there. It might have been a Catholic home but we were treated like animals and it put me off religion for life. We had to rise every morning at six for Mass and then attend lessons throughout the day. We ate in a communal stone room with stern-faced nuns standing guard like sentries. At our first meal, we were served a plate of stew. Then they came around with the pudding and plonked it on the same plate, on top of what was left of the stew. We slept in dormitories and many children cried themselves to sleep. Poor John would wet the bed and for that they would beat us all. I had to look after him and sit with him at night. Yet we were better off than most of the children in there because my father subsidised our board. Many of our fellow inmates were penniless war orphans and they took terrible abuse. They beat you with sticks on the slightest pretext. They even threw us down stairs.

After a few weeks, the rebel inside me could take no more; I plotted our escape. The home was beside the Bridgewater Canal and I knew that if we followed the canal south it would take us in the direction of home. So one day we scaled the wall and set off. I did not realize we were on the wrong side of the canal and heading in the wrong direction. We were soon picked up and taken back for another beating.

We endured several months of hell before we returned home. It affected us all: we became anti-social. Perhaps it was no coincidence that, soon after, I committed my first real crime. Mum sent me to the local chemist to collect something. As usual it was busy. As I stood in line, I noticed a glass case full of cigarette lighters. I quietly slid open the glass, palmed half a dozen lighters and stuffed them into my pockets. That was the start of a sixty-year life of villainy.

Did my ordeal in St Joseph's turn me into a criminal? I cannot say – perhaps it was already in me. But certainly from then on, it was as if I was born to be a thief. I raided allotments and gardens for apples, pears and tomatoes and sold them to neighbours. I stole bicycles and flogged them or broke them up and swapped the parts. I sneaked money from the headmaster's office. I nicked batches of school dinner tickets and sold them at half price. Anything for money. I was eventually caught stealing apples from the back of a pub that my mother cleaned and ended up at juvenile court, where I was ordered to spend twelve Saturday mornings scrubbing school floors.

My anti-authority attitude also led to problems at junior school. Going into the dining hall at lunchtime break, I saw two long queues, chose one, went to the back of it and picked up a plate off the pile. Without warning, a teacher cuffed me around the head, then grabbed my ear lobe and lifted me onto my toes. Apparently I was in the wrong queue, although I did not realize. He gave me a bollocking and then walked off, no doubt pleased with himself for scaring a young kid. I threw my plate like a Frisbee and it skimmed off the floor and hit him just below the knee. He howled and went down on the floor. I legged it out of the grounds but was made to surrender back to school a few days later.

My first proper burglary soon followed, when I was about ten. Playing on the local fields, I noticed two men loitering at a disused air-raid shelter. The shelter had metal doors sealed with heavy padlocks. After they left, I had a snoop and noticed that there was a new lock on one of the doors. I went back that night with my brother, armed with a crowbar, hammer and chisel, and smashed off the lock. Entering the dank shelter and peering about with a torch, I noticed a stack of boxes. We opened one and it was full of American cigarettes. Others contained bottles of spirits. Bingo. We helped ourselves and got out of there.

The following day we kept watch to see if our theft had been discovered but nobody turned up, so that night we went back in for another load. We later found out that the stock had itself been stolen from the American military base at Burtonwood. It was in the papers, which said this black market fiddle had gone on for years. Anyway, after selling off everything we had pilfered, I was the richest kid in the neighbourhood.

I graduated to breaking into shops. It was easy. There were no alarms or reinforced doors, while nobody seemed to have thought that burglars might go in through the roof. Wythenshawe was patrolled by bobbies on bicycles but the estate was so vast you had to commit murder to get a policeman out. We would play at the rear of the shops, which had yards where they stored their stock, and it was easy to sneak over a wall and take a case of lemonade. Any goodies we pilfered were hidden until they could be sold or consumed, and if they were found we just lied. If my mum asked me where I got something I would say I had done a swap with another kid.

An even bigger target than the local shops was the Brookes Biscuits factory near our house. Some builders left their ladders outside it one night, and Arthur and I were on the roof in seconds. Opening a fanlight, I looked in to see the night shift at work among hundreds of cases stacked up to the eaves. We watched as a couple of the workers, a man and woman, wandered from the main packing area into a secluded spot among the labyrinth of boxes below us. The next thing, they were having sex. I am sure when they got home to their respective partners, they said what a hard night's work they'd had! Once they had finished and left, we dropped down onto the top of a stack and helped ourselves. For a few weeks we got away with numerous boxes of biscuits, until the 'Night of the Chocolates', when we opened our stolen boxes to find that they contained large bars of dark cooking chocolate. I sold them around the playground the following week, and within a couple of days the whole school had gone down with the shits. Most of them dobbed me in. I was hauled back to juvenile court and put on probation.

Another bit of work was at the local Co-op shop. Instead of cash tills, they had a system of 'flying machines': they put your money in a little box with your bill, it went upstairs on a wire to an office and then it came back the same way with your change. The shop had a fanlight, and once you got into the roof cavity you could drop down through the false ceiling. We could help ourselves and be out in minutes. Sometimes we even went through the brickwork into the next shop or would chisel through the door panel, cut around the edge with a hacksaw blade and then push through. But usually we entered in such a way that nobody knew we had been in; that way we could go back again at a later date. By this time I had a few regular punters who I left my booty with. I would call back every day to see what had been sold. Cigarettes and bottles of spirits always went well.

Every Saturday morning, I would be on the railway tracks. I built a cart with two bike wheels, an axle and a packing case and picked up any coal that fell from the trains. Once I had filled a couple of old sacks, I would sell it around the neighbourhood. One lady, Mrs Wolstonecroft, never paid her bill and the coal man would not give her credit, so she would often wait for me on a Saturday and I would always have a hundredweight or two. The firemen on the trains got so used to me that they would throw a couple of shovel loads over the side as they passed by.

By the time I moved up to St Columba's, the local Catholic senior school, I was both a dedicated thief and an up-and-coming tearaway. Though I was small for my age, nobody frightened me: not the teachers and certainly not other pupils. I started boxing at the age of eight, so had learned how to use my fists and would fight anybody. One of the lads in my class, Colin Cross, was a lot bigger and a bit of a bully. We must have fought twenty times over a couple of years. He won some, I won some, but I would never let up. If he looked the wrong way at me in school I would wait for him on the way home, hide in the bushes, jump out and attack him. The next day at school he would assault me in the playground. In the end I had to have the edge. He was too big, so I decided I needed a tool of some kind. I made a cosh at home and started carrying it inside my coat, burying it in a spot near school and picking it up when I left. I caught my tormentor a couple of times and battered him with it.

Later on, after I left school, I met my old foe outside a pub called the Benchill. He had a go in the car park but by this time I was fighting for fun and I really hurt him. The next I heard he had joined the army. Then by chance I bumped into him again. He had lost all his hair to alopecia and I felt a bit sorry for him. We had a drink and buried the hatchet. One thing I was good at in later life was making friends with people I had previously crossed swords with. It was a trait that would serve me well.

By the time I entered my teens, I was a total streetfighter. I left out nobody: all the bullies, all the so-called tough kids, I would have them all, I didn't care. Even at five foot nothing, nobody got past me and in the end it paid off with a lot of respect. My brothers were the same; if anyone picked on us we were all in it together. I would not take abuse off anybody. When the headmaster, Mr Fitzpatrick, tried to hit me with the cane, I wrapped it round his neck. He tried to throw me over his desk but he got a few kicks for his trouble and I was out of the door. In fact the only teacher I remember fondly was a housemaster called Greenhalgh who ran the sport, a former sergeant in the Commandos who came into school on special days in his green beret. Through him I made the rugby and football teams and also boxed for school. My sparring partner was often my pal Jackie Veron, who was small like me. He went on to box for England and later became a good trainer.

At thirteen or fourteen, I joined the Army Cadets at Sharston Hall, mainly because they had a recreation centre with table tennis, snooker and boxing. After six months, I was kitted out with a full uniform in the Manchester Cadet regiment. We learned to drill, read maps and fire a gun on the range. My favourite was the .303 Lee Enfield rifle. I also got to fire a Sten gun and a Bren gun; perhaps that's why, later in life, I was comfortable with any firearm. In summer we went away to camp. It was good fun, until one night we found a pub that was prepared to serve us because were in uniform. We got drunk, had a row, I battered one of the other kids and was sent home. But I had learned from my army training, not least how to be part of a unit.

Severe asthma sadly stopped me from pursuing my boxing ambitions. I was forced to take a lot of time off school and eventually went to a convalescent home in North Wales. Today professional athletes can have asthma and still reach the top level, but in those days if the ring doctor saw it on your medical card, he wouldn't let you box. It broke my heart. The only thing that cheered me up was receiving a 'get well' card from Johnny Sullivan, the British middleweight champion, after my sister wrote to him to tell him about my illness.

At least I was a natural entrepreneur. I was selling motorbikes when I was thirteen, khaki BSA Bantams out of the war supplied to me by a family of villains called Davies. There was lots of army surplus gear around, including Lugers and other military firearms. Bayonets, we had by the dozen: long Japanese ones and the shorter German ones. I also acquired a solid silver ring with an eagle on either side and a swastika on the front that must have belonged to a German officer. I wore it for years; it made a handy knuckleduster.

The result of my junior crime empire was that I had money to spend, much more than the average Wythenshawe tyke. I could go to the pictures whenever I wanted. Saturday was 'spends' day, when we would get sixpence pocket money, but I would be going to the flicks with half a crown in my pocket earned from my various scams. I felt like a king. There were two cinemas within walking distance, at Northenden and Gatley, and while I enjoyed the movies, I soon spotted another opportunity. I would wait until a film started, when the projectionist was in his room and everybody's attention was occupied, then would slip out of the screening room and into the foyer. By then there would be nobody about, bar the ice cream girl getting her stock ready in a side room. I would dart into the ticket office, grab a handful of change and stroll back into the movie without anyone noticing. It was just so easy to get a few quid.

At school I was no academic, but I did have talents. In practical subjects like woodwork, I could draw a joint in seconds, whereas others took ages. I was a magician at it. The teachers were astounded but they could not get me to apply myself. The end result was that I left school at fifteen with no qualifications. That was when the Davies family came into my life.

THE DAVIES CLAN were on their own when it came to money: if anybody had it, they thought it was theirs. They had interests in car dealing, haulage and pubs but were always ready for any bit of villainy that came along. They were really my introduction to the underworld: wheeler-dealers with a dangerous edge. Albert, or 'Ginger', was the oldest. He drove Bentleys and other flash cars around the neighbourhood and was always buying and selling, a proper wide boy. When I was still at school, he gave me two BSA Bantam motorcycles to sell for him. Ginger became my mentor. I watched him deal and absorbed it all. In fact I wanted to be like him.

His siblings were Annie, Betty, George and Ronnie. George was particularly notorious. When I was fourteen, and he was twenty-four, he was jailed for seven years for pulling a gun on two detectives in Liverpool. Six months later, he busted out of HMP Strangeways with the London criminal Teddy Rice and four others by climbing through a workshop skylight and dropping over a wall. The police caught him within a couple of weeks. I did a bit of work with George when he finally left prison and we became friends. We would cruise around in his Jowett Javelin and committed a few burglaries, but there was a scary side to him. He had a terrible temper and often carried a gun, which is a bad combination, so I eased myself away, though we remained pals. He later shot his next-door neighbour. George had a furniture business and this guy was one of his van drivers. He had just finished a twelve-hour shift when George told him he had to go to London with another load. He refused, so George put a bullet in him. He got five years for that.

The other Davies of note was Albert Davies Gibbons, Ginger's nephew and namesake. 'Little Albert', as we called him, was particularly close to my brother Arthur, and they both served four years jail with a guy called Ray Carding for tying up a jeweller; Carding's wife was a little too friendly with a policeman and gave them away. Little Albert was a walking psychopath. He always carried a knife, and we knew he would kill one day. One Friday night, in the summer of 1965, Albert was queuing in a fish and chip shop when his cousin Norman came up to him to change the order. Two big guys behind Norman grabbed him and threw him to the back of the queue. Like a flash, Albert reacted and thrust his knife into both of them. Pat Fallon, a doorman at the Stork Club in Manchester, died where he was. The other man ran out of the chippy with Albert still stabbing him; he suffered nineteen wounds and barely survived. Everybody thought Albert would get ten years, but when the background history of Fallon and his pal came out at trial the judge called them thugs and bullies, and Albert got just three years for manslaughter.

Many of the Davies family would come to tragic ends. Little Albert died at thirty-eight of a heart attack. Ronnie hanged himself when he was about twenty-one. Ginger committed suicide, as did a brother-in-law, Jimmy Broom, while Ginger's two sons died from drugs in their early forties. In fact just about all the family passed away young: only George lived to his sixties. Yet to me the Davies family were role models. While other kids wanted to be like Stanley Matthews or Tom Finney, I wanted to be like them. Leaving school at fifteen with only a basic education, I was out in the wide world and looking to make money any way I could, and they pointed the way.

I did take a straight job as an apprentice toolmaker in Altrincham but lasted only a few months, until I was caught running a card school during lunch breaks. The boss did not like me relieving the other apprentices of their wages. 'This is not the sort of thing we like here, Donnelly,' he said, as he showed me the door.

Then I took the step that would change my life.

2

THE MARKET MOB

SMITHFIELD MARKET was Manchester's main clearing house for fresh produce of all kinds, a noisy, bustling sprawl based on Shudehill in the city centre. At its heart sat a vast covered area selling meat, fruit and vegetables, with separate annexes for poultry and fish, as well as storage warehouses and offices. Hotels, restaurants, cafes and stores all bought their provisions at the wholesale market, while the retail stalls sold to the public. Over the years the market had spread into the surrounding streets, with barrows seeping across Swan Street and into the neighbouring district of Ancoats. You could buy everything from shoes to puppy dogs, and find a pub or drinking den open virtually around the clock.

A pal of mine told me it was easy to find work on the market if you were prepared to rise early, so one day I went along. I walked down the three or four alleyways of tables laid out with fish and asked if anyone had work.

'Can you ride a bike?' someone asked.

And that was it: I was taken on by H.R. Wood, Fish Merchants, as a bike boy.

They gave me an adapted bicycle with metal baskets attached that could hold several stone of fish. The bike was not the easiest thing to ride but once I had mastered it I was twisting and turning between the stalls and off through the streets like Eddie Mercx. My job was to deliver fish and poultry to restaurants, hotels and shops. My regular stops also included the railway stations at Victoria and Piccadilly, where we supplied the dining cars on inter-city trains. I would start at about 6.30 every morning, still in the dark in winter, and would be back and forth to the stations once an hour all through the morning to serve the London trains.

I immediately loved the atmosphere of the market: the masculine banter, the clamour and the camaraderie, the clatter of wooden-soled clogs worn to keep out damp, nails and fishbones, the pungent smells, the shouts and the arguments. And I loved the money. The market was flush with ready cash. Meat rationing had ended in 1954 and Britain was finally emerging from post-war parsimony. The pay was good for a teenager and the perks were even better. Customers would tip you for loading their wagon and breakfast often came from the first tip of the day. I also discovered fiddles all over the place. This was made for me: I was like a kid let loose in a sweet shop.

Customers ordered their fish by weight, but it was quite easy to slip some aside. After taking a bit of cod or plaice out of every box, I could steal up to a stone of fish a day and maybe the odd chicken or two, and soon found a buyer who ran a chip shop in Moss Side. My wage was just under £3 a week but I was soon making that in a day, while my father was only on £8 a week as a bricklayer. Another fiddle was the daily stocktake in the fruit market. The lads would offload from the farmers and might stack seven or eight 'leg' of potatoes in a pyramid. They would arrange the sacks so the stack was hollow in the middle, giving the impression of more than there actually were. The stocktakers would count them, not realising there were sacks missing. We did the same with boxes of oranges. By the end of the week, the clerk in the office was scratching his head because the numbers did not add up, while we were counting the extra cash in our pockets.

I sometimes went out on a wagon from the fruit and vegetable market and discovered yet another fiddle further along the supply chain. We would untie the string on the sacks of potatoes, scoop a few pounds in weight out of each and put them into our own empty sacks. This was known as 'milking it'. Soon you had a couple of full sacks of your own, which you would sell to a shop or a chippie. The wagon driver and I would split the proceeds.

After a few weeks, I went to the number one fish stall – I worked at number two – to collect a case of chickens. A new kid was there who had started work for H.R. Wood that morning. He was a good-looking lad, younger than me, with a full head of hair in a crudely cut quiff. We got to talking. He said he lived just a short walk away from the market.

'What's your name?' I asked.

'Jimmy Monaghan,' he replied.

JAMES PATRICK MONAGHAN was an Ancoats lad, and in Manchester that meant something. Ancoats was a special area. A hundred years earlier, its cotton mills had driven the Industrial Revolution and made Manchester the workshop of the world. The steam-powered engines of its huge factories had thumped away all day long, flanked by row after row of terraced houses for the thousands of families drawn in by the promise of a living wage. Ancoats created riches for the mill owners and merchants, but its inhabitants were the poorest in the city, living in cramped, over-crowded slums. Many families were Irish or Italian, descended from immigrants who had arrived with just the shirts on their backs, looking for work. They formed a huge casual labour force, and many ended up at Smithfield Market or as street sellers and hawkers.

The first Italians settled in Ancoats more than a hundred years before I was born. They included many skilled craftsmen such as carvers, gilders and instrument makers. Some played box or barrel organs with dancing monkeys, others made and sold ice cream. The mill workers' houses they settled in were little more than hovels but were luxurious compared to the shacks many of them had left behind, and the area between Great Ancoats Street and Oldham Street became known as Little Italy. The Italians tended to have large families, and to escape the house the men would stand in the street gossiping or meet up in the Green Dragon pub, where the vaults were known locally as the 'Italian room'. It had a great football team for many years and a few players made it onto Manchester City's books. Ancoats was chock-a-bloc with people, and pubs formed the bedrock of the social scene. There was a pub on every corner and often the sound of an organ or piano accordion could be heard through an open window.

Ancoats was also a very tough place. In the late Victorian age, young gangs called scuttlers fought mass battles in the streets. The most famous, the Bengal Tigers, came from Bengal Street, while their sworn enemies, the Prussia Street gang, were just a few hundred yards away. In the period between the Wars, another gang appeared called the Napoo, a military slang word that meant 'no more' or 'never again': it meant they took no shit off anyone. They wore navy blue suits, trilby hats and pink neckerchiefs, a style borrowed from American gangster films, and met at a dance hall in Belle Vue. They were said to wield straight razors against shopkeepers and publicans who refused them protection money, or indeed against anybody who crossed them. Their leader was the boxer Pokey Flynn, who fought in the 'blood tubs', small arenas which were often little more than the back rooms of pubs, many of which were so cramped that the boxing ring had to be the smallest available to leave room for spectators. After hanging up his gloves, Flynn was a common sight outside the Angel pub, offering to take on all comers in street fights.

Many of what would later be called the Quality Street Gang were born in Ancoats of Irish or Italian extraction. I was myself adopted by the place when I was sixteen years old and I live there now, nearly six decades later. The area bred a certain type of person: tough, self-reliant and clannish. It was my kind of place.

Jimmy Monaghan was a typical Ancoats urchin, brought up near the canal on Woodward Street. I learned that he'd had a very hard upbringing. His father, a foreman at a timber yard, had died a few years earlier, leaving his mother, Flo, to raise four children: Jimmy, his older brother and sister, Chris and Mary, and a younger brother, Joe. Flo was a tough woman and a real character, in the pub drinking a Guinness every night, but she had little money and the kids grew up with nothing. Jimmy had little schooling and ended up in children's homes and approved schools. He was raised in the streets, did some boxing and knew how to look after himself – how well, I would soon find out.

We got on well from day one and within a few weeks we had formed a tight group of pals with some other market lads. Our working day usually finished around noon, after which we were free to do what we wanted, with money to spend. If someone was skint, we clubbed together and sorted them out. Every day we earned and every night we enjoyed ourselves. The Edwardian dress craze was sweeping through Britain and rock and roll was infecting the jive, jump and dance bands of the youth clubs and halls. Drape suits, duck's arse haircuts and crepe shoes became our uniform, complete with studded belts that could be used as weapons when required. A new suit every month was not uncommon, made to measure from John Colliers or Weavers to Wearers or Burtons for less than a fiver. At sixteen, in my powder blue suit, I was the smartest kid in Wythenshawe.

Wythenshave was a hotbed of teddy boys. The meeting place was Charlie's, a kind of amusement arcade in Northenden that had cafes and a boxing and wrestling booth on Saturday nights. I got nicked there for being drunk and disorderly when I was sixteen with a teddy boy gang. I was never a big beer drinker but it was only sevenpence for a pint, mild, mixed or bitter, so for a nicker you could have fifteen pints if you were so minded – and a lot of the market men were very heavy drinkers. I was bound over to keep the peace. The biggest ted in the area was Erm Derbyshire – we called him 'Erm' because he had a stammer. He was a handsome kid who looked and dressed like Elvis Presley and in later years he built a shrine to Elvis on the back of his house. Erm was the bee's knees: all the lads wanted to dress like him and all the girls, even my sisters, swooned when they saw him.

In September 1956, the film *Rock Around The Clock* came to town. It had been causing a sensation and igniting riots at cinemas across the country, which made everyone want to see it even more. So for its first showing, a mob of young market lads piled onto the back of a lorry at Smithfield and arrived at the Gaiety Cinema in Peter Street like a band of pirates. Of course, it ended in another riot. One lad went over the balcony and hit the deck, someone grabbed a hosepipe and sprayed the cinema manager, others danced in the aisles in between fighting the police, and the film was stopped for eighteen minutes. It was great.

Unlike my younger brothers, I had somehow managed to avoid approved school and borstal, but it was only a matter of time before I was locked up for something. It happened after a chef at the Queens Hotel had set about a pal of mine. Some of us younger lads from the market went looking for revenge and steamed into the hotel kitchen through the back door, which they kept open because of the heat. We threw the potato pies all over the place and beat up a couple of chefs. Somebody phoned the police and I was charged with assault.

As I was sixteen, I was remanded to Rose Hill, a remand home for juveniles in Northenden. It later became notorious for sexual abuse, and rightly so. I wasn't sexually abused but I was certainly physically abused. As soon as I arrived, a house master made me go straight to the bathhouse.

'Take your clothes off, Donnelly,' he said. 'Run the bath. Get all your clothes off.'

'Why?'

He punched me in the nose and I fell back into the bath, hit my head on the taps and briefly lost consciousness. From then on, this same brute kicked the daylights out of me every chance he got. There were some sadists in those places.

Again I was bound over at court, so I did not have to serve a custodial sentence. But the remand in Rose Hill had been bad enough. It was not until years later that the systematic abuse both there and at other Manchester children's homes was uncovered. Scores of former inmates, including a good pal of mine, were awarded £15,000 compensation each for the sexual assaults they had endured. It was a disgrace. I was tough enough and bloody-minded enough to fend for myself but many were not, and it scarred them for life.

JIMMY MONAGHAN'S reputation as a fighter was earned at daybreak one morning when he wheeled his porter's truck to the ice works. Fresh fish came into Manchester on wagons from the docks at Fleetwood, and the first job of the day was to offload it and ice it up to preserve it. The market had a big machine to break up slabs of ice and Jimmy was sent for a barrelful. There was usually a rush to get there first and avoid the queue, though it never bothered me, I was content to go for a cup of tea and a bacon butty and wait until the line had gone.

The boss at the ice works was a surly bloke in his mid-twenties known as Big John. On this day the wait seemed longer than usual, so Jimmy asked why the delay.

'Fucking wait your turn,' was the answer from Big John.

Jimmy gave him some verbal back, so Big John, who was not accustomed to young whippersnappers giving him grief, threw a punch at him.

The first I heard of it was a shout: 'Get round to Edge Street! Jimmy Monaghan is having a fight with Big John from the ice works!' I hurried round to see them squaring off in the middle of the street, with seventy or eighty porters watching. Fights were common on the market, as the porters were always falling out, accusing each other of stealing customers or whatever, but this one looked a total mismatch. Big John was a powerful man and towered over his opponent, who was only in his mid-teens. Nobody gave Jimmy a chance.

Then he went to work.

Jimmy beat Big John to a pulp. His fists were a blur and you could clearly hear the thud of his punches even through the shouts of the crowd. The scariest thing was, he would not stop. Some of those watching had to step in and haul him off. Big John was in a bad state and went for medical treatment.

The next day, Jimmy went for ice again. Big John came out of his office with a heavily bruised face and said to his worker, 'Serve this feller first,' then shook Jimmy's hand. They became friends, and James Patrick Monaghan became a name.

I soon realised what a fighter this kid was. At weekends, some of the market lads started coming to Wythenshawe for dances. The dance halls were little more than youth club huts but we were still too young to drink in pubs, so this was our social scene. We soon bumped up against a nasty fellow called Sutton, who was a few years older than us and who ruled the roost in the local dance hall, where he had a habit of threatening people. We had a bit of a row with him and some of his cronies, a few people got arrested and Sutton ended up with a fine.

Not long after, I went to the annual funfair in Wythenshawe Park with some of my market pals: Jimmy Monaghan, Jimmy Specchio, Charlie Pearson and Dave Grant. We were fooling about, checking out the girls, when we spotted a few fellers watching us. Within minutes, twenty of them were glaring in our direction. The ringleader was unmistakable for his huge head and fair ginger hair: it was Sutton. We knew it was on top, so we slowly made our way out. They followed and, as we reached the main gate, they broke into a charge. We had little choice but to scatter. I cut off the main track and headed for a small fence. This was my manor, so I knew where I was going. I was just about to clear the fence when a blow on the back of the head made me stumble. I turned to see a guy with a bat about to hit me again.

Suddenly an arm wrapped round his neck, then another hand with a blade came over and round his face. He gave a terrible scream as the blade tore his cheek, cutting from his ear to his chin. Then the blade was stuck up his arse. It was Jimmy Specchio to the rescue.

We fled together, leaving my attacker writhing on the ground.

'I was last and saw you with this cunt behind you,' said Jimmy. 'I couldn't leave you.'

We crossed the fence and found the others. Everybody had got away.

'Where the fuck have you been?' said Jimmy Monaghan.

I told him what had happened and showed him the lump on my head.

'Right,' he said. 'Find out who the guy with the big head is.'

A few weeks later, I had the information I needed. His full name was Derek Sutton and he went every night to a café called the Boxtree. The plan was laid to go after him: me, Jimmy Monaghan and Dave Grant.

We met at my mother's and at nine o'clock we headed for the cafe. I went inside and spotted Sutton. Nobody took any notice as I walked back out. We split up and waited.

About an hour later, he came out alone. We regrouped and followed him.

'Hey, Sutton,' shouted Jimmy.

This monster turned around and quickly took in the situation.

'Do you young pups want some fun?' he growled. 'I'll fight you all.'

'No,' said Jimmy. 'Just you and me.'

Sutton closed in on him. He was as strong as an ox but he could not put punches together like Jimmy. A lightning flurry put him over a wall into a garden and he was at Jimmy's mercy. That was not a good place to be. Jimmy hit him with everything.

With the commotion and the yelps of Sutton, windows opened and someone shouted, 'Phone the police!' I told Jimmy we had to go but Sutton had hold of his legs and was screaming, 'I'm holding you for the police.' So Jimmy reached into his pocket and pulled out a small blade. He jabbed it into Sutton's face, then slashed him across the head for good measure. Sutton let go, Jimmy got back over the garden wall and we were off. I grabbed his blade and another one off Dave Grant and dropped them down a grid.

We put some distance behind us and were trying to walk nonchalantly down a road when we were surrounded by police. There was no escape. They took us to the local nick, Sutton identified Jimmy and he was charged with causing grievous bodily harm. However, when it came to court the case against Jimmy was slung out because of Sutton's actions in the witnesses box: he ranted, raved and threatened barristers and even the judge.

Jimmy and I had a conversation afterwards.

'I want you to come with me and watch my back,' he said. 'I am going to batter every hard man and doorman in Manchester. Anybody with a name. I am going to take them all.'

He was deadly serious. And for the next three or four years, that is what he did. He went on a mission to take on anyone in the city who fancied himself as a fighter, with us as his back-up.

We always travelled at least five-handed. Charlie Pearson was a good boxer, Jimmy Specchio was another tough lad and Dave Grant was a lunatic who carried a blade and was not afraid to use it. We fought every weekend. Each area had its local mob and they were rarely slow to take us on. Whenever we went outside our area, be it to Collyhurst, Miles Platting, Clayton or Openshaw, someone would fancy having a go. One regular battleground was Chick Hibbert's dance hall on Ashton Old Road. We soon made a name for ourselves, and became known as the Market Mob.

One night we were on the corner of Queens Road and Rochdale Road at chucking out time, waiting for a taxi, when a this big feller and a few pals walked straight into us. A row started and Dave Grant stuck him with his knife. We ran off, chased by a policeman who had seen the commotion, and I ran around a corner straight into a lamp post, knocking myself spark out. I woke up in the nick. The police told me that the stabbed guy might die. Hanging had not yet been abolished for murder, so I felt pretty miserable. Fortunately the guy recovered and said the person who stabbed him was over six feet tall. As I was only five foot four, I was off the hook – and the scaffold.

One of the Davies clan was responsible for my next bust-up with the police. I had been out in Manchester and had caught the last bus home to Wythenshawe. As I crossed the road, a police car pulled up and the officers pounced on me. My brother Arthur saw it from our house and he and my mother came out into the street. It went off and they even arrested my mother. They battered me, hauled me to the cells where I was handcuffed to a radiator, and charged me with stealing a motorbike. Arthur was also charged.

It turned out that the police had been chasing two kids on a motorbike and had found it dumped in a garden. They then saw me crossing the road, assumed I was involved and jumped on me. The two lads who had actually pinched the bike were Albert Davies Gibbons and his mate. They came to court and made a statement to my solicitor admitting guilt, but instead of letting me go the cops now stuck all four of us in the dock: Arthur and me for assaulting the police and Albert and his mate for pinching the bike. If I had been a bit older and wiser and had better legal advice, I would have sued the police, but at that age I had no idea. I got a fine in the end, while the local *Wythenshawe Recorder* carried the headline 'Brothers Attack PCs With Studded Belts'.

I guess it didn't hurt my reputation. It was also around this time that I acquired the nickname that would stay with me for the rest of my life. Most people think I was nicknamed 'the Weed' because I am only five foot four. In fact I got the name when I left H.R. Wood and moved to another firm on the market called Bold Aldred. I was not everybody's cup of tea when I started there, as I wouldn't take any shit, but after a couple of weeks a fellow called Lol King said to the other workers, 'You know, he grows on you this Jimmy, like a fucking weed.'

And that was how I became Jimmy the Weed.

3

REPUTATION

MY OWN REPUTATION was made one Sunday night when I was eighteen. I walked into my local pub in Wythenshawe, ordered a bottle of Guinness and felt a tap on the shoulder.

'I hear you are a bit of a villain,' this fellow said, 'and were involved in doing Derek Sutton.'

'Well, if I was, what has it got to do with you?'

He introduced himself.

'I'm Jim Hancock. I'm the guv'nor in Wythenshawe and I don't like you or any of your market mob. So if you don't fuck off, I'm going to do you.'

I had heard of Hancock around the neighbourhood, but our paths had not crossed: Wythenshawe covered a vast area and he lived a couple of miles from me. Now he was in my local with five mates, while I was on my own, but I was not going to back down. This was a direct challenge and there was no way out.

'If you want a row, get in the car park, man to man,' I said, loud enough so his pals would hear it was to be a fair fight.

Out we went, and what a fight it was. We could both use our fists and were both fit young men, and neither of us would quit. We fought for three-quarters of an hour, with no-one getting the edge, until in the end, with both of us virtually at a standstill, someone said the police were coming.

'Okay,' gasped Hancock, who was as knackered as I was. 'I think we have both had it. What do you say we go and have a drink?'

'Sure,' I wheezed, 'but you could have said that half an hour ago!'

We went back into the pub, where a fellow called Jack Shaw bought the beer.

'Fucking hell, Jimmy,' he said, 'I was meant to fight you. I'm glad I didn't.'

From then on I was made in Wythenshawe. The fight was the talk of the estate and I got big respect both for taking on Hancock and because of my market and Ancoats connections.

Even so, there were other people who wanted to have a pop at me. Not long after, I was walking home from the pub with a guy called Peter Tranter when we were approached by a few blokes.

'Hey you, I want to talk to you,' said one.

I thought he was talking to Peter but he went on, 'You, Donnelly, you think you are a clever cunt with your market pals. How are you without them?'

I knew the guy speaking, a feller named Pat Strap. He and his brother had reputations. Peter Tranter said something about me being with him, but Pat said, 'Stay out of it, it is between me and him.'

Once again there was no way out, so before any more was said I belted Strap on the chin. He fell into a fence that collapsed under his weight. I jumped on him and hit him with a brick that was lying in the garden. It was over in less than a minute; I could not believe how easy it had been. My instant action had caught him unawares.

As usual after a fight, I became pals with Pat Strap, even though I had put the skids under his reputation. The street fights with Hancock, Strap, and another I had with a local boxer called Steve Murphy, meant that I was now known as someone who could and would look after himself. I was able go into different manors, drink with the local faces and be accepted as someone not to mess with, while on my own patch everybody wanted to buy me a beer or ask about my market mates and, in particular, Jimmy Monaghan. His reputation was growing far and wide as he battered every villain, streetfighter and doorman who crossed him.

You had to earn your spurs to run with the Market Mob. One night, one of our pals had his face slashed in a fight, so five of us went out to find out who had done it: me, Jimmy Monaghan, Denis 'Urmo' Maher, Frank Platt, and a friend of mine called George Fletcher, who I had first met in the brutal St Joseph's home in 1948 and who worked on the market. George could have a fight but only I had seen him in action. To the rest of the boys he was an unknown quantity, and that meant he would have to prove himself.

After rows in a couple of bars, we called into the Cheshire Cheese public house, then owned by the Italian Mancini family. No sooner had we ordered our drinks than Ronnie Mancini, the landlady, confronted Jimmy.

'I want no trouble in here from you and your pals,' she said. 'I have got Scotch Dave on the other door, so behave yourselves.'

Scotch Dave was a bull of a man, born in Aberdeen but living in Hulme. He was one of the most feared fighters in Manchester but that cut no ice with Jimmy.

'Go and get him,' he said.

Scotch Dave came charging over like an angry ox, but Jimmy simply said to George Fletcher, 'You take him, I am not going to dirty my hands on him.'

With that, Fletch hit Dave full on the chin and down he went. There was a stunned silence.

'There's your bouncer,' said Jimmy to the landlady. Then he knocked out Scotch Dave's pal.

The place was in uproar. People were trying to get out of the way and shouting for the police. As we made our exit, Ronnie Mancini picked up a handful of wooden darts used for pub games and threw them at our retreating backs, shouting abuse. Embarrassingly, one stuck in my arse and another in my shoulder. So we threw a couple of bins through the pub windows. We later became great friends with the Mancinis, but a point had been made: we were not afraid of any doorman, and George Fletcher got his brownie points.

One of our regular Friday night haunts was the Newton Heath Palace dance hall. What happened on this particular Friday I do not recall, but somebody went at the mix and I ended up having a few cross words with Jimmy in a pub. By the time I got to the dance hall, I was seriously pissed off with him. *Fuck it*, I thought, *I don't care*. I spoke to Jimmy again and what I said did not go down well.

'Do you think you are a hard case?' I asked him. Then I threw a punch. The others jumped in and stopped it.

'I'll see you in the market tomorrow,' said Jimmy.

I had already fallen out with another pal, Tommy Wimpleton, another street fighter, and had arranged a straightener with him at eleven o'clock the next morning. Now I said to Jimmy, 'I will see you at ten.' So that would be two fights, with two of the best, in one morning. I must have been mad.

But come Saturday morning, I was there. Jimmy gave me the chance to leave it out but reputation and your name was everything and I refused. We climbed over a wall onto a bomb site and squared up. I never stood a chance.

When I had recovered, I went to see Tommy. His eyes widened when he saw the mess I was in.

'Fuck me Jimmy, leave it over,' he said. 'I am not going to fight you in that state.'

I still carried a grudge against Jimmy, and was in a pub with Tommy not long after when he came in with some of the lads. I saw him go to the toilets, followed him in, and launched a punch at him as he was relieving himself. It had no effect. He simply turned and flattened me again. Fortunately Tommy had followed me into the toilets and pulled Jimmy off me. All Jimmy said was, 'You brave little bastard.'

That was the last time we ever fell out, over fifty years ago. We laugh about it now, though the memory still brings me out in a cold sweat. But at the time it let people know that I would not walk away from anybody, even the hardest. There is no shame in losing, I have lost a few, but your word, your reputation and your honour are everything. And whenever we went out to challenge somebody after that, Jimmy would say, 'I want the Weed there to watch my back.'

I also realised that I was not big enough to take on certain people with my fists, so I had to even things up. The knife, the axe, and later the gun came into my life – and I would use them when called for.

JIMMY MONAGHAN was now the guv'nor. Behind him was a wild crew of market boys who were fast with their fists and scared of no-one. Alongside myself there was Charlie Pearson, Dave Grant, Frank Platt, Jimmy Specchio and Denis Maher, another good amateur boxer who was fearless on the cobbles. With every fight we added to our reputation.

We were out drinking one day in the pubs on Ancoats Lane and walked past the landmark *Daily Express* building, made largely of black glass. We could see the workers inside at the printing machines.

'Look at them idiots,' somebody said.

The workers spotted us looking in and gave us the finger. We returned the gesture. The next thing we knew, about twenty of them were pouring out of the door, spoiling for a fight, and it went off royal in the street. When it was all over, Denis and a pal called Tommy Leary had been arrested. Jimmy was picked up later. I was lucky: my girlfriend at the time was passing looking for me, and I grabbed her arm and walked off with her.

The 'inky-oilies', as we called newspaper printers, suffered all sorts of injuries and the lads were charged with Section 18 wounding, otherwise known as grievous bodily harm with intent, a serious charge. In all there were eight counts of wounding and one newspaper labelled it the 'Battle of Ancoats Lane'. All three of the lads arrested ended up going to borstal. Jimmy was sent all the way to the Portland in Dorset, which housed the most violent and troublesome young offenders in the country. He did every hardcase in there and finished up the 'daddy' of the place. To keep him quiet they put him on the boxing team and he won a stack of trophies.

Tommy Leary went on to be in and out of the nick in later life. Everybody liked Tommy, he was a good-looking guy and had a nice way with him, but he never had any luck. We called him 'Biffo' because he hit so hard that he was always breaking his hands. When he was skint he would just walk into a shop, punch the owner on the chin, help himself and then get off. He felt the need to commit a crime every day. 'I can't go home yet, I haven't had a tickle,' he used to say. Denis Maher took a different path. He trained to be a bricklayer in borstal and tried his hand at it when he came home but did no good, so he got a ticket to work as a steel erector. He worked straight in the steel business and became one of the top trade union delegates in the country.

ALWAYS LOOKING FOR opportunities to make a quid, I met a family called Moran in a market pub, the Glue Pot. They had a fruit and vegetable stall. Soon I was supplementing my income by helping them out. The Morans would give me a couple of bob to push their barrow from an overnight storage depot down to Market Street, then the same for pushing it back at the end of the day. The fish stall where I worked closed after lunch, so in the afternoons I was free to start serving on their stall as well, to give them a break. Soon I was doing the same for two or three other stallholders.

Pushing the barrows out was backbreaking work but there are ways and means of moving a heavy cart laden with produce. Once you found the middle weight, or centre of gravity, of the barrow you could bounce it and then skip along the cobbles, so that at times your feet were lifted off the ground and you could hitch a ride on its forward momentum. It was fine going downhill to Market Street but pushing back up was the problem – you had to travel the streets in a zigzag to reduce the gradient. There was an art to it. Those Smithfield market porters were fit: old Jake Winters famously carried a hundredweight sack of spuds on his back from the city centre to the Old Cock pub in Stretford without stopping, to win a bet. I don't think anyone has done it since. I would have the barrow back for six o'clock, get changed in Maggie Moran's house and then go out to meet the lads.

Always hungry for that few quid in my pocket, I left the market for a while and went hod-carrying for my dad. I also drove an overhead crane at the railway sidings at Ancoats. The fiddle there was incredible: security was non-existent so we would nick whole cases of whisky and sling them over the wall. Within a couple of months, I had enough money to buy a Francis-Barnett motorbike so I could get to see my Ancoats pals more easily.

A few of us hit on another angle to get money. Every night, American soldiers from the Burtonwood military base, near Warrington, would ride the train to Manchester to go to the Ritz dance hall and the pubs on Oxford Street. It was like a football crowd every night and all the girls on the game would make a beeline for the area. One night we followed a G.I. and a prostitute into a back street. As they were at it in a doorway, the soldier's trousers round his ankles, Jimmy Specchio grabbed him.

'What are you doing to my sister?' he shouted.

He gave the Yank a bit of a crack, demanded money and took his watch.

We repeated this a few times. We knew we were out of order and that if we were to get any respect we should not be pulling such cheap stunts, but we were what we were, up-and-coming villains, and anything went. Eventually we left it out. At least to the girls of the night we were thieves and not 'pudding-eaters', our term for ponces.

The most popular dance hall in town, especially for the younger crowd, was the Plaza in Oxford Street. It opened lunchtimes and evenings and had DJs like Jimmy Savile and Dave Lee Travis as well as live bands. We would finish on the market at about noon, go to the Plaza for a couple of hours, then go to the cinema, have some tea, then return to the Plaza for the evening dance. It was a good time. The Plaza did not sell alcohol so we would drop into the famous Tommy Ducks pub beforehand: the story goes that the original owner was called Tommy Duckworth but the signwriter ran out of space, hence 'Ducks'. The Moss Side mob of the Lyons brothers frequented there too and it went off with them a few times before we became great friends.

Walking back to Ancoats after one afternoon dance, we passed through Piccadilly Gardens, where a gang of about fifteen men started having a go, obstructing us and hurling insults. They were looking for a fight and must have seen us as easy prey, as there was only half a dozen of us, including Jimmy, who was now back from borstal, Denis Maher, Charlie Pearson and Dave Grant, the usual suspects.

'Keep going,' said Jimmy. 'There are too many of them.'

It was not like Jimmy to walk away from a fight, no matter what the odds, but he already had a plan. Crossing the road, he led us into the Woolworth's department store, where he headed for the gardening section. We had no idea what he was doing until he selected a two-bob axe and paid for it at the counter. We did the same.

'Now we're even,' he said.

We slid the axe handles down our waistbands and headed back towards Piccadilly Gardens. The mob was sitting on the small wall. Their leader, a man with a Scouse accent wearing a cheese-cutter cap, shouted, 'Oh, they're back.'

Jimmy ran forward, leapt the wall while pulling out his axe, and hacked it into Cheese-cutter's shoulder. We steamed in behind him. I got my victim still sitting on the wall, in shock. We did four or five of them, while the rest ran for their lives. I can still picture the diabolical scene of Jimmy Monaghan, standing in the fountain in the middle of Piccadilly Gardens, sticking an axe in a fellow's head as the water turned blood-red around him. How we did not get nicked for that I will never know. There were hundreds of witnesses but no police, as they were all on duty at a football match.

From then on, Jimmy always carried either an axe or his trusty

Gurkha knife, although he enjoyed fist fights the most. You had to be prepared because you never knew what you might come up against. On another occasion, he and I were in Woolworths buying new axes – having already slung a couple that had been used – when I spotted the gardening master from Rose Hill remand centre buying plants. This bastard had been one of my tormentors. I set about him right there in Woolworths and kicked him across the shop floor like a dog. I also caught up with the headmaster from there when I was coming out of a cinema one afternoon with Jimmy and a couple of the lads. He had apparently been a champion boxer in the Middle East but it didn't save him from a belting.

In truth, the only thing that has ever really frightened me in life is me, because I have no compunction. I could hurt someone and not feel a bit of remorse. I have been like that all my life. It is not temper, it is calculated. And I won't forget.

ONE SUNDAY afternoon, I arrived at Jimmy Monaghan's house on my motorbike to go to Newton Heath Palais for the rock and roll dance. His mother opened the door.

'Am I glad to see you,' she said. 'Jimmy's gone to Newton Heath for a drink and there have been about six men at the house looking for him, all big bastards.'

'Do you know who they are?'

'One of them is Brian Dunn,' she said. 'The Bear.'

My heart thumped. Brian Dunn was a beast of a man, feared throughout Manchester. When he walked into a bar, people ran out. He and his cronies were hunting Jimmy because of an incident at the Plaza dance hall. Jimmy and Peter King, an ex-boxer who worked there as a doorman, had exchanged a few words and Jimmy had stuck the nut on him. Now King was out for blood.

'Okay,' I told his mum. 'I'll go after him and call a few people.'

I set off on my bike and found Jimmy with a few of the lads in the Copenhagen Tavern, our regular Sunday afternoon meeting place on Oldham Road. I blurted out the news.

Jimmy's eyes hardened.

'Let them come,' was all he said.

Word spread, and by the time we left the pub for the dance hall there must have been twenty of us. If there was a gang of them, we needed a gang of us.

We reached the Palais and stopped outside, just as a car pulled up. The doors opened and the car creaked on its axles as half a ton of beef alighted. In the lead was the Bear. I had never seen anybody with arms and fists so big. The men with him included Micky Lennon and Mick Tierney, two other terrors, and Peter King, a black ex-boxer who had twice fought eliminators for the British welterweight title.

Micky Lennon was a scaffolder and a very tough man. He did the talking.

'Right, lads,' he said. 'We're only here to see a straight fight between these two.' He nodded towards Peter King and then Jimmy.

What Jimmy said next will stay with me as long as I live.

'If you want to fight me,' he hissed, 'I'll take your fucking eyes out.'

There was a silence

Give King is due, he was made of stern stuff. He had fought nearly fifty times as a pro, was ten years older than Jimmy and was never going to back down.

'Let's get on with it,' he said.

He and Jimmy walked out of sight to a strip of land behind the dance hall.

We stood waiting, straining our ears to hear what was going on. The Bear and company looked unconcerned. They had heard about Jimmy, he was making waves, but had complete confidence that King would take him apart.

After what seemed like an hour, but was probably a couple of minutes, a figure appeared from around the corner. It was Jimmy. He walked up to Mick Lennon.

'You'd better get an ambulance for him,' he said.

We hurried behind the building. Peter King was lying on top of a mound of coke that was used for heating the dance hall. He was semi-conscious and his face was a bloody mess. Jimmy had punched him senseless, then grabbed him by the hair and ground his face into the coke. He looked like he had been slashed by a thousand razors. The Bear and friends picked him up and drove off. Once it was over, it was over. There were no comebacks. Each side respected the other.

Brian Dunn and his crew were a few years older than us and were the heavy mob of their day. Dunn had hands like shovels, big arms, a huge chest and torso and this deep, growling voice. 'Hey you,' he would growl to some unfortunate stranger, 'get me a fucking pint.' He drank around the Harpurhey area and could often be seen sitting in the corner of the Bottom Derby pub on Rochdale Road, supping free beer and keeping the young hooligans in line. He was on backhanders from a lot of landlords to 'mind' their pubs: basically a protection racket. I watched the Bear have a few fights over the years and, for a man his size, he was lightning. Not many in the country could have taken him on but with Jimmy Monaghan he knew it would be to the death, so he never had a bad word to say about us. Mick Tierney was another fearsome man. He was boss-eyed, had scars all over him and put fear in anybody he met. He lived in Moss Side among the black firms and earned his money minding shebeens, so he was always tooled up. He was once supposed to have a straight fight with Jimmy but it never happened. Mick told me he did not fancy it.

You only had to mention a name to Jimmy in those days and he wanted to fight them: 'Who is he?' he would ask. 'Where does he live? Where does he go? What nights does he go in there?' By now he was doing it all. If we faced another gang, he would point to them one by one and say, 'I will fight you, then I will fight you, then I will fight you.' If they were foolish enough to take him on, he cleaned up. Eventually even businessmen in the city, the car dealers and the club owners, wanted Jimmy around them, and with Jimmy came us.

4

LEARNING THE ROPES

AROLD MACMILLAN SAID the country had never had it so good, and we wanted in. I had no schooling or trade, nor did Jimmy Monaghan. For all that we were making money on the market and through other work, we were basically unskilled and uneducated labour, with criminal records. My brothers, Arthur and John, and Jimmy's brother Joe had all been through approved schools and borstal and were in the same boat. All we had to look forward to was what we could do ourselves. The post-war boom had brought plentiful work, even for the likes of us, but we wanted more than a living wage. We wanted a future.

I started to make contacts that would stand me in good stead. I stayed for a couple of months with Ginger Davies in Leytonstone, east London, where he had met a woman, and helped him with his furniture van. Then I went down there again, this time with Tommy Wimpleton, who was wanted by the police for something in Manchester. We called in on a pal of his from borstal, and he and his little gang put us up in a flat in Crystal Palace. We did a job for them, hijacking a lorry load of smoked salmon. I was impressed by the suits and cars of the young South London firm. 'This is for me, Tommy,' I said. After a couple of weeks we returned home and Tommy was arrested, but I had got a taste of criminal life in the capital.

When George Davies came out of prison, he took me down there again, and this time I met a few of his high-profile pals from the nick. He introduced me to Bobby Warren and 'Mad' Frankie Fraser, who had just done seven years each for cutting up the gangland boss Jack Spot. I was young and very impressed: this was first division stuff. You never heard of Bobby Warren after that, but he was always well respected and stopped a lot of aggro between firms in London with his common sense. George Davies had served time with these guys, who called him Manchester George, so there was a connection between the two cities that would later become important for me.

I then took a construction job at the Llandarcy oil refinery at Swansea, for a change of scene. The money was good but I was on the lookout for a bigger score. I noticed that the weekly wage delivery to another firm on the site always went to the same wooden cabin where the workers clocked in and out at the start and end of every day. There was no security and no burglar alarm. The following week, I watched again. In came the money. I casually asked a couple of the workers what day they got paid and they said Fridays, at lunchtime. The pay packets were delivered every Thursday, so that meant they were kept on site overnight.

I called our Arthur and another pal and told them to get the train to Swansea. Then I took them to the site, showed them the cabin and waited for the Thursday night. It was easy: we levered off the padlock and were in. We jacked open a metal cabinet and there was the stack of wage packets. We were back in the pub within the hour with a haul of £2,800 in notes and a few pounds in change. Most of it we put in registered letters and posted home, then Arthur and his pal caught the train back. After waiting a decent period so as not to arouse suspicion, I packed in the job and followed them back to Manchester.

Ginger Davies had also returned to Manchester and had a pub in Ancoats called the Saint Vincent, which he asked me to run for a while. One Friday night, a few girls came in and, having never been short of something to say, I chatted them up. I soon had a date with a petite blonde called Rita Wilkinson. We hit it off straight away. Rita was an Ancoats girl, born with her three sisters in an apartment in the historic Victoria Square flats complex, the first municipal housing in Manchester. Her dad had been a submariner in the War and survived being sunk a couple of times. He was not too keen on me when he heard I was a bit of a rogue and a gambler, but in the end we got on well. He was a nice fellow.

At around this time, Jimmy Monaghan decided to turn his fighting prowess into money. He entered the professional boxing ranks, adopting the ring name 'Swords', I think because his father came from the town of Swords, near Dublin, and had boxed under that name himself. From then on, he would be known to all as Jim Swords, though his close friends often shortened it to 'JS'. In October 1961, at the age of nineteen, he made his debut against fellow Mancunian Brian Ellaby at the famous Free Trade Hall. He lost on points after four rounds. Jimmy clearly had potential, but with little amateur experience he was raw and untutored.

What he did have was a wicked punch and a natural ferocity that, once unleashed, was almost impossible to tame. Over the next five months he cut a swathe through the local middleweight scene, winning six fights in a row, all inside the distance. Jimmy fought as he did in the streets, an explosion of speed and fury, and was so thrilling to watch that even as an undercard fighter he was packing out the Free Trade Hall and the King's Hall at Belle Vue. In fact he went through opponents so quickly that people started saying that his promoters were matching him with pushovers. So Gus Demmy and his son Selwyn, who promoted at the Free Trade Hall, went to the other extreme and put him up against a fighter called Maxie Smith in a main support bout. It was a daft choice of opponent for someone with only seven contests under his belt, as Smith had already beaten some of the best middleweights in Britain. Then Smith suffered a training injury and pulled out, only to be replaced by a top prospect called Joe Leeming, who had been ABA light-heavyweight champion and was unbeaten as a pro.

Boxing was a different sport in those days. Good young fighters were not brought along carefully to nurture their skills and confidence or to build up a long unbeaten record to make them more attractive to a TV audience that anyway did not yet exist. If you showed promise you were expected to get in there and mix it against quality opposition at the earliest opportunity. It could be the making of a fighter but it also ruined some promising careers as young boxers were overmatched too early.

Leeming had won all his fights inside the distance, so this one was never going to go to the judges. It was as exciting as everyone expected and in the end Jim just could not contain the streetfighter in him. 'In three hectic rounds of non-stop punching with much blood flowing, there was little in it when Swords was sent to his corner for butting his opponent in the face,' *Boxing News* reported. 'The Manchester man had previously been warned for the same illegal tactics and lost his head when he found his taller and faster opponent fighting back after taking a hammering to the body.' Jimmy was disqualified for sticking the nut in.

Back in action a month later, he once again found himself up against a bigger guy. Julius Caesar, from South Africa, was basically a light-heavy, while Jimmy was not even a big middleweight. By the time they got in the ring, Caesar must have outweighed him by nearly a stone and actually had to pay a forfeit for not making the weight. 'Swords tried his usual quick fire punching but it had no effect on the rugged Caesar and the lighter Manchester boy made the mistake of not using the ring against a slower moving opponent,' reported *Boxing News*. 'Instead he tried to slog it out toe-to-toe and paid the penalty.' Jimmy was knocked down four times in round four but refused to quit. The ref was forced to stop it.

ON 25 AUGUST 1962, Rita and I were married at St Anne's Roman Catholic Church in Ancoats. She was pregnant but it was no shotgun wedding; we wanted to marry. It was a plain affair: our reception was at the Brown Cow pub and our marital home was a rented bedsit above a doctor's surgery on Oldham Road. It wasn't fancy but it was a start.

A month later, it was Jim Swords' turn to get married, to Pam, who he had been courting for a while. A gang of us met on the Friday before the wedding for his bachelor night. It was a rowdy evening: we did all the bars and inevitably a few people got a crack here and there. Late on, about eight of us decided to go to the Wilton Club in New Cannon Street, where the comedian Bernard Manning was performing. We breezed past the queue and into the foyer, where a doorman put his hand on Jimmy.

'It's two-and-six,' he said. 'Anyway you can't come in. You're not wearing ties.'

Bang, it was off. The main doorman, Andy Partington, who was six foot six, started fighting our pal Frank Platt. Jimmy went for a guy called George Ashton, who had joined with the doorman. I seized the opportunity to grab a handful of cash from the open till.

Within seconds there was blood everywhere. People were screaming and the staff were trying to lock us in the club.

Somebody said, 'Let's go,' and we scarpered, leaving chaos in our wake.

By 2.30 a.m., we were back at a house in Ancoats and had cleaned ourselves up. Jim Swords, however, was still raring to go.

'I am going to get that fucking Partington,' he said.

So three of us – me, Jimmy and Denis Maher – walked back to the Wilton Club. Big mistake. We had just reached the club door when we were surrounded by police. Jimmy and I were nicked but Denis managed to slip away. They hauled us off to Bootle Street nick and let us stew in a cell. Then a burly sergeant came in and told us, with a look of satisfaction, that we were in serious trouble. Ashton was in hospital with numerous injuries, the worst of which was that his nose had been bitten off.

We refused to say anything and spent what was left of the night trying to sleep off the booze on hard wooden benches. Despite the seriousness of Ashton's injuries, we managed to get police bail later that morning when the duty solicitor explained that Jimmy was actually getting married that day. It cast a bit of a pall over the wedding at St Anne's Church, and the reception that evening was muted. Copies of the *Manchester Evening News* were surreptitiously passed around, with a story under the headline 'Police Hunt Gang After Man's Nose is Bitten Off' being of particular interest. The newspaper reported that Ashton, who was thirty-four years old, needed thirteen stitches to repair his snout and nine more in other wounds.

A few days later, the police came for us at dawn. This time they charged us with wounding with intent. 'This is all because the guy lost his nose,' I said to Jimmy once we were back in the cells. 'Why couldn't you just get a hamburger like the rest of us?' We were put before the magistrates and remanded in custody.

A prison van drove us the short distance to HMP Strangeways, the big house, where we were taken into reception for induction. We immediately got into an argument. Remand prisoners, having not yet been convicted, did not have to wear prison clothes. With Jimmy being only nineteen, and me fibbing about my age, we were to be put in a cell on the young prisoners' wing, but the authorities liked to assert themselves over the YP remand prisoners by forcing them to wear uniform. They also had the remand YPs sewing mailbags, which was again against the rules. Jimmy decided he wasn't having it. There was a bit of a row and one of the guards hit me on the napper with a stick.

We were put in the cage before being removed to our cell. I spotted Billy Able, an old pal who had done years for fraud. He came over and warned that the heavy mob would be waiting for us. The warders did not like young tearaways who wouldn't conform and were going to teach us a lesson.

Sure enough, we had not been in our cell five minutes when a mob of guards arrived. Four or five of them crammed around the doorway. Jimmy and I faced them.

'I don't want any trouble out of you two,' said the leader.

I could see that cold glint in Jimmy's eye.

'No trouble,' he said, 'but we do no work and we keep our own clothes. And if you ever come in this cell again, I'll break your jaw.'

He was unbelievable. Yet they just looked at us. They knew who Jimmy was and how he could fight.

'Oh, and if you touch him again,' said Jimmy, indicating me, 'you are going to have a hard time with me. I will knock you out one by one and throw you over the landing.'

The guards clearly did not fancy it, and withdrew. I guess they also knew they were in the wrong and could not force us to work or wear uniforms. Still, I could not believe we had not taken a hiding.

The next day, another screw came to see us. 'You can stay in your cell,' he said. 'We will leave your door open when the other prisoners are working so you won't be banged up. But will you at least clean the landing?'

Before Jimmy could open his mouth again, I said, 'No problem, we'll do it.' And from then on they left us alone.

Strangeways was a hole. Jimmy and I were two-ed up together but most cells held three inmates. We had two tiny single beds and a toilet bucket in the corner that had to be slopped out every morning. They would come round with a straight razor for you to shave and then return for it ten minutes later. Because Jimmy refused to let us work it did mean the days were pretty boring. Still, things weren't too bad: in those days you could have food brought in and were even allowed half a bottle of wine a day.

The four wings in our block fed into a central aisle or grid, like the spokes of a wheel feeding into the hub. The quickest way to get from one wing to another would be to walk straight across the grid, but prisoners were not allowed to, they had to walk around it. Screws stood around the grid and you risked being disciplined or even beaten if you crossed it. Strangeways legend had it that only one man, Malcolm Rance, had ever done so. Malcolm was a teak-tough Londoner who lived in Manchester. His thing was robbing the late-night goods trains; he used to hit them as they came into stations. Nobody would take him on in a fight: he was like a god. He was a lot older than us, but he had a lot of respect for us. Well, once Jimmy learned that Malcolm had walked across the grid, he had to do it too.

'Hey you,' shouted a screw, 'get fucking back here, *now!*'

Jimmy ignored him and carried on walking, and the screw did nothing. They say Mad Frank Fraser later crossed the grid when he served some time in Strangeways. I am not sure it is true, but I saw Jim Swords do it.

We met some tough boys inside. Vinnie Carroll, a bodybuilder known as 'the Buddha', was about ten years older than us and worked as a minder for Bobby Critchley, the Mr Big of Manchester in the forties and fifties. Vinnie weighed twenty-five stone and they could not find a prison uniform to fit him, but he was fast as lightning. He was also renowned for violence. When a copper cycled to his house over a trivial complaint, Vinnie put a hose on him and then locked him in a cellar for two days. Another great friend I made inside was Joseph Walford McNelly, known to all as Wally. He was thirty-three then, thirteen years older than me, and was finishing a four-year sentence. He moved to our wing because of overcrowding. What a character. We got on great and would work together in years to come.

Both my Rita and Jimmy's new wife, Pam, were pregnant. With fatherhood imminent, we talked about the future. Jimmy wanted to go as far as he could with his boxing, while I knew I would end up making money by any means necessary, legitimate or not. Then one day I took a phone call to say I had a baby son. Naturally I was delighted, and we had a bit of a mini celebration in our cell. Seventeen days later, I got another call. My son had died. Two weeks after that, Jimmy was summoned to the telephone to find that his wife had had a daughter who was stillborn. You could not bet on such a tragic coincidence, the odds would be too great. It was a very difficult time, not least because we were inside and could not console our wives.

Finally we were driven to Manchester Crown Court for our hearing, and put in the holding pen to await our turn. Already in there were five very tough-looking men, all older than us, immaculately suited and booted and wearing Crombie overcoats. They looked like Chicago gangsters. One of them, a broad-shouldered man we knew slightly, beckoned us over. His name was Les Simms. His friends included Roy Copeland and Bert Mills, names we had heard.

'How are you doing?' one of them said to Jimmy Swords.

Simms and his pals were car dealers and had been charged with taking the licence plate numbers of Corporation buses and putting them through as cars to finance companies, thereby fraudulently obtaining loans for non-existent cars for non-existent customers. They had mugs to go in for the 'drip', or finance, so their names would not be associated with it, even when the finance companies started screaming. What finally got them was that they took the plate number off a hearse. Anyway, they came over to us, asking Jimmy about future boxing fights. I was impressed. They looked the part and we knew they could walk the walk as well as talk the talk. Les Simms in particular had a real air of authority.

In court, we faced a young prosecutor called Ivor Taylor, who later became a top judge on the Northern Circuit. He said we had carried out 'a most brutal attack' and added that it was a pity that only two of those involved were in the dock. We both denied the charges and were committed for trial. The police were winding us up, saying we were going to get a three-stretch apiece. Biting off noses was not the done thing. But Gus and Selwyn Demmy were very influential in Manchester, and Jimmy was their star attraction, a potential champion. Gus made a case to the judge, saying that Jimmy had a successful boxing career ahead of him and what a shame it would be to jeopardize it with a long custodial sentence. When we came to trial, they lowered my charges and I pleaded guilty to common assault. They did the same with Jimmy and we both walked free that day.

George Ashton sued us for damages but it never reached court. He moved to Australia and, I heard, died young. Partington, the doorman, would later feature again in the folklore of gangland when he took a crack off Reggie Kray at the Portland Lodge. In truth, we got off lightly. More importantly, we now knew some of the real players in the Manchester underworld, and they knew us.

*

THE MEN WE met in Strangeways taught us that the city was divided. Each area had its hard men. Around Collyhurst and north Manchester, Brian 'the Bear' Dunn held sway. In Cheetham Hill, Mick Lennon and his pals ruled the roost. Salford was led by Ronnie Camilleri and Danny Danson. South Manchester had Bert Mills, while on the east side was Big Jim Evans. In the city itself, the top men included Les Simms, Billy Ingham, George King, Billy Kerfoot, Wally Downs, Jimmy Coulter, Scotch Dave Wilson, Ginger McAllister, Harold Brown and Don Toney. Then there were the three Foley brothers, George, Gerry and Brian, all big men; Albert and George Davies; Bobby McDermott, the so-called 'King of the Barrow Boys', who ran many of the pitches around Piccadilly; Malcolm Rance; and Johnny Thunder. All good men.

George King was black or, more accurately, mixed race but you could not mention it in front of him: he thought he was white and adopted the accent, dress and mannerisms of an English gentleman. Yet he was feared by many and served a ten-year term for violence. When he came out he went into the car trade, with a pitch in Hulme. He was particularly pally with Wally Downs, a top armed robber, while in later years he socialized with us a couple of nights a week. He finished up a wealthy man, with an export company shipping engines to the Caribbean and a home in Barbados, where he indulged his love of golf.

Bert Mills was a photographer by trade and had a pitch beside a register office in Rusholme. Ornamental gardens at the front served for wedding photos and Bert had the concession. If you hired your own photographer, he would chase them off. Bert was a rough customer. He came in the Barley Mow pub one day and started sounding off at me.

'You are a pal of Jimmy Swords, aren't you? I cou
him with one arm.'

'Listen Bert,' I said, 'you have had a good drink. Nov
out. You are going on and people are listening and word v
back to Jimmy. So I am going to have to tell him, because if I
don't, others will, and then he will come to me and want to know
why I kept quiet.'

'Fucking tell him what you want. You tell him.'

I asked the barman for some change and went to the phone box
but I only pretended that I was phoning Jimmy. Then I came back.

'It is on you,' I said. 'You told me to tell him and I have.'

I went to the toilets, came back and Bert was gone. It was a sen-
sible decision. He was a handful but he wasn't in the same league
as Jimmy.

The Salford mob were another breed. Salford and Manchester
are basically twin cities separated by the narrow River Irwell, and
Salford was once the third largest port in the country thanks to its
ship canal. Many of its hardest men were dockers. They could
legally carry dockers' hooks on their belts, which made terrifying
weapons, and had numerous fiddles. That was why you did not
see many Salford villains robbing banks in those days: they had
their own 'bank' on the docks.

Eight out of ten of them were huge: I swear nearly everyone in
Salford seemed to be six foot four. It would make me chuckle in
later years to hear people go on about the Kray twins: they were
small men. Ronnie Camilleri would have picked up the pair of
them and banged their heads together. Originally a merchant
seaman, he was built like Adonis and would fight anyone who
upset him. He had his earns on the docks but was basically a
straight person, much in demand by publicans and club owners, as
his presence would stop any would-be idiots from kicking off.

Danny Danson, his close pal, was only five foot six inches tall but about five foot wide. I saw him hit a man in the Glue Pot pub in Smithfield Market and put him straight through the window. Danny also had a famous pre-arranged straightener outside Bobby McDermott's Cellar club with Scotch Dave, a big name from the Hulme area. Danny won when he bit off a piece of Dave's ear.

In the late seventies, Ronnie Camilleri had a savage row with a huge doorman called Bernard Sullivan, who was about six foot seven. Sullivan, a bully, had once tried to have a go at me in Nick the Greek's twenty-four-hour cafe when my wife and I called in for breakfast on our way home. He said a few words, so I picked up my knife and fork and told him, 'If you open your mouth to me again, I will stick this straight in your eye.' Another doorman got hold of him and asked him what he thought he was doing. Well he made a big mistake when he gave Ronnie's pal Alfie Olbiston a hard time in Sid Otty's spieler. Word reached Ronnie, who went round to see him. Sullivan offered to fight him in the street and Ronnie flattened him. Sullivan later died of his injuries in hospital. In court, it came out that he had a steel plate in his head from a car crash and this had contributed to his death, so Ronnie was cleared.

Most of the Salford mob were about ten years older than us. I would later own a couple of bars on their manor and never had one problem with them. Ronnie, who sometimes worked for Les Simms on the door of the Theatre Club, would call in every Friday on his way to a weekly meet in Cheetham Hill. He thought the world of Jim Swords, it was a meeting of minds. Les and Bobby Harper were two more highly respected Salford guys, as was my future doorman Tommy Cunliffe, who could have a terrible fight. These lads, and others like the two Norbury brothers, were all giants; I don't know what they feed them over there.

It was useful for us to know men like these. Many of them came to Jim Swords' fights and were among his biggest supporters. In some ways, they 'ran' the city, and in the years to come they would prove to be invaluable friends or associates.

AFTER PRISON, JIMMY resumed his boxing career against Willie Hart, a prospect from Glasgow. Several months in lock-up had hardly been ideal preparation but it was another terrific punch-up. They shared ten knockdowns before Hart's eye split open and the ref stopped it in Jim's favour. It confirmed his reputation as the most thrilling fighter around. A month later, he knocked out another leading Scottish middleweight, Willie Fisher, at the Free Trade Hall, then went on to stop the well-regarded Sid Parkinson and beat a tough Tunisian on points. Tickets to his fights became the hottest in town.

In June 1963, he was rewarded for his victories with a step up in class against Harry Scott, for the Central Area title. Scott, a Scouser, was a gentleman outside the ring but a rock inside it, with a concrete jaw and a pile-driver punch. He had twice Jimmy's pro experience and, though he could be outboxed, fancy ringwork wasn't Jimmy's style: he was toe-to-toe all the way. Jim ordered hundreds of tickets to sell himself and the press played up the Manchester versus Liverpool angle: *Boxing News* called it one of the most highly anticipated 'local derbies' in years.

Once again, Jimmy was giving away weight. Officially Scott was seven pounds heavier but by fight time it was certainly much more than that. Nevertheless, Jimmy stormed into him from the opening bell. Scott kept his cool and came back with brutal body punches. The pace was blistering as they tore into each other, with no quarter asked or given. Eventually Scott's extra weight told, and he won on a referee's stoppage in the ninth round. Jimmy pissed blood for several days afterwards. Losing to Scott was certainly no disgrace: he later fought several world champions and beat the ferocious American contender Rubin 'Hurricane' Carter, which shows how good he was. At least Jimmy's younger brother made a successful pro debut as a welterweight on the same bill. Joe knocked around with us now and was a chip off the same block.

Despite the Scott defeat, Jim Swords continued to top the bill every time he boxed. He had charisma, he went forward all the time, in fact he was a bit of a god in Manchester. In January 1965, he won an eliminator for the British middleweight title when he outpointed Willie Hart at the Free Trade Hall. He was warned early on for butting (again) but pulled away with a big effort in the last few rounds. The win put him next in line for a title shot against the champion, Wally Swift of Nottingham, and a bout between them was pencilled in for November. The money and glory that he had trained so hard for was now within reach.

First, however, Jimmy accepted a warm-up bout against Johnny Cooke. It was a mistake: Cooke was a classy boxer who had fought more than forty times and had miles more experience. His style was just not right for Jimmy, who lost on points. The British title fight was cancelled and his chance slipped away. Disappointed, Jimmy made a poor show against Nat Jacobs for the Central Area title, then lost his next two bouts after that. A year that had promised so much turned lousy. We all thought JS was going to win a title, but it was not to be. Today he would be a world champion, no question, but in those days you couldn't fight for a title after only twelve or fourteen fights. And his manager, Jack Edwards, did not bring him on the way he should have. Jim was often left to his own devices to get up and do his own roadwork. The only time Edwards saw him was in the gym sparring.

*

WHILE JS CONCENTRATED on his boxing, I was the first of the market lads to make my mark in business. Working in the building trade for a Birmingham-based company called North Worcestershire Construction, I hustled and bustled and, within a year, I bought them out. I was too ambitious and independent to work for other people for long, I had to be in charge of my own destiny, and with my natural aptitude for dealmaking, the business took off like a rocket. By the mid-sixties, I had thirty men working seven days a week on one job alone, at the ICI plant at Runcorn. Rita and I were able to move from our bedsit to a little terraced house in Openshaw, then to another, more modern house in the same area. I bought the freehold of a grocer's store with a flat above it and ran my business from there, while Rita ran the shop. Jimmy did the same for his wife. In 1964, our son Tony was born, and the following year he was joined by a brother, Dominic. Rita now had her hands full with two babies and a shop, while I went on the money trail.

My firm built the Comet discount electrical stores and demolished many of the pits in Scotland for the National Coal Board. The miners had previously had to go down the lift shaft to a storage room to get a new light bulb, battery or helmet and it became impractical, so in the end Lord Robens, the chairman, designed a new storage facility in Alloa and scrapped everywhere else – and we got the work to do it. Steel shelving was replacing wooden shelving and I was in at the beginning of that too. We worked for United Glass, Coventry Climax, in fact lots of major firms. I had a six-year stretch when I was a straight businessman, and I made money hand over fist. In the late sixties I was able to buy my first house outright, in Miles Platting, for £800 cash. I was also going out every night. Manchester had the best nightlife in Europe, and I threw myself into it full on.

5

CLUBLAND

MANCHESTER WAS A mecca for clubs in the fifties and sixties. It had cabaret bars and spielers, supper clubs and afternoon drinkers, gambling dens and late-night dives, and hundreds of pubs. Listed under the letter 'A' alone were the Astor, the Abdullah, the Athanaeum, the AG Club, the Auto Club, Annabelles, the Arizona, Ali Baba's, the Afrique and Amigos, and they are just the ones I can remember. Live music was the norm and every decent venue had a resident band. The musicians rarely received the kudos of more glamorous, pop-orientated bands but were every bit as good, with top-quality jazz, beat, soul, ballads, skiffle, jive and even reggae. The city's nightlife was second to none.

Certain licensing rules were meant to be observed. Pubs had to close at 3 p.m., then opened again at teatime and could serve until 10.30 or 11 at night. Night clubs were permitted to open until 2 a.m. provided that cooked meals were served: a chip butty often sufficed. Most clubs were members-only and had to keep a signing-in book. Many had gambling tables, as the gaming laws were a grey area. Casino gaming officially became legal in 1960 but the law was poorly regulated and large numbers of villains were attracted to the club industry. The Gaming Act of 1968 tightened things up but numerous illicit spielers remained in operation.

Among the cream of the city's venues was the Cromford Club, just around the corner from the Wilton, where Jimmy and I had been arrested. Owned by two tough, dapper guys, Owen Ratcliffe and Paddy McGrath, the Cromford had a casino and a restaurant, featured the top acts of the day and was the place to be seen. Its clientele included everyone from Matt Busby to high-ranking police officers, judges, surgeons, newspaper columnists and politicians. The doorman, an ex-boxer called Shep, was a pal of ours and when we first got married Rita and I would dine there every Saturday night and watch the show. Owen Ratcliffe later branched out and opened a club called Mr Smith and the Witchdoctor in Catford, south London. Two gangs of local heavies had a dispute over who was 'minding' the place and in March 1966 it was the scene of a fatal gangland battle between the Richardson and Haward clans and their associates. Dickie Hart was killed and Eddie Richardson, 'Mad' Frankie Fraser and several others were badly injured. The affray ultimately led to the downfall of the Richardson gang, many of whom received long jail terms the following year. Whatever happened down there, the Cromford in Manchester was a high-class establishment and rarely saw trouble.

Les Simms, who I had first met in the holding pen at crown court, was another of the best-known club owners. Simmy became a great pal. Hard as nails, he recognised that we were the up-and-coming firm and that, if he played his cards right, he would have us all with him – and he did. His most successful club was Annabelles on Wood Street, off Deansgate, where one of the DJs was a local kid called Dave Lee Travis. Everybody went there: footballers like George Best and Ian Storey Moore, famous actors and personalities from Granada TV, and all of what became known as the Quality Street Gang. Les also had the Normandy, a late club where the VIPs from Annabelles went after it closed; in those days you did not find many places still open at 4 a.m. The Theatre Club, which Les had with Roy Copeland, was another moneymaker serving late afternoon drinkers and the racing mob. He also opened a seafood restaurant called Simms and bought a fabulous place called the Kersal Cell, a fifteenth century manor house where Oliver Cromwell had once slept, which he made into a restaurant and disco. He went on to buy what was left of Belle Vue, the famous sporting venue, and I partnered him there in the eighties to promote boxing and dinner shows. Les became a Manchester legend.

Dougie Welsby, another hard man, worked with Les. Dougie had the Queens Club, first in Queen Street and later in Chinatown. He was a very straight owner and had his own ways. He would not have bad language in the place, and everything had to be just right. He always drank gin and tonic with a slice of lemon and if he went in a bar and they had no lemon, out he walked.

Joe Plant was another larger-than-life character. He came from showman stock and was related to the Silcocks fairground family by marriage. Joe had boxed in the booths and could more than look after himself. He opened Chez Joey, a classy joint with red flock wallpaper and expensive fittings. Tony Hulme, who went on to work for me, was his compere while Billy Ingham manned the door. Billy looked the part, with a big chiv scar down his face, and was a bit like the well-known heavy John Nash at the Astor in London: people went there to see him, not the owner.

I was in Chez Joey one night when in walked Billy Two Rivers, a well-known Canadian wrestler with a Mohawk hairstyle who was often billed as the 'Last of the Mohicans'. He was a bit worse for wear and had a go at some of the staff. Billy Ingham told him to cool it, so Two Rivers told him to fuck off. Billy tried everything with him but Two Rivers kept going on until Billy hit him over the head with a champagne bottle. There was murder. Two Rivers' pals, all wrestlers, later threatened to come in the club to sort out Billy. Instead, after a few words from the right people, Two Rivers went back to Canada and wasn't seen again. The incident was very much a one-off, as there was rarely trouble in Chez Joey; Joe Plant would not stand for it.

Wrestling was popular then and a lot of club owners dabbled in it, in fact the wrestling mob were a bit of a mini mafia in their own right: 'Big' Bill Benny owned the Cabaret Club, Billy Kerfoot took it on after him, and Jack Dillon owned the Lonsdale Club, all wrestlers. Billy Kerfoot eventually had a string of clubs. He sold one to the Moss brothers, who owned clubs in Stockport, on condition that he would not open a rival venue nearby, but then went ahead and opened Ocean's Eleven on Upper Brook Street, in breach of their agreement. The Moss brothers gave him some grief and it turned nasty. As a result, Billy approached me and asked me to burn down the club he had sold them. He knew I was up for most things, provided there was something in it for me.

I knew the club in question, in fact Jim Swords had battered the doorman there, a well known character called Big Mick Duffy. Not long after, the club was indeed badly damaged by a mysterious fire. Billy Kerfoot then opened a casino. I went to see him there with my wife, expecting a bit of wages, but he mugged me off with a pint of Guinness and some casino chips. I was furious. It was a bad night all round: I skidded on black ice on the way home, crashed the car and Rita went through the windscreen and nearly died. She had thirty stitches across her forehead and later needed plastic surgery.

A while later, I went to Kerfoot's Cabaret Club. The doorman said we had to pay fifty pence to get in. This was the last straw. 'You have got to be joking,' I said. 'Go and get Bill Kerfoot.'

When he arrived, I grabbed him by the hair and his wig came off. It was comical really. Eventually he extended the olive branch and that ended any problem between us. His wife later ran off with a policeman, of all people, and all his money.

Another place I called in at a lot was the Stork Club on Mosley Street, owned by Eli Rose, a big gambler. It was a private members' club but was easy enough to get in. All the faces went there, as it opened late, and there were always bits you could earn. Over the years some of its doormen would be on our 'firm', including 'Wingy' Jimmy Lyth and Tommy Tarby, while George Derbyshire, another rum lad, often sang there. Also on the door was Pat Fallon, who died at the hands of my little pal Albert Gibbons.

Around the corner was another good club, the Chanteclair, run by Ted Barry, who also had the Mancunian Club and the Silver Moon. Pop Fitz, another pal who socialised with us, had a famous fight at the Silver Moon against a half-caste doorman, Ralph Somerville. Ralph wouldn't let Pop in and it kicked off. The Silver Moon was at the end of an alley and they slugged it out all along the alley and all down Shudehill. Pop Fitz, whose real name was Peter Fitzgerald, was a 'take-on': a soft spoken, mild mannered man who, if you crossed him, became a demon. In the same club, I saw Jim Swords hit a steel erector called Johnny Quirke so hard that he literally flew through the air and collapsed through a drum kit on the stage. When JS hit them, they stayed hit.

By now Jimmy was no longer flattening doormen: he didn't need to, as no-one would take him on. Nobody wanted a taste of his knuckles or indeed of 'Freddie', his trusty Gurkha knife. Most of the bouncers instead became our good friends, men like Tommy O'Neill, a barrow boy and former lightweight boxing contender, who worked at Arthur Fox's Revue Bar. Tommy was always the gentleman, whereas the doorman at the Astor Club,

Jimmy Burns, was a lunatic when riled. He carried a newspaper with an axe wrapped up in it and if you upset him you got the 'Evening News', as he put it.

With scores of clubs in little more than a square mile, the city was wide open for our firm. We had made waves for several years as Jimmy took on all the hard men. Now we started to mix with the real players, the men who ran the clubs or who controlled the gambling and fruit machine rackets. We began to mix in higher circles, in which the likes of Simmy, Dougie Welsby and Billy Kerfoot were established players.

One well-known club owner we did not see eye-to-eye with was Dougie Flood, another hard man from the north side of Manchester. I first met Flood in 1965, after I had fallen behind with the payments for a car. It was parked outside my house when a knock came at my door in the early evening. Two men stood there, one of them Flood.

'You Jim Donnelly?'

'Yes.'

He pulled out some papers.

'I have come for the car.'

'Fuck off.'

I picked up a poker from behind the door.

'Listen, there's no trouble,' said Flood. 'We just want the car back. Give us the keys, close your eyes, blink, and it's gone.'

My mind was working overtime.

'Let's go to the nick,' I said. 'If they say what you're doing is legal, then okay.'

I made a quick phone call, then off we went to the local cop shop. The police confirmed that their paperwork was in order and that they had a right to repossess the car, so we returned to my house. Flood looked up and down the empty street.

'What's going on?' he said. 'Where's the car?'

'Blink, it's there, blink, it's gone,' I said. 'Now fuck off.'

Flood went on to open a string of clubs across Greater Manchester and made a fortune. However, he developed a terrible reputation for taking liberties. When he opened Quaffers, at Bredbury Hall in Stockport, in the seventies, one poor feller who straightened out the extensive grounds for him was owed twelve grand, but Flood would not pay. The guy was faced with having his digger repossessed, so on opening night he drove his machine into the foyer, demolishing it. He was charged with malicious damage, got three months in the nick and lost his digger. A similar thing happened at the Broadway Club: the builder got knocked so he took his truck one night and rammed Flood's Rolls-Royce. Flood used to batter his staff if they spoke back to him and once banned the whole of an amateur boxing team from coming in his club for not wearing ties, even though they were fighting in the club that night. He was crackers, but he earned millions. I later bought a house near him and I saw him a lot around the town but never said hello.

Jim Swords hated him. One night we were at a boxing dinner at the Piccadilly Hotel put on by Alan Kay, a casino owner and fight promoter who formed the Anglo-American Sporting Club with Micky Duff and Jarvis Astaire, when JS spotted Dougie Flood at the next table.

'That cunt over there is going to spoil my night,' he said. 'I want to batter him.'

Once the meal was served and we were about to eat, Jimmy got a pea on a spoon and flicked it at the back of Flood's head. Childish, I know, but that's how we were sometimes. Flood ignored it, so he did it again. Flood must have known that this was a direct challenge and that Jimmy was responsible, but he said nothing. After the meal, Flood got up and walked out. We thought he had gone for a piss but he never came back for the boxing.

His three children later fought a bitter contest over his £14 million will. One of them declared in court that their dad had been a member of the Quality Street Gang and was a gangster. Well, he never was with the QSG and he was no gangster either. He was a bully and a tough guy, a rich one at that. An equally untrue claim about Flood is that he was a part of a group of Manchester heavies who chased the Kray twins out of Manchester. The story goes that they were met at Piccadilly Station, told they were not wanted in the city and were put on the next train out. What a load of cobblers.

The myth grew out of a real incident. In the mid-sixties, the Krays were involved in bringing the former boxing champion Joe Louis to the UK for a tour. The old Brown Bomber, one of the greatest ever, was paid to meet-and-greet at clubs and casinos to help attract custom. The Krays were invited to bring him to Manchester by a Jewish kid, 'Diamond' Joe Marlow, who ran the casino at the Piccadilly Club for Alan Kay. A photo survives of the trip and shows Ronnie and Reggie posing with Joe Louis, the London gangster Joey Pyle, his partner Alex Steene, Joe Marlow and Nat Basso, who became a famous boxing MC. They booked into the Midland Hotel, then went out to the Piccadilly, where Diamond Joe had laid on a private party. Afterwards they had a walk around the town. They visited the Portland Lodge, where the doorman was Andy Partington, the guy involved in the infamous fight with Jim Swords and me at the Wilton Club in 1962. Partington apparently said something and Reggie Kray flattened him, which made me laugh when I heard about it: Reggie didn't know he had done us a favour.

We were in the Cabaret Club when a couple of club owners

made phone calls to pass on the message that this heavy-duty
Cockney firm was in town and to stick about in case of trouble. I
had briefly met the Krays when I stayed at the Majestic Hotel in
north London in the early sixties. It was next door to the
Glengarry Hotel, which they were said to have an interest in. I had
no beef with them, but we told the club owners no problem, we
would be about if needed.

I later did some work with Joe Marlow and he told me that he
heard the 'Jim Swords firm' was on standby that night – we were
not yet known as the Quality Street Gang. He was right, but there
was no team of villains against the Krays, no meeting at the train
station, no ultimatum. Instead they were confronted by the police,
who told them to behave themselves and that they were being
watched. They left the city peacefully the next day.

The Krays were finally brought down by the Metropolitan
Police in 1968. Ronnie and Reggie got life and never saw the
outside again, except when they were let out for funerals. To set
the record straight, the fact is they would never have gotten a hold
in the clubs or indeed in any illegal activities in Manchester. Of
course they were very dangerous men, and could have a fight, but
man-to-man, either or both, with or without tools, they could
never in a million years have beaten Jim Swords.

Alan Kay, who hosted them, was known as 'the man who
broke the bank at Monte Carlo', apparently because he did. A
charismatic person, he owned a string of casinos and clubs with a
guy called Melvyn Davies. They staged shows every month at the
Piccadilly Hotel and also put on concerts at the Poco-a-Poco, a
former cinema outside Stockport where the likes of David Bowie
performed. In those days nowhere, not even London, had the
nightlife we had in Manchester. Alan earned fortunes but was a
prolific gambler: I saw him lose twenty grand in one night, and

that was in the early seventies. His minder was Butch Lyons, a very tough man from a big family from the Hulme/Moss Side area. Alan turned out to be a good pal and gave me a lot of advice. Once, when I was in trouble and wanted by the police, I called into a casino and was having a snack when he came over with Sandy Busby, Sir Matt's son, another gambler. He stuck a grand in my hand and wished me well. Alan is still talked about in Manchester and rightly so.

His partner in the Buckingham Club was another great gambler, Cladinoro Sadotti, known to all as Sid Otty. Sid was George Best's mentor; they went everywhere together for years. People do not know that George was as much a gambler as an alcoholic: he used to do in his dough gambling and then get pissed. He once did four after-dinner spots in Manchester, got paid twelve grand, then turned up back at Sid's spieler having blown the lot. He had to sleep on Sid's couch because he couldn't pay his hotel bill.

Clubland was a magnet for the city's football players. Manchester United and City were both enjoying success at the time and the stars of the day were often in our company. That did not go down well with some of their managers. One night, a crowd of us were in the Cabaret Club with the City player Tony Coleman, who won championship and FA Cup winners' medals. Tony was quite a feisty lad and liked a drink. In walked Malcolm Allison, who was then City's assistant manager. Allison was loud and brash, and to be honest few people liked him, unless they were diehard Blues and did not know him personally. When he saw his player drinking, he went into a rage, effing and blinding and telling him to get out of the club. Jim Swords stepped in.

'He is with us,' he said. 'Don't speak to him like that. If anybody leaves here it will be you.'

Allison was a cocky so-and-so and did not take kindly to being put down in front of one of his players. 'I'm not frightened of you,' he said.

So JS told him the facts of life. It was not the time or place for anything to happen but Jimmy said, 'Listen, you cunt, I will meet you tomorrow anywhere you want. On the centre spot at Maine Road if you fancy it. Now fuck off.'

The next day a phone call was made and an apology passed on to Jimmy. Mysteriously Coleman and his drinking habit did later hit the newspapers. Someone with a grudge had obviously leaked in to the press.

JIMMY REMAINED THE biggest crowd-puller in Manchester boxing until the end of his career. He never got that elusive title shot but he did fight five men who at one time or another were British champions: Johnny Cooke, Les McAteer, Johnny Pritchett, Bunny Sterling and Wally Swift. For me he was beating McAteer until he fell through the ropes, which were loose. He struggled to get back into the ring and the ref counted him out. It was a liberty; they should have allowed him to get back in. He also should have won the decision in at least one of his fights with Cooke. He had a real dingdong against the Danish world title contender Tom Bogs and put him down in the second round, only to lose on a cut. In all, he had a great career, but not much luck.

When he wasn't training, he started working at Sid O'Brien's car pitch on Hyde Road during the day. He soon wanted his own business, so Sid advised him and he opened his own pitch on Great Ancoats Street. I started to buy all my company vehicles from him to help him out, and other friends did the same. That would be his bedrock for the next twenty years or so.

Jimmy also developed a sideline settling disputes between various factions. We knew a lot of volatile characters, and often they would fall out with each other for some ridiculous reason or other. The next thing, they would be at war. Jimmy's role was to give advice and, if necessary, say that heads would be knocked together if they did not resolve their differences amicably. In one case, the Lyons family had a legendary punch-up with a young Ancoats firm, the Barlow brothers, who had just turned pro boxers. People were hurt on both sides. They all became pals and shook hands after a few of us got involved and arranged a truce. Quite a bit of that went on and it became more of a private thing on Jimmy's part. He was the key man. He would go in and settle things but made sure he got paid in return. 'Put me on the earn,' he would say. He did that for years. For example, in the eighties a wealthy Iranian friend of ours owned an upmarket club in Mayfair, London, called Blondes, which was fronted by George Best. Our friend's partners tried to take the club off him, so JS was brought in to sort it out. The partners ended up leaving rather than our pal, and Jimmy was rewarded with a Rolls-Royce for his trouble.

Eventually, people who wanted to do all sorts of deals came to JS first. He might respond, 'It's not for me, but have a word with so-and-so.' Then if they did the deal, JS was in the middle all the way. Through this he had his share of many things. With him involved, both sides would be too afraid to rip each other off or grass each other up, so things went smoothly.

Violence was always a last resort with us, but when needed it was swift and brutal. Big Frank Platt, our pal from the Market Mob, now ran a building site for me, while in the evenings he was a doorman at the Regency Club. I got the needle with him over some job expenses, so on a Friday night I tooled up with a hammer wrapped in a bandage and went to the Regency to find him. Another doorman let me in and I went upstairs into the bar. It was not yet ten-thirty and still quiet. Jim Swords was in and bought me a drink.

'You look a bit serious,' he said. 'What's wrong?'

'I've come to speak with Frank,' I said.

He shouted Frank over.

'I am out of this Frank,' he said. 'You had better speak to the Weed.'

I told Frank straight he was bilking me on expenses. He started laughing.

'Fuck me, Jimmy, I thought it was something bad. Here, I've got a bank bag I have been saving for you.'

He handed me the bag and I looked inside. There was £150.

That settled things between us, but I still had the hump. As chance would have it, at that moment three people came into the bar. I knew one of them, Vinnie Hamilton, a barrow boy. Vinnie was one of seven brothers, a couple of whom were in the nick for slashings. People were scared of the Hamiltons. Vinnie, in a jokey way, gave me a smack on the back of the head as he walked past. It was not a serious smack but he did it to the wrong person at the wrong time. I pulled out my bandaged hammer and hit him on the head with a terrible thud. He fell back and I was on him, while Jim Swords moved in to stop anyone from interfering.

I left Vinnie in a bad way. Jimmy gave me a lift home and I calmed down but we both knew there would be comebacks. So at noon the next day, Jimmy was at my house.

'Come on,' he said, 'let's go to the pub and see if they want some more. I've brought "Freddie" with me.' He pulled out his massive Gurkha knife.

We sat in my local, the Little George, for an hour but no-one said a word. On the following Monday, I called in again for a beer with my pal Brendan Withers. He was tooled up and I was armed with a little surprise of my own. We ordered drinks, then I heard a voice.

'Hey you, you little cunt.'

I turned around. Vinnie Hamilton was sat there, his head bandaged like a mummy.

'I have had twenty-seven stitches,' he said. 'Now fucking get outside, I have got something for you.'

Nobody else in the pub said a word as we stepped outside. From inside his coat, Vinnie brandished a length of metal wrapped in some sort of material.

'You're getting this,' he snarled.

Not likely. I pulled out a Beretta handgun and let a shot go into the air.

'No, Jimmy,' said Vinnie, holding up his hands. 'You're crazy. Let's leave it out.'

I told him I was sorry, that I'd had the hump with Frank Platt and it was unfortunate that he was on the receiving end, but it had to end now. We went back in the pub and it was over. We became friends and remained so until he sadly died of cancer. His son is a good man and a friend to this day.

EVEN WITH A thriving construction company, I found myself with time on my hands. Though I might travel for a couple of days to a building site somewhere, once I had made sure the lads had a van, expenses, tools for the job and their design drawings, there was not much more to do. My brother Arthur ran most of the sites, while my other brother John ran the offices in Booth Street. The excitement of doing deals was more appealing to me than the chores of day-to-day management.

The business brought me into contact with some of the London mob, mainly through an Ancoats lad I knew who had fled to the capital in fear of his life. Bert 'Cert' Davis had worked as a night man for McFisheries in Smithfield Market. Most of the fish companies sold poultry too, and one Christmas an enforcer called Ray Vickers and the armed robber Terry Jeffreys informed Bert that he was going to be tied up and robbed of the yuletide stock of turkeys and chickens. They said he would not get hurt if he kept his mouth shut. Bert did not like the idea but what could he do? On the night, they went in, tied up Bert and loaded a wagon with stolen food. Vickers then decided to hit Bert over the head a couple of times to make it look realistic. Poor Bert ended up in hospital. From then on he was mortally terrified of Ray and got a move with his firm to Finsbury Park, to be away from Manchester.

I hooked up with Bert when I stayed on Seven Sisters Road on company business. He was a funny man and could get on with anybody. Through him I got to know a few 'faces' around the Blackstock Road and Finsbury Park area, including Ronnie and Reggie Kray, as well as sportsmen like Ken Buchanan, who became the world lightweight boxing champion, Bobby Arthur, who was a British champion, and Dick Plume, who played football for Millwall. Bert also delivered fish to the stables where Frankie Durr was head jockey. Since jockeys were not allowed to put on bets, Frankie would give Bert brown-envelope money to have a punt for him and would share tips. Bert started wiring money up to me to put on the horses or phoning with the tips – hence why we called him 'Bert the Cert'. We made a few bob together.

Gambling was also rife in the clubs and here I seized on another opportunity. Most of the gaming tables were not owned by the clubs but were concessions: a third party would buy the right to set up the games and take what was called 'the mains', which was about ten per cent of each winning pot. I started to do deals to put my own tables and card dealers into the clubs. There was a fair bit of violence involved. If someone already had a sixty-forty deal with their local club and I stepped in and offered the owner fifty-fifty, there would be trouble. Jim Swords and the lads came in handy on those occasions. There could also be trouble with the punters, even ones I knew well. Chopper McGarrick was notorious for kicking over the table and trying to snatch back his money if he lost; you could not keep him down no matter what you hit him with.

The undercurrent of violence in the spielers, or illegal gambling dens, was something you had to live with. Tommy Harrold, later to be my partner in a nightclub, and Ronnie Muir, who was Jim Swords' brother-in-law, owned the Rooster drinking club, and I went in there one afternoon to see who was running the concession for the card table, as I was interested in taking it over. After talking to Tommy, I sat down to have a game.

There were some heavy people at the table, including Mick Lennon from Cheetham Hill, his pal Jim White, and Danny Fielding, who had just finished a long sentence. Danny, a Manchester United nut, was quite friendly with Bobby Charlton, who used to write to him in the nick. He was a game man and well respected.

I had been playing for about an hour when I spotted that one of the men was palming cards.

'Is this guy with you?' I asked Mick Lennon.

'Yes, he is.'

This put me in an awkward position. I did not want to fall out with Mick. He was a big man and in a fistfight I would have had no chance. You would have to shoot him to beat him. But I could not just sit there and get fucked. I waited until the card sharp had a pile of money in front of him, then leant over and grabbed it with my left hand. As he bent forward to protect it, I hit him with my right. The table went up in the air and money flew everywhere. Danny Fielding grabbed me and pulled me out of the way while everybody else was busy trying to snatch back their readies. In the melee, we slipped out of a fire door.

'Don't worry,' Danny said, when I explained why I had done it. 'I will ring Mick tomorrow and tell him what happened. He wouldn't have known about the guy who was at it. Mick is not like that. He will probably give the geezer a crack himself.'

True to his word, Danny rang me the next day and confirmed Mick had not known what was going on and now had the needle with the other feller. Mick also asked would I go in the club again, as he had finished up with more from the floor than he had started out with. For years after, we would laugh about it. 'You have got some bottle, Jimmy,' Mick used to say. 'There must have been ten of us and you still kicked the table over.'

My love of gambling proved to be my downfall. I played everything: poker, blackjack, dice, roulette, the horses, the dogs. Though I was earning probably a grand a week, a lot of money in the sixties, it went as fast as I made it. I frequented not just the top clubs like the Portland and the Cabaret but also the spielers, many of them run by Greeks. The most 'in' place of all was Deno's, one of the great clubs, with a floor show every night. All the firm went in there a few nights a week and got VIP treatment. The owner, Denos Kitromilides, was a Greek Cypriot involved in clubs with his brothers, Panos and Takis. Denos famously refused entry to Mick Jagger of the Rolling Stones for not wearing a tie. They were a great family, very well liked, and the club was a place you could relax with the wife or girlfriend – and lose a lot of money.

Inevitably the gambling put an intolerable strain on my finances. My bank manager was a fellow called Mitchell. He had stupidly advised me that, because I was driving around the country so much, I should get a bigger company car. So I bought a brand new XJ6 as soon as they came out. I owed the bank fourteen grand, which was a lot then, and I was in no hurry to pay it back. Now Mitchell began to feel the strain. There was an advert on TV at the time in which someone opened a broom cupboard and out came a bank manager saying, 'Can I help you?' One of the firm joked to me, 'I've just seen Mitchell, he's gone fucking grey with the grief you've caused him. He didn't jump out of the broom cupboard, he fell out!'

I was so busy being a night-time fellow that I took my eye off the ball, delegating the running of the construction business to my brothers. I eventually had to put up the deeds to my house as collateral and ended up losing it to the bank. Rita and I moved into a Corporation house in Ancoats. In 1968, my brother John took over the business and bought me out, as by then I was desperately short of money. I fell out with him for a while over it, but in truth I was not cut out for spending seven days a week on building sites.

So by the late sixties, I was at a crossroads. At the same time, Jim Swords' boxing career was coming to an end. He had his last fight in March 1969, in South Africa, and retired at just twenty-six years old. Of the fights he lost, eight were to either British, Irish or European champions. Had he been handled and trained better, he would have gone much further in his career and today he would have been a champion, no question.

Jimmy now became lethal in his dealings. Money was his god. He took over a car pitch on Great Ancoats Street and had also acquired several barrows selling fruit and veg. Joe Swords loaned me some money and I got a barrow too with my pal Denis Crolla on Tib Street. I ended up with four barrows and JS with seven or eight. We just marched in and that was the end of it; stallholders who had been selling fruit on certain pitches for fifty years had no choice but to move over. Nobody said a word. I even put one in Cheetham Hill village, the first one there. The local shopkeepers moaned but it was on private land, so they couldn't stop it. Then I put two by the gates to Alexandra Park in Moss Side. I worked them for about three years and they kept me in spending money but eventually I felt the return I was getting did not justify the work I put in, so I got rid of all but one, which exclusively sold mushrooms. That was daily cash.

Around this time, my outlook changed. I met some older guys, men like Stan Ritchie, Jimmy Coulter and Wally Downs, and started planning a different future. Stan Ritchie was known as the 'old master' and was an experienced safeblower. He sometimes worked with Wally McNelly, my pal from Strangeways Prison. Stan showed me diagrams of safes and told me what tools to use to open them. In those days there were no battery-operated drills, so if you wanted to do any drilling you had to tap into the electrics. Jimmy Coulter was the brains: we called him 'the teacher' or 'the doctor'. A motor dealer by trade, which was the next best thing to robbing banks in those days, he knew where to put money, what to do and what not to do. If you found yourself on trial he would sit in court, observe and tell you how to play it. A wise man.

Coulter was great pals with Wally Downs, another great villain out of Ancoats. Wally was the real thing: he dressed in Savile Row suits and carried a nine-millimetre Browning in a shoulder holster. I first came across him when he was palling about with Davie Wilson from Glasgow; they both got ten years for blowing a post office safe in Longsight. He later got eighteen years with Terry

Jeffreys for jewellery robberies. His last sentence was eight years, topped up to twelve because he was on parole at the time. When he wasn't in jail, Wally lived a lot of his life in London and a crowd of us began to travel down there on the train for the boxing, the Ali fights and such, then go on to the clubs.

Jim Swords and I still had our market pals but we drifted into this new circle. I was getting educated, turning from a young tearaway to a serious villain, still getting money straight but looking for the right time to do a bit of villainy. I had been a thief since childhood. Now, nearing my thirties, I faced a choice. I could choose a life of crime, with all the risks and rewards that entailed, or I could go straight and put myself at the mercy of a system that I felt was stacked against people with my background and temperament. To be frank, the former was more attractive to me than the latter. In the event, I did both. For the next thirty years or so, I would simply go where my nature took me.

One Sunday afternoon, a pal rang to see if I would lend him a car, as he wanted to look at a 'bit of work'. He had been with me since we were sixteen and I trusted him.

'Okay,' I said, 'but be careful.'

I was going out for a few drinks, so I left the car keys with my wife.

Later on that day I met my pal, Brendan Withers. He told me he and a friend had screwed a shop, Avery Scales, and had taken some expensive weighing scales. I was stunned when he told me that not only had they used my car but also they had driven it back to my terraced house, unloaded the scales in my yard and hidden them in the old outside loo, which we never used. I gave Brendan a bollocking for putting me in this position but the damage was done. When I got home that night, Rita was in a state. A neighbour had seen my pals in the alleyway at the back of the house and had phoned the police. They had been round, found the scales and taken them away. She said they were coming back to see me. I was in it.

I was arrested and charged with handling £10,000-worth of stolen scales. I pleaded not guilty and went before Manchester Crown Court. My defence was that somebody had got the wrong house and had hidden the scales in my toilet by mistake. My pals were sick that they had put me in it but said they had nowhere to put the gear. The damage was done. I was more embarrassed than anything else: it was not professional at all.

I was convicted and received a suspended sentence. I was lucky. I think the judge half believed me that somebody dumped the gear in my yard, and Avery got their scales back. My pals paid all my court costs and a bit more. I let them off and told them in future to leave me out. Brendan Withers stayed with me for forty years looking after the construction side of my business and paid me back many times.

That summer, we travelled abroad for a holiday. Denis Crolla and I stole a caravan, hired a mobile home, hooked up the box and off we went, two families. After a month or two we headed back, leaving the caravan in Calais on a campsite. A month later, we got a call from the owner of the site. He wanted to know if the caravan was for sale. That was it, we were in the caravan business.

Temptation was the one thing I found hard to resist. I saw my future. I was going to earn money, whatever it took.

6

THE QUALITY STREET GANG

THE GROUP THAT became known as the Quality Street Gang began to gather together around 1967, when I was twenty-seven. A band of eight or ten close friends became twenty, then thirty. Most of us had known each other for years. Some were straight businessmen, some were rogues, some were a mixture of the two, leaning more in one direction or the other depending on circumstance or opportunity. Many had backgrounds in similar occupations: the markets, car sales, scrap metal, door security. We could all look after ourselves and some were very hard men indeed.

At heart, we were a bunch of mates, many from the Ancoats area, who both enjoyed each other's company socially and had dealings together in business. Really, that is all there was to it. We were not a 'gang' in the usual sense. There was no initiation, no membership, no hierarchy and no rules. In fact, had it not been for the jokey comment one night which gave us our name, I do not think we would ever have been labelled a gang at all. A better word to describe us might be 'network': the QSG was a web of interlocking and mutually beneficial friendships between men from poor backgrounds who were trying to make something of themselves. Outwardly, we appeared little different from any other group of blokes out on the town: a few more flat noses and scars, perhaps. We even had our own Sunday football team for a while, known simply as the QSG. But our bonds were deeper than normal. In a sense, we felt it was us against the world.

The original core of our little band consisted of no more than a dozen men, many of immigrant descent. Perhaps that was why we felt like outsiders. There was Jim and Joe Swords, both Ancoats Irish; Vinnie and Louis Schiavo, Ancoats Italian; Joe Leach, Ancoats Italian; Mick Brown, English from a Cockney father; Denis Crolla, Ancoats Italian; Jack Trickett, English; Jimmy Riley, Ancoats Irish; and me, Jimmy Donnelly, Wythenshawe Irish adopted by Ancoats. A younger face who came along a little later was another Ancoats lad, Ricky Gore.

The leader – figurehead might be a better word – was undoubtedly Jim Swords. We gathered around Jimmy. He is a great example of why the police and press misunderstood the QSG. Jimmy was not a thief. He was first a market lad, then a professional boxer, then a stallholder, then a successful car dealer and finally a property developer. He made money legitimately, if you could call the car game in those days legitimate, and invested it shrewdly. Yes, he had a criminal record, but mainly for fighting when he was younger. He did not rob banks, demand protection money or sell drugs. He was simply his own man, living not by society's rules but by his own. 'Jim,' he once said to me, 'even if you are wrong, you are right. So what are we all about? There is no wrong.' It was his way of saying, never complain, never explain.

Jimmy also used to say, 'Never put a mug before your family,' and his closest companion was his brother Joe. They looked alike and as a pair they were a bit like the Kray twins: two ex-boxers who could fight for fun and took absolutely no crap off anyone. They reminded me of the Krays in another way, in that they could both wind each other up or calm each other down, depending on their moods. I did not meet Joe until he was sixteen, as he had spent a lot of his childhood in approved schools and borstals. We eventually became great pals and would share in many ventures. Joe was utterly trustworthy, a deep thinker and a dangerous man if he had to be.

Vinnie and Louis Schiavo were also brothers. We met in the late sixties, when my construction company was on a site in Stockport facing Alan Kay's Poco-a-Poco club, where they were working as electricians. We gelled. Vinnie and Louis had a more stable upbringing than most of us, as their family ice cream business was one of the best-known in Little Italy. They were both tall, slim men, and very fit. Louis was madcap while Vinnie was more formal, a plotter and a planner, a cool head. Their dad, Carmen, was a lovely, generous man. In the late sixties, when I was having money problems, he would send an envelope over to my house with a tenner in it; I would see him in the pub at night and have to force it back on him.

Joe Leach was Italian on his mother's side: her maiden name was Rossi. Joe was a harum-scarum type and totally fearless. He had never bothered much with school but he had a sharp mind and great ideas. Joe could figure out things, ways around what we were trying to do. His younger brother, Peter, who we called 'Peter Perfect' because he didn't drink or smoke, later married one of Rita's sisters, so we became brothers-in-law by marriage. Completing the Italian contingent was Denis Crolla, from another big Ancoats family. He and I would work very closely together over the years; we were almost a firm within 'the firm'.

Jimmy Riley was one of the original market lads, having worked on a flower stall. He was only five foot seven but powerfully built – we later nicknamed him Urko after the gorilla general in *Planet of the Apes* – and he could fight. Jimmy was always beautifully dressed and later had his eyes lasered and his teeth fixed. He even went for elocution lessons. He could sell snow to the Eskimos and was very astute. He went into the scrap metal business in a big way, was in that job for twenty years and made a fortune.

Jack Trickett was about ten years older than most of us. He had boxed on the booths as a lad and worked as milkman, delivering to clubs and restaurants in the city, when I was a market boy. He also worked for a car sales business on City Road and eventually went into the motor trade on his own, financed by a wealthy Stockport family, the Dignams. Jack was a boxing enthusiast and met us in the early sixties through following Jim Swords' career, like a lot of car traders. A straight businessman, he had an endearing personality and was great company.

Mick Brown, on the other hand, was a criminal: a proper, hands-on robber. His father was a London gangster who had had an affair and Mick was the result. Safes, tie-ups, country houses, you name it, he knocked them off. He worked with a kid nicknamed 'Silent Night' and they burgled countless places. Mick was a big fellow, six foot two, and a bit deep. He was one of the few from outside Ancoats to be on the firm from day one.

Those guys and myself were, I suppose, the 'inner circle'. Most of our dealings with each other were on the level. If I needed money for a new business, I would go to one of the lads rather than to the bank. By the same token, if I had money, one of them might be launching a business or have a deal that I could invest in. We trusted each other and backed each other. We stood united, one for all and all for one, out to make our mark in the world together. Between us we would develop a wide and lucrative range of interests, from market stalls to pubs and clubs, land, property, car sales, scrap metal, boxing, entertainment and security. And yes, in my case, criminality too.

Standing with us was a much wider ring of close friends and acquaintances. On any given night there might be thirty or more of what we called 'the firm' out together. The likes of Les Simms and Billy Ingham, who were older and already established in the city, rightly saw us as the next generation, and knew if they got on board with us it would strengthen them too. Others who were always with us included faces like Ronnie Earl, Jimmy Lythe, Mark Klapish, Dessie O'Connor, 'Paki' Pete Khan, Ray Parry, Honey Boy Zimba, Frank Laws, Mick 'the Golly' Friend, Jimmy 'the Liar' McDonald, Sean Kenny, Sean Nugent, Stuart Codling, Alf Osbiston and 'London' Ronnie Baker. Each of these guys could write a book on his own, they lived such varied and interesting lives.

Ronnie Earl was a pub owner around the Piccadilly area, a handsome man who had been a chief petty officer in the Navy. He opened a boozer in Chinatown with a private bar upstairs, perfect for us to meet and talk away from prying eyes. For years it was our unofficial office. Ronnie was later my partner in a massage parlour and a night club. Micky Friend was known as 'Golly' because of his permed hair. He was Jewish and a proper car trader, a master at the art of minting up an old banger to look brand new. The Golly eventually emigrated to South Africa, where he stayed for twenty years. He owed JS money, which was why he could not return, but he made a killing out there in the car game.

Paki Pete was an Asian lad who had a small club in Chinatown in the mid-seventies. He never minded you calling him 'Paki'. Pete was a one-off. He always carried a blade and did not give a fuck for anybody. He had a very quick temper that was a little bit much at times but we got on very well and for years he watched my back. He was also good if we needed someone to speak the language when doing deals with members of the Asian community.

Pete was a good earner but he could not keep out of the casinos. I think he is barred from most of them even today.

Frank Laws came from Newcastle way and worked the doors in Manchester. He had a flat nose, wore a wig and was only a little man, but was brave as a lion. He was a face around town for twenty years and he could talk anyone into anything. One of his scams was putting adverts in newspapers offering to sell your car for you, best prices obtained, then he would sell the car and keep the money. He even started getting Rolls-Royces on loan and then selling them on. One day he disappeared from Manchester: too many people were on his case and he fell out with the firm, telling lies. Jimmy Riley set about him in a casino and he got the message.

Honey Boy Zimba was one of the most popular heavyweight wrestlers of the day. From Sierra Leone, he was originally billed as 'Nigel the Wrestler', which didn't quite have the right exotic ring to it. Zimba loved a good time. He was also immensely strong, with muscles on top of muscles, and was famous for his headbutts. Jimmy Riley once hit him over the head with the heavy end of a snooker cue in Jack Trickettt's hotel and the cue splintered like bamboo. Zimba, who was usually very good natured, picked him up and slung him across the room like a rag doll. Jimmy came back with an axe and we had to keep the two of them apart, which wasn't easy. But it was rare for us to fall out among ourselves.

Ray Parry was another straight goer who grew up among us. His dad Tommy, a lovely man known as the 'Gentle Giant', owned pubs and clubs in Salford. The two Seans, Kenny and Nugent, were very tough Irish lads who worked the doors and knew all of the Dublin mob. Another tough lad, Stuart Codling, has been around us socially all his life. A non-drinker and non-smoker, Stuart was a car dealer, owned a couple of night clubs and is now in the insurance business: he owns The Mortgage Point and is a multi-millionaire.

My father, James Donnelly (*left*) with Harry, one of his seven brothers. Notice the size of Dad's hands: he could flatten anyone he hit.

The Donnelly men (*left to right*): my brothers John and Arthur, me and my dad. From humble beginnings, we all did pretty well for ourselves.

A publicity photo of Jim Swords in boxing pose. He fought five British champions and today would have won a title. On the cobbles he was unbeatable.

With my first-born son, Tony, in the mid-sixties. His brother Dominic came along a year later, and I went on the money trail.

On holiday with Rita in Jersey in the sixties. We met and married young and stayed together through thick and thin for more than twenty-five years, until her tragic early death from cancer.

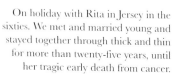

A rare shot of the Quality Street Gang and friends. The two at the back (*from left to right*) are Vinnie 'the Buddha' Carroll and his brother. In the middle are Denis Crolla, Louis Schiavo, Vinnie Schiavo, the comedian Jerry Harris, Tommy Tarby, Jimmy Lythe and Jim Jones. The front row is John Steele, Peter 'Tut-Tut' Walsh, Stan Ritchie, Joe Leach. Jimmy 'the Liar' McDonald and Joe Swords.

Jimmy Riley and Vinnie Schiavo discuss a bit of business. Jimmy made a fortune in scrap metal, while Vinnie's family had a well-known ice cream firm in Ancoats

Joe Leach, the inspiration for the Thin Lizzy song 'Waiting For An Alibi'. Joe was a great pal of Phil Lynott's and many other musicians. He was also a great gambler.

Mick Brown, the illegitimate son of a London gangster and one of the few 'outsiders' on the firm. Mick often worked with a burglar known as 'Silent Night'.

Denis Crolla, my pal and partner in crime. Denis was another Ancoats Italian although his base was Blackpool for many years.

Joe Swords, Vinnie Schiavo and Jim Swords with kids and dog at the car sales lot in Ancoats. Much of our working day revolved around car pitches.

The old school: ex-jailbird Bunny Charles, Bobby Critchley pointing in the middle and the thirty-stone bulk of 'Wingy' Jimmy Lythe. Critch was the original guv'nor of Manchester in the forties and fifties. He befriended us in later years.

(*Left to right*) Dessie O'Connor, who handled my security, Dublin Alan, wrongly arrested with me on suspicion of the murder of a policeman, Jonathan Young, singer with the reformed Bachelors, and the dangerous George Davies, one of my criminal mentors.

Being 'crowned' with a gold disc by Phyllis 'the Godmother' Lynott in her Showbiz bar in Whalley Range. The Showbiz was our second home and the scene of many an all-night drinking session.

Sangrange Motors, one of the QSG car pitches that was put under heavy surveillance by the police. We were usually one step ahead of them.

My breaker's yard, Donnelly Auto Spares, where I had my own method of dealing with customer complaints, involving a one-ton crusher.

With Vinnie Schiavo and Tommy McCarthy in Soho, west London. Tommy, a boxing trainer and club owner, was our introduction to many London underworld characters.

John (*left*), me and Arthur in the seventies. John took over the running of my successful construction firm, while Arthur ran the scrap metal site.

The deadly Rab Carruthers, leader of the Scottish firm based in Manchester. We nearly had a war with them, only to later become friends.

Our even wider circle of close friends included the likes of Tommy Tarby, Ray Mancini, Eddie 'Jaws' Barber, Tommy Dawson, Gino Chiappe, David 'Sundance Kid' Proudfoot, Crazy Horse, Jimmy Jones, Peter 'Tut-Tut' Walsh and Polish Janis. Then there was Bob Spanner, known as 'Bob the Jeweller' because he bought and sold jewellery for a living, as well as working the doors. His pal Jimmy Shaw, an Ardwick heavy with big shoulders, was a safe blower and armed robber but never had any luck: he got fifteen years for a robbery and then two equally long stretches for drugs. A lot of the fellows who knocked about with us were doormen. Peter Tut-Tut worked doors for Les Simms and Dougie Flood, while Johnny Steele, whose nickname was the 'Pink Mouse' – I don't know why – was another doorman for Simmy and also ran the College Club. Polish Janis, who came to the city as a refugee, worked at the ICI as a chemist during the day and as a doorman for the Greeks at night.

Tommy Dawson was known as 'Tommy the Coon', which was not very politically correct but he never seemed to mind. He pulled off a couple of armed robberies and was convicted of one when a witness claimed to be able to identify him from the bottom half of his face, which was partly covered by a mask. He got eight years but on appeal the judge said there was no way he could be recognised from that and overturned his conviction. He later got involved with a transport firm and ended up being embroiled in a drug importation, which led to a few more years inside. Crazy Horse was a big nutter of a doorman who worked for Jack Dillon at the Lonsdale Club. Jimmy Jones was never a villain; he came from a big Irish family and was in the popular Strand Showband in the sixties. He knew all the club owners, hung out with the firm and was a good storyteller. Eddie Barber was a typical fast-talking car trader, if he shook your hand you had to count your fingers, and was always about with us for years.

A lot of tough Salford guys would join us too, men like Ronnie Camilleri and his brother-in-law Brian Swarbrick, Arthur Atkins, Tommy Cunliffe, John Malloy and the Norbury brothers. Brian Swarbrick was a bouncer extraordinaire, he could do the job of any three doormen. Stan Bowles, the footballer, and his brother Steve were also part of our crowd. Stan, a mad gambler, first hung around with us when he was in his teens, living in a corporation flat in Ancoats and playing for Manchester City. He tells of some of his exploits with us in his autobiography, including various scams to rip off betting shops. Stan was especially friendly with Joe Leach and says Joe would 'think nothing of spending £300 a night, which made my twenty pounds a week wages look a bit pathetic'. That is how we were. He goes on to say, 'The QSG became hugely respected in Manchester, and in some ways, they were greater celebrities than the rock stars and footballers they knew and partied with. But they never hurt anyone too badly, and were never arrested for anything major; so I could never understand why they ended up with such a big reputation. However, they were legendary characters, and remain so to this day. Maybe they did something that nobody else knew about ...'

No comment, Stan.

Add to that lot various other footballers, entertainers, actors and musicians who were often in our company, and you have 'the QSG'. We rarely drank in pubs, preferring to meet in hotel cocktail bars, which were more private. Our favourite for a while was the Grand Hotel in Piccadilly. Word would just go out, 'The Grand tonight', and we would gather there, then move on to one of the many clubs whose owners we knew. Wingy Jimmy, who weighed over thirty stone, never moved once he sat down, so he would hold the fort and tell any late arrivals where we had gone. In those days, numerous clubs were within walking distance of each other. We had favourites: the Cabaret, for instance, was always on the walkabout and attracted all the gamblers, the likes of Sid Otty, Sandy Busby, Alan Kay, Melvyn Davies, Kevin Taylor and George Downing, a legendary highroller from Liverpool. George, a wealthy lad from the scrap metal game, often came to Manchester to gamble and was well respected by all.

When we walked into a club, Wingy would have already phoned the door to say we were on our way and the waiters would run over, drinks at the ready. But we were not bullies. We never had a row with management or staff. We did not have to. We did not want the owner's money, we had our own and found it hard to spend what we had. We were waited on and looked after but we did not get paid and we did not ask to be. Protection racketeers were not proper villains to us, going after a man's money who might have been on the pavements to get it, buys a pub and then gets told he has to pay every week. That was not for us, and anybody going at the demand was fucked off good style. The club owners were all friendly anyway. They knew that where we went, there would be no trouble; if there was, the perpetrators would get hurt. The odd mug might be thrown out or given a caution, and if they persisted, they would get a knock on their front door. A final warning when they were sober and on their own with no bravado was usually sufficient.

It would be easy, forty years later, to get the wrong impression about us. We were not some bunch of thugs turning up in clubs, intimidating customers and throwing our weight around. Quite the opposite. There was always fun and laughter in our company and people from all walks of life would join us. Some of the banter might have been a bit rough and ready, but that was us. Louis Schiavo, for instance, was a crackpot who was always fooling about and could cause chaos on a night out. He would think nothing of suddenly grabbing your shirt and ripping it off, or wrestling you to the ground in the middle of a smart club. Louis also got drunk very quickly and would invariably pass out at some stage. Many a time we would go for a nice Italian meal on a Saturday night, Louis would have been drinking, and by the time we sat down he would be asleep with his head in the soup dish.

Few of the lads were beer drinkers; they might have the occasional bottle. We mainly drank spirits, and quite a few did not drink much at all. We ate out at least five nights a week and by the time we hit the clubs at midnight we all had a meal inside us, so there was no lager lout behaviour. Jim Swords was not a big drinker, nor was Joe Leach. Vinnie Schiavo stopped drinking at a young age, so while others got inebriated he kept a cool and sober head. Wingy Jimmy, on the other hand, could drink for Britain and I was also a heavy drinker. My tipple was cognac and I could handle a couple of bottles in a night. Joe Swords liked a drink too, and many a Tuesday night, when no-one else was out, me, him and Mick Brown would go to a Greek restaurant and have dinner and a few drinks. Joe liked his cigar and a cognac after a meal and Mick was the same.

Wherever we went, we took centre stage. After pub closing time, various doormen would join us, then the bar owners and staff. We were often out until seven or eight in the morning; how we did it so often I do not know. Manchester was a great city, with well over 100 clubs in and around the centre, and we could fill a place on our own. When all the boys were out, we would each throw £20 in a kitty and when that was gone we would replenish it. The next day we'd hold a mock inquest to uncover who had finished up with the last of the pot. Of course everyone would deny it.

As for the name, there was a television advert for Quality Street chocolates in which a limousine pulls up outside a bank and a group of gangsters emerge wearing coats, fedoras and dark glasses. One of them walks up to a terrified cashier, slips his hand inside his overcoat and pulls out not a gun but a box of Quality Street. Jack Trickett tells the story that one night we walked into the Cabaret Club team-handed and Billy Ingham, who was on the door, remarked, 'Here they are, the Quality Street mob.' And that was it. We became the Quality Street Gang, later shortened to QSG or simply 'the QS'.

AS I HAVE said, most of the wide group referred to as the QSG were not criminals at all. Some, like myself, Mick Brown and Denis Crolla, were. We saw where the money was and decided to get it, and for us anything and everything went down from the late sixties onwards: blowing post office safes, robbery, long firm frauds, insurance scams. We eventually built up such a reputation that all the thieves would come to us. If you had a tip about a wage delivery, you came to us. If you wanted to offload a parcel of stolen jewellery, you came to us. If you had a wad of travellers' cheques, you came to us.

Those of us involved in crime each had our own personal little crews that only we dealt with. For example, my childhood pal Tommy Wimp, a great thief, came only to me. Another crew did nothing but blow safes. Their hauls often included postage stamps and postal orders as well as cash. They might then give me the work on the selling side. You could shift stolen stamps at half price, while postal orders went to the kiting mob at perhaps twenty pence in the pound. Their main targets were post offices in isolated rural locations, with poor security and old-fashioned safes. They divided them into 'livers' and 'non-livers': a shop with someone living above it was a liver, a shop that was empty at night was a non-liver and could usually be easily accessed, sometimes simply by going though the wall next door. One person on the firm spent his time driving around the country looking for non-livers, making notes and drawing diagrams of getaway routes. Then you had your 'safety valve', who would take the stolen money or loot off the burglary team immediately after the job was done and leave by a separate route, perhaps with his wife in tow to avoid suspicion.

Others had different specialisms. Mark Klapish, for instance, was heavily involved in frauds of various kinds. Another guy was the armourer. You might ask him for some guns for a job but you would not know where he kept them and you would not want to know; that was his business. The fewer people who knew, the better. Recycling money was a further challenge. You might pay someone £200,0000 for a parcel of stolen tom, then they might give you some of the money back and ask you to invest it for them. That was where the wider circle of the QSG came in: there were lots of opportunities to invest a bit of cash, no questions asked.

I cannot go into detail about many of the 'jobs' in this period, for the simple reason that those who did them were never caught. This is why some elements of my story must remain secret. In any case, it would be impossible to say how many crimes I was involved in. Post offices were getting done at least once a week, all over the country. People still talk about the Great Train Robbery, which took just over £2 million, but I have had that in gold alone out of a couple of robberies. Even more slipped away. The men behind a raid on the Kendals department store one Christmas were three minutes away from getting their hands on £3 million, and that was around 1970, when eighty grand was considered a major score. This team had the money, which was packed into Army kitbags, and were crossing a walkway from Kendals to the car park next door when a straight member spotted them and they panicked, dumped the bags and fled. Sadly my pals on that work have since passed away.

What we called a 'working' jeweller was a mobile gem salesman who carried stock around with him all week. They would be followed to their homes, sometimes tied up (hence the phrase 'a tie-up') and relieved of their stock. My brother Arthur was caught over a tie-up and served a few years for it because the wife of one of his accomplices blabbed. Generally, however, we didn't expose ourselves to outsiders. Certain things were only discussed with certain people, and we never talked business in the pubs and clubs at night. Anything work-related would be 'put to bed' before we went out. A lot of others sit in pubs talking about their escapades, but not us. There was no proper criminal intelligence in those days and you could usually spot the Old Bill a mile off. Now you cannot speak in the car or even near a mobile phone because they can be turned into transmitters.

One case that was publicized involved the arrest of Joe Swords and Vinnie Schiavo over a £16,000 bank robbery in Ilkeston, Derbyshire. The police also put out a warrant for Joe Leach after they found ammonia and a road map at his house linking him to the crime. Joe Leach went on his toes to Spain, where a bar was bought for him outside Alicante. Vinnie and Joe Swords strongly denied the charges and were cleared at Shrewsbury Crown Court. However, Dave Proudfoot, who was on the firm and was known as the 'Sundance Kid' because he looked like Robert Redford, was convicted and got ten years for it with another guy, while Joe Leach eventually got eighteen months. A club owner we knew also got three years for setting it up.

I was arrested myself over a job with a Scottish friend, John Shearer. An electrical goods shop in the Lake District was burgled and some of the goods were sold to a guy who worked in a scrapyard owned by Louis Schiavo. He turned out to be a dog, and I was raided by the police. They found one item, took it away and put me on police bail. Two weeks later, I was working on one of my barrows when the Old Bill grabbed me, cuffed me and drove me straight to the motorway, where I was transferred to another waiting police car. I finished up in a cell in Kendal. Initially the charges, including breaking and entering, were quite serious, a typical police ruse. I eventually pleaded guilty to a minor charge of handling one item and received a wrist slap.

One lesson I had absorbed was that it was valuable to have legitimate businesses if you also wanted to pursue crime, as it gave you a cover and an explanation for your income. So in 1971, I borrowed some money off a friend and started up in construction again. At first it went well, but as the months went by the companies we worked for began to struggle. The country was going down the pan, with strikes, blackouts and the three-day week. The trade unions were militant and impossible to deal with: we had one big job at Cammell Lairds, near Liverpool, where the Scousers would not let us on site. It took longer and longer to get paid and all the while the bank was screaming at me. I grew sick of waiting six months for cheques from big firms. In any case, with the top rate of income tax peaking at eighty-three per cent it was hardly worth trying to earn legitimately. In 1973, having accumulated substantial debts, I was made bankrupt *sine die*. The judge called me an 'utter gambler' – on other people's money, of course.

I decided to go into all-cash businesses. As a bankrupt I could not be a company director, but it was never a problem finding someone to front for me, and in the future many of my business interests would be in my wife's name. I still had the barrows, which brought in cash, and next I opened a scrapyard just off Great Ancoats Street, a couple of hundred yards from Jim Swords' car pitch. I squatted on what was derelict land, started paying rates to the council, then did the same with the land next door and ended up with about two acres. I bought scrap cars, broke them up and sold the parts, while any car that was any good went for sale on the site next door. Vinnie Schiavo and Joe Swords set up around the corner from Jimmy in Canal Street and then later opened Sangrange Motors. Over the years we all went into ventures together: Vinnie and Joe Swords, me and Vinnie, Joe Leach and Louis. Jimmy mainly kept his own car business to himself though.

By the early seventies, everybody was working together but also had their own things going. The main heads had regular meetings to sort out any problems and most decisions were reached within a group of ten people. A typical day would begin with the workers getting up early. The bosses were night-time people and would have been out until the small hours, so they were still in bed. My brother Arthur was not a drinker, so he would open up the scrap-yards for me. At around two in the afternoon, the other guys and I would meet at one of the car pitches, perhaps in a caravan on site. There would be a lot of banter, the day's work to get through, different firms coming on the pitch wanting to discuss this and that. All the business was around the car pitches or my scrapyard.

As the day drew to a close, someone would say, 'Right, where's the meet tonight?' It was often in the cocktail bar of the Grand Hotel. Twenty or thirty might turn up, then we would drive to Deno's, or the Cabaret Club, or wherever. Nobody bothered about drinking and driving. We liked good food and jokingly referred to ourselves as 'the gourmet society'. When Jack Trickett bought the Acton Court Hotel in south Manchester in the mid-seventies, we would all go there, maybe fifteen-handed, then on to Deno's late, then to Phyllis's Showbiz bar in Whalley Range for the all-night session.

We were all making money and needed to put it to work. Having previously installed gaming tables in clubs, and laid off bets, I now dabbled in bookmaking. The friend of a friend had been through a costly divorce and was stuck for money. He had a couple of starting price shops as well as front line pitches at every race track in the north of England, and was looking for a partner with cash. I met him and we did a deal: I would put up the money and we would split the profits down the middle. We worked Haydock Park, Doncaster, Catterick, Wetherby, York and the Grand National at Aintree.

It started well, but as I got into it I began to see all the fiddles and moves. We had our own tic-tac men and a clerk we called Dancing Albert. He could dance all right – with the books. Our workers were having free private bets through the tic-tac men: if they won they would collect the winnings, if they lost they would put it down in the books as a bad bet. Unless I travelled with them to keep an eye on them, they never seemed to have a winning day. I won in the end: I sold the front line pitches to another bookie who was on the back line and moved onto his pitch. I certainly received an education, but it all went into my head and I became better for it. The main lesson: never give a mug a chance unless you hold all the aces. I had a good run for a couple of years until my partner passed away and so did the pitches. I would later finance a couple of other bookmakers.

In 1972, the UK was put on a three-day week and homes were without power for up to nine hours a day due to a national miners' strike, which lasted for about two months. The following year, the miners imposed an overtime ban and the three-day week was reinstated, and in January 1974 they staged a second all-out strike. During one of these blackouts, I came across a bit of a conman called John Davidson. He spoke fluent German and had made contact with a small town in Germany that was twinned with a district of Manchester. All they did in this town was make church candles; the priest there showed John mounds of them. He rang from Germany to tell me.

'Buy them up,' I said.

I put a scrap dealer called Tommy Bulger into the deal, he raised some of the money and we arranged for two wagons to go over there. On the first day of the blackout, our wagons arrived back in Manchester with the candles. It was mayhem. We sold up in one hour and were straight back on the blower to John in Germany to buy every candle he could. Two more wagons arrived the next morning. We had a queue a mile long, not just members of the public but dealers from all over the north-west. The manager of the Piccadilly Hotel ordered a hundred cases and other hotels took candles by the barrow. We even worked the bus queues on Oldham Street at rush hour, with a barrow loaded up, selling to commuters to take home, at £1 each or six for a fiver. Few shops stocked large candles, the only ones they had were for birthday cakes, and as the days went by little firms were selling out of suitcases on every street corner. I supplied them all. Some pals of mine from Blackpool came over and told me they were getting £2 for one six-inch candle. Another pal bought all the remaining candles just as the strike came to an end. I think he still has some of them, but I made a lot of money.

John Davidson was later embroiled in another incident which showed the influence Jim Swords now exerted in Manchester. Our pal Joe Cash had loaned Davidson some money and took three cars as collateral: a Rolls-Royce Silver Cloud, a Jag and an Austin. Davidson eventually wanted the cars back but could not repay, so he enlisted the services of a heavyweight firm of Mick Lennon, Chick Devoy and a couple of others to help him.

A worried Joe Cash rang and asked me to come over to the scrapyard urgently. There he told me about the demands.

'How much have you lent out?' I asked.

He told me. I said I would give him the money and take the cars, and the problem, off his hands. He protested that he had also been 'on a drink' from Davidson for loaning the money and wanted that as well.

'Fuck me, Joe, you are going to lose your money and the cars if you don't do this deal. Forget your drink.'

I said there would be no problems and he could tell this heavyweight firm that he had sold the cars already. Then I went to see Jim Swords and put him in the deal.

'No problem,' he said, 'but when we collect the cars, we go to see Mick Lennon and tell him we now own them and to leave Joe out.'

Jimmy and I drove to the Cheetham Hill pub where Mick Lennon drank every day. JS told me to wait in the car. 'I am going in on my own to see him, man to man,' he said.

Now Mick Lennon was a real man who had a lot of respect in Manchester. Very few, if any, would have walked alone onto his turf and told him he was out of a deal. But JS was JS. Into the pub he walked.

After a while, he came back out.

'It's okay,' he said. 'Mick's agreed to stay out of it. Not only that, he has got a buyer for the Rolls for big money. If we want to sell it, he will give us the punter's name.'

We got good money for all three cars and gave Mick a drink out of the deal, so everyone was happy. All except Davidson: he got a smack for putting Joe Cash in trouble after he had helped him.

With JS at our head, the QSG were now the main faces in town. We were welcomed everywhere we went, and our circle of friends, of all ages, grew bigger and more interesting by the week. We were young, energetic, ambitious, and game for anything. Best of all, the ride was just beginning.

7

THE BOYS ARE BACK IN TOWN

ANCHESTER WAS CHANGING. In 1972, work began in Market Street on the Arndale Centre. Seven years later, when work was completed, it was Europe's largest city centre shopping mall. It was also the worst abortion I have ever seen. A vast, ugly, modernist box, it wiped out the old manor where I had worked and played for so long, and took with it much of the character, and characters, that made Cottonopolis what it was. Smithfield Market itself was relocated several miles away, marking the end of an era, and the old clubs were demolished: Bobby McDermott's Cellar, the Wilton, the Central, the Cromford, the Rooster Club, the Cinephone, the Stork, the Chanteclair and many more. The social scene, in which you could walk from den to den and drink from dawn to dusk, was lost.

One relic of the past still going strong, however, was the original guv'nor of Manchester. Bobby Critchley was about thirty years older than most of the QSG. He had been in the car game for years and the heavy game for just as long. Critch was the city's main face in the forties and fifties, when he was said to drive a bulletproof car. He did not give a running fuck for anyone. He had served three years in the fifties for having his henchman, Harry 'the Savage' Hilton, leather a guy in the Stage and Radio Club and put a red hot poker up the arse of one fellow who owed him money. Yet though he was still feared, he was very witty and great company. I got to know him well. To us he was a dapper old gent who wore beautiful suits, always light-coloured – pale blue, cream or fawn – matched with silk ties. He was also always covered in scent and smelt like a lady's boudoir. He even had a pet poodle. But Critch, Harry the Savage and the rest were ruthless. They would sell you a car on private drip but miss a payment and they were at your door. They would take the car back but you still had to pay.

Critch seemed to fall into our group after I bought a car from him. He would come for a drink with us with his partner, Wingy Jimmy, and then opened a car pitch next to my breakers yard. I would often have a coffee with them in the daytime. Jimmy Lythe was thirty-five stone and had a crippled arm from a childhood accident, hence his nickname 'Wingy'. He and Critch were like a cabaret act, they would have you in stitches all afternoon.

I was sat with them one day when a police car pulled up. Two young officers got out, a woman and a man, and came into the caravan office.

'We believe you have been selling stolen MoTs,' the WPC said to Critch.

He did not miss a beat.

'I am sorry love,' he said, 'I have just sold the last one. Come back tomorrow and I will sort you out. And not only that, I like girls in uniforms. If you want to do a little show I will only charge half price.'

She went beetroot-red and fell out of the office.

Wingy Jim also worked as a salesman for Joe Swords and Vinnie Schiavo on their pitch. He could keep you going all day with his jokes. On one occasion he was signing up a couple for drip on a car when Joe Swords noticed that one of his bollocks was hanging out – he had been to the toilet and forgotten to zip up, but did not notice because of his massive gut. Joe nudged Vinnie and they both tried to catch Wingy's eye. In the end Joe walked over, threw a towel over his lap and whispered in his ear. Wingy let out a roar of laughter.

'Is it the right one or the left one?' he asked. 'If it's the left one it's a sure sign of rain.'

Wingy was a monster drinker. He could do three bottles of gin in an evening. 'I have got to give up the gin,' he announced one night. 'The doctor says it is killing me.' He went on Mateus Rosé instead and drank twelve bottles!

My most memorable trip with Critch and Jimmy was when we took a mini cruise to Copenhagen with several of their cronies: Bunny Charles and Billy Higgins, who had both done a twelve-stretch on the Moor, and Tommy Harrold, later my business partner. When we got to Denmark, Wingy stayed in the hotel drinking; he would not move because of his bulk. The rest of us went to a club called Napoleons, where I asked this beautiful half-caste girl to join us. We had a great evening, and at the end of the night I asked her to come back with me. She said okay but nothing kinky and she wanted money up front.

Wingy and I were sharing a two-bed suite, sort of L-shaped. I took the girl back and let us into the room. She gave out a scream. There was all thirty-five stone of Wingy in a string vest, splayed out on his bed like a wounded whale, snoring. He must have been out shopping: on the table were two whips. I ushered the girl into my part of the suite, reassured her and we peeled off. We were playing games for about twenty minutes when she froze, jumped up and put the light on. There was Critch and Bunny Charles, both stark-ers except Critch had his underpants on his head. This time the screams from the girl brought the night porter. She grabbed her clothes, gave me some heartfelt abuse and fucked off. Some night.

The car game in those days was like the Wild West. Anything went. Widespread car ownership was relatively new and the trade was booming. There was straight money in it, but almost everyone was a bit bent. Few people knew what they were buying or what to look out for: so long as the oil was clear when they dipped it, they were happy. We used to put sawdust in the sump to stop an engine knocking. Warranties were rare. Many cars were 'rung' or 'clocked'. Consequently you occasionally got one or two 'screamers', complaining about faults with their cars. If they were particularly troublesome I would ask them to drop off the car for us to look at, then have someone steal it overnight and run it into the nearest wall, or even chop it up. When they came back for it, I would just say, 'Oh dear, we left it parked on the street, it must have been stolen. How terrible. I do hope you were insured.'

One day a black guy pulled onto the site. He said the car I had sold him was 'shit' and he wanted his money back. I told him truthfully that I had never seen him before but he kept going on, so I went in the office to go through the sales book and find the deal.

'When did you buy it?' I asked.

'Three weeks ago,' he said.

I told him I had been on holiday then and he must have dealt with Denis, my partner, who did look a bit like me. Now this fucker was getting agitated and abusive. I told him to come back in a week and Denis would sort it out. With that, he told me he was going to do me. He did not get the chance. I picked up a half-full petrol can and hit him on the head. He went down with his head split open.

My brother Arthur was watching from the gate of the scrap-yard and rushed over.

'Fucking hell, Jimmy, I think you've killed him. You'd better fuck off and let me handle this.'

The guy spent a couple of days in hospital: he had twelve stitches and an x-ray for a suspected skull fracture. A few days later, Arthur got a phone call. This guy wanted a lump of money or he would make a statement to the cops. After a few threats both ways, I told him I would give him two grand compensation. He was to meet me at the yard.

He arrived on time and I invited him into the back office, which had a side door into the yard. And as he walked in, I hit him with a rubber cosh. Arthur had the crane with a crusher already running. We threw this ponce into the bottom car and then Arthur dropped the one-ton weight. After a few bashes the car was like a pancake and the guy was screaming for mercy. I looked in through what was left of the window.

'Do you still want your two grand,' I asked, 'or do you want to go in the crusher?'

We dragged him out. The guy had soiled himself and stank. We sent him on his way and he never came back.

The staff could cause as many headaches as the customers. I kept a fully equipped caravan on the yard that a guy called Tommy Bird lived in. He acted as an oddjob man and a bit of security at night. One evening I was having a drink when a fellow asked me for some new parts for his car.

'You've got them in your shop on Ashton Old Road,' he said.

I told him he had the wrong man. He responded that Tommy Bird had served him an alternator from this shop one night, and gave me a business card. The address was a two-storey warehouse which I rented out to a notorious fraudster named Frank Crawford, who also had his own breaker's yard.

My suspicions were aroused. Why did this guy think I was

selling car parts out of this warehouse? I got hold of Wally McNelly and Denis Crolla, my little firm within the firm, and went over to the pub where Tommy Bird drank. We grabbed him, dragged him out and threw him in the back of the car.

'Jimmy, Jimmy, what have I done?' he screamed.

I hit him on the legs a couple of times with an iron bar to shut him up.

'We know all about your fucking scam,' I told him. 'You are stealing nearly new cars and stripping them in my yard for Frank Crawford.'

We headed for my yard. I hit Tommy a few more times on his kneecaps and by the time we got to the yard he had told us everything. He and Crawford would steal a car and bring it into my yard late at night. Within two hours, it would be stripped and the parts put on a wagon and driven to the warehouse they rented from me. From there, the parts would go to a shop or be advertised in the newspapers for sale. By the time I came onto the yard in the mornings, all of the evidence had gone.

These cheeky bastards could have landed me right in it. Part of me admired their nerve, but it was not something I could let go. We kept Tommy all night and went to Crawford's shop the next day. It was loaded with every make of car part. I hit Crawford on the head with a heavy rubber truncheon and flattened him, then we took the two of them to the warehouse. It was piled high with engines, gearboxes and parts; they had been busy. They would not admit how long it had gone on for but Tommy had lived in the caravan for two years, so it could have been that long. Denis and Wally set about the two of them and gave them a proper hiding. I told Crawford I wanted twenty grand off him and eventually let them go.

The next day Crawford's wife came to my yard, going on about the beating her husband had suffered. She was lucky he was still alive. Anyway, I got my readies off him. The man did have brass balls. He went on for years, fucking people over and telling lies. Vinnie Schiavo later got six months for buying one of his ringers that turned out to be stolen. He was also done for one fraud that I heard brought in £4 million. How he was never killed I do not know. The last I heard of Tommy, he was selling American cars. It just shows you have to be on the ball.

With all the strokes we pulled, we naturally expected some attention from the police. Even so, I was taken aback when I became the first man I had ever heard of to be charged with selling cars with no MoTs and no tax on private land. So far as I or anyone else knew, if a vehicle was off the road it did not need a current MoT or tax disc. Well, according to the court, I was wrong. I was found guilty and had to pay a heavy fine. I still haven't worked that one out, to this day.

WITH THE SCRAPYARD and car pitch going well, I took over a café around the corner called the Black Cat. I had been over to Hamburg and Amsterdam and seen the knocking shops there, and that gave me the idea of turning it into a sauna and massage parlour with an upmarket interior. I spent a lot of money on it, with Habitat furniture in the lounge bar area, an eight-person sauna, steam room, sunbed room, small training room with a running machine and weights, private rooms for the 'massage' and a private car park. I advertised for masseuses and was inundated.

I called it El Corrida and it created a sensation. There was only one similar place in Manchester at the time, owned by my pal Don Toney in Moss Side. I put a bar in for 'the chaps' to have a drink after it closed and kept a private room for pals from London who sometimes stayed over. It took off so quickly that I decided to go into the escort business as well. Even major companies used to requests escorts at trade meetings and seminars in those days, in fact one of our biggest clients was Green Shield Stamps. The girls were chauffeur driven and serviced many of the major hotels. We advertised in the *Manchester Evening News* until one of the managers there got the hump and stopped it, so we had to switch to smaller papers that were glad of the advertising, as well as weeklies like *Reveille*. About twenty girls worked shifts at its peak. I often wonder where they are today.

Rita was upset about it and I got a bit of earache. It was difficult, but as I told her, 'Bottom line, it's money.' What convinced her to accept it was that I refused to take money off the girls. I took a percentage of the call out charge but whatever the escorts charged after that was theirs. The same with the sauna: I took only the £5 entrance fee and what was made in the bar. The girl on reception gave the customers clean linen and booked them in and they passed through into the lounge and got a sauna. There was no need for a minder because people were very shy about it. A good few famous faces went through, a lot of well-respected professional people too. I never had a problem off the vice squad, they were more concerned with punters on the streets and girls working the clubs. I had a great run, but while I was in Spain on holiday the place was mysteriously torched. The insurance paid me thirty-five grand for fixtures and fittings but nothing for loss of business, as I had not kept proper books. There were a few 'Jewish fires' in those days.

In 1974, I acquired my first nightclub. Nitos was next door to Stockport County football club. The owner had a couple of other places and was sick of the hassle Nitos gave him, while the kid who managed it for him was fed up as well. I went in originally to give him a bit of rent but after a few months I gave him nothing. He was eased out, so to speak. Nitos held 400 people, the restaurant seated eighty and the cocktail bar forty, and it had a 4 a.m. licence, which was unheard of. It clearly had potential. To front it I had Tommy Harrold, who already had a couple of clubs and a clean record, so he could get a licence. I brought Tommy Cunliffe from Salford to work the door. Tommy was a 'take-on': you would think him easy meat until he got into gear, then he could fight for fun. Topping the bill for me was Maxton G. Beesley, a great drummer and impersonator who appeared in a couple of TV shows. Rita helped to run the place on Friday and Saturday nights, while Sunday was 'stag' day with striptease, so she stayed at home. It boomed: a lot of working people struggled to have even a black and white telly in those days, so live entertainment was still a big draw.

Despite its success, Nitos caused me headaches. In fact it was the scene of the first serious attempt on my life. Some of the locals did not like the fact that I had Manchester doormen on the club. They did not give a fuck for Manchester names: they were still wearing teddy boy clothes and having razor fights down in Stockport. Early one evening, I went to the club to collect something and was turning around to drive out of the car park when a couple of bullets shattered the front windscreen. Fortunately it was a left-hand drive American car; if I had been sitting on the right, I would have been hit.

At around the same time, my brother had blue paint thrown over his yellow XJ6. This seriously pissed me off. We knew it must be local heavies trying it on but we did not know who was responsible. The QSG could handle trouble from anyone, but they couldn't be everywhere at once, and in Stockport I was vulnerable to a sneak attack. Alan Kay, who owned the nearby Poco-a-Poco and was a very experienced club owner, came over for a drink and I told him about my problem.

'You have done it wrong, Jimmy,' he said.

Alan sent over a couple of his local doormen, including a guy called Joe Walsh, who was the top man in Stockport. My problems vanished and I became one of the local chaps.

There was still the unpredictable to deal with. Mick 'the Beast' Clarke was a big slob who lived in Wythenshawe and knocked about with Mick Tierney and Brian 'the Bear' Dunn. They tolerated him because he put himself about and would befriend landlords, then bring them in to demand protection money. He was not a big drinker but on this particular night he was in my club knocking back sherry. As he went to the toilets, he passed through the restaurant and saw Jack Trickett sat with his girlfriend. The Beast went over and insulted him. There was a bit of a row and Jack's girl said, 'Let's go.'

I was in the cocktail bar when a doorman came over and told me Jack was leaving because the Beast was having a go at him. I slipped into the kitchen, grabbed a knife and hurried outside. Jack was in the car park. The Beast had snatched his glasses off his face and slung them away.

'What the fuck do you think you are doing with my pal?' I asked.

Before the Beast could answer, I went for him. He saw the knife, turned white and ran back into the club. He made for the toilets and locked himself in a cubicle. The cubicle door had a gap at the bottom so I bent down and stuck the knife in his leg. He screamed like a pig.

'I didn't know he was your pal, Jimmy,' he pleaded.

After a while the doormen coaxed him out with the promise he would not get hurt further. They got him a cab and off he went.

A couple of days later my brother rang, saying Mick Clarke was going to do me and would bring the Bear and others with him. I got in touch with Brian Dunn and asked him the score.

'Fuck him, Jimmy, we are sick of him sticking our names up. Do what you want with him.'

I sent a message to the Beast to ring me at the club. He phoned full of apologies and said to tell Jack he would pay for new spectacles for him. He asked was there anything he could do for me.

'You have a tipper truck, don't you? Well I have tons of rubbish at the back of the club. Move it and we are all square.'

True to his word, he cleaned up the club yard. A week later he turned up at the club asking if I would let him back in. I did and he sat there all night drinking sherry and giving the bar staff big tips. We also found Jack's glasses in the car park.

I never had another problem with Mick the Beast.

BY THE EARLY seventies, the QSG were *the* faces about town. We could be seen out every night at regular hangouts such as the Portland Lodge, the Cabaret Club and Annabelles, but probably the two places we became most associated with were the Showbiz and Deno's. Our links with these clubs would even be immortalized in song by one of the all-time great rock bands.

The Showbiz was run by Philomena Lynott, or Phyllis, as she was known to all. Phyllis had left a poor area of Dublin in her teens to work in England, and at eighteen becoming pregnant to a man she met at a dance. Even worse, in those more prejudiced days, than having a baby out of wedlock was the fact that the father was black, from British Guiana. Phyllis was thrown out of the hostel where she was staying and had to ask her parents to take in her baby, Philip, while she stayed in England working. She eventually arrived in Manchester in the early sixties.

In 1966, Phyllis and her latest boyfriend, Denis Keeley, took over the running of the Clifton Grange, a Victorian hotel in

Whalley Range with a showbusiness clientele: cabaret artists, dancers, magicians, actors and singers. After six months, they bought the place, and would remain there for the next fifteen years. Phyllis had an unconventional attitude that suited the hotel's bohemian guests: if you wanted breakfast any earlier than noon you had to get up and cook it yourself. She also turned the bar into an after-hours club known as the Showbiz, the Biz, or simply 'Phyllis's'. It was a shebeen really: I am not sure Phyllis ever had a drinks licence. You walked up steps at the back to get to the door and pressed a buzzer to get in. Denis would be in a kind of crow's nest on the roof, looking along the street to see if the police were about. The Showbiz rarely opened before 2 a.m., when the other clubs had shut, and became a favourite with the QSG. We called Phyllis 'the Godmother'.

They were crazy years, great years. George Best was a regular: I have seen him party at Phyllis's all night until 8 a.m., then go to the airport to fly to London to play football. George Carman, a heavy drinker and smoker who was making his name as a brilliant young barrister, was often in there chasing young birds. He used to arrive on Friday nights when he was defending the politician Jeremy Thorpe against a charge of conspiracy to murder and tell me fascinating stories about the case. You never knew who you would meet in there. I had a drink with one young lady who I suspected was gay because she had such a gruff voice. She turned out to be Helen Shapiro, the singer. Michael Parkinson used to come in, and Bob Greaves, who was then Granada TV's main presenter. In fact a lot of TV cameramen and directors were regulars, as were many club owners who would arrive after they had locked up. Even the Sex Pistols stayed at the hotel, and for once were on their best behaviour.

Phyllis's son, Philip, grew into a tall, lanky kid with a wild mess of hair. He loved music and formed a band, the Black Eagles, in Dublin in 1965; it was not until 1969 that he put together a group called Thin Lizzy. In the meantime he would come over to Manchester to stay with his mum. Summer and Christmas holidays meant he was over for weeks among the crazy customers of the Showbiz. He was just a nice boy. No-one realised how talented he was, until Phyllis pushed him up on stage at the Cabaret Club one night to sing a song. Although he was mortally embarrassed, it was clear that he had some voice.

Thin Lizzy eventually got picked up by Decca Records after a gig and started recording. Their first hit was a version of the traditional Irish song 'Whiskey In The Jar', in 1973. Phil was also writing his own lyrics, many of them based on people in his life. That included the QSG, who inspired one of his greatest songs, 'The Boys Are Back In Town'. We had been in Italy visiting relatives of Lou and Vinnie Schiavo and had just got back.

'Come in the bar tonight,' Phyllis told Phil, 'the boys are back in town.'

Like all great songwriters, he took that one phrase and made it into something special. He also namechecked one of our most popular haunts: 'Friday night they'll be dressed to kill/Down at Dino's bar and grill/The drink will flow and blood will spill/And if the boys wanna to fight, you'd better let 'em.' Dino's bar and grill was, of course, our pal Denos' club. 'The Boys Are Back In Town' became Thin Lizzy's biggest international hit, reaching number twelve in the US charts and breaking the top ten in the UK and several other countries in 1976. It was on their great album *Jailbreak*, which also went top twenty in the USA.

Their next album, *Johnny The Fox*, had a direct reference to me: the song 'Johnny the Fox Meets Jimmy the Weed'. I still have the gold disc that Phil gave me on my wall: it was to mark 250,000 sales and is one of my most prized possessions. Phil wrote the album while recovering from a bout of hepatitis in a Manchester hospital. The track itself is about underworld characters in an American city, but it was not hard to see where he got the idea for lyrics like, 'Jimmy the Weed won't use no muscle/That cat's so sly, slick and subtle.' I was chuffed with the result.

Another great song was inspired by Joe Leach, who loved the music scene – he later managed a Manchester punk band called The Drones – and was very close to Phil. Joe became embroiled in a legal dispute over some cars he had bought and sold, and the police got involved. Three of the cars, Daimlers bought from a funeral director, had been supplied to Thin Lizzy and their entourage, and Joe needed a statement from Phil Lynott confirming that. But Phil, who was in Los Angeles working on a single, was a bit late in sending it. So Joe rang him and said, 'Phil, I'm waiting for this alibi statement.' Phil, a genius at turning events from his life into lyrics, came up with 'Waiting For An Alibi', another hit.

I had many happy times with Phil. He was such an approachable guy, modest and friendly and always helpful to other musicians, many of whom idolised him. On one occasion when he played the Apollo in Manchester, he held his private after-party at my hotel. The doorbell rang and there was Paul Young, then the lead singer with Sad Café. Paul was a Wythenshawe lad.

'Sorry Paul,' I said, 'but you're not on the guest list.'

'Fuck me, Jimmy,' he said, 'we're pals.'

'Okay, I'll let you in. Go into the small bar.'

'Can you introduce me to Phil?'

Paul had done me a couple of favours so I said, 'Leave it with me.'

I went over to Phil and told him I had the Sad Café band and

Paul Young was with them. 'Where are they?' he immediately asked. 'I am a fan of theirs.'

I took Phil into the small bar and introduced them. They were in that bar for hours and were still chatting away in the early morning. I got a kick out of watching these two great singers get on so well together.

I saw Paul Young a few months later. He and Phil had become good friends. 'I owe you Jimmy,' he said.

Paul later joined Mike & The Mechanics with one of the founders of Genesis. It was very sad when he died of a heart attack in 2000.

Another memorable occasion was Phil's wedding to Caroline, the daughter of TV presenter Lesley Crowther, at the Hilton Hotel in London. All the Cockney firm was invited. I stayed at the Cumberland and arranged to go for a drink with Bobby Dixey, a well-known face. We finished up in Chinatown, where Bobby did his bollocks in gambling. He asked if I had any money on me. I told him I had two grand but would need most of it for my hotel bill and limo the next day.

'No problem,' said Bobby, 'give me the two large, I will drop it in to you at the hotel tomorrow.'

The next day, panic. My limo arrived and I had to leave for the wedding but I had no money and there was no sign of Bobby. Then the hotel's public address system sounded.

'Will Mister Donnelly come to reception.'

There was Bob, sweating like a Turkish wrestler. He had sprinted two blocks with the dough.

It turned out to be a lovely day. Rita and I sat at the reception next to Bob Geldof, a great friend and admirer of Phil's. P' would later be deeply upset when Geldof left him out of the Aid concert in 1985, but all that was in the future.

Phyllis's hotel was close to Moss Side, which was another lively nightlife destination. Moss Side was the home of the shebeen, or unlicensed drinking den, usually found in the basement of a large house. They would knock through adjoining cellars, put in a bar and perhaps some palm trees or other exotic plants, serve Jamaican food and play reggae. I became friendly with many of the guys who ran the shebeens, men like Scarface Shine and Little Roddy, who had the Nile and Reno clubs. A big fellow called Don Toney was the power behind many of them and I suppose was the 'godfather' of the area. Surprisingly he was white, though all his partners were black.

Moss Side later became notorious for gang shootings but in those days there was little trouble. On one occasion I was with Albert Gibbons, my brother Arthur and Brendan Withers when we had a fight in a shebeen off Great Western Street and ended up being chased out by a mob. We went back the following week and fire-bombed it: they were jumping out of windows to get away. They thought a rival shebeen up the street was responsible, so they raided it in retaliation and it caused a turf war. My pal John Shearer and I also had a bit of fun in the shebeen on Cheetham Hill Road run by a guy called Banjo. John let off a couple of shots into the ceiling from a handgun that fired shotgun cartridges. We had to get off before the police came. But generally we got on well with the shebeen owners. We would often go in places with our pal Honey Boy Zimba, the black wrestler, and he was like a god in his own community.

Deno's was another of our main hangouts for years, until one New Year's Eve things did not go right. There were four tables of s, about forty-handed including women. One of the firm had a words with his wife, to which some people on the next table ted. We knew them very well, they were in the scrap busi-father and his sons and their wives. Unfortunately it got out of hand and the next thing, it went off royal. There were no heavy tools as such but Tiny Brown of the QSG suffered a broken leg, a few heads were split and the place was wrecked. The next day, it was sorted in the proper manner and the two firms shook hands, but Deno's was never the same again. Denos himself held no grudge and until he died we used to meet for a drink.

That sort of violent confrontation with the QSG was rare. By the mid-seventies, we had proven ourselves time and again and our name was usually enough to deter any would-be hard men. Only the biggest hitters would even think of taking us on. But they did exist, and over the course of the decade we had a few encounters with men from outside the city that threatened to unleash serious bloodshed.

8

TROUBLE

RAB CARRUTHERS WAS a dangerous man. The rising star of the Glasgow underworld, he was forced to leave his home city in the early seventies to avoid questioning over an unsolved murder, and arrived in Manchester with a young firm of fellow Jocks. Fit, fearless and violent, he was the unchallenged boss of his men and would hurt you very badly if you crossed him. Rab soon teamed up with some young local villains and went on a nation-wide robbery spree, hitting jewellery stores as far afield as Cornwall and Wales. They were eventually caught and jailed.

When he came out of prison, Rab continued to make waves. In one fight, he hit the formidable Mick Tierney with an axe; Mick turned up at hospital with it stuck in his head. But a Jock mob in our city did not bother the QSG. There were always up-and-coming teams flexing their muscles. So long as they were not a nuisance, we did not care. We were too well established to be affected and were all preoccupied with our own things – until one afternoon they went too far.

I had driven to the Barley Mow pub to meet a pal about a bit of business. It was busy inside and I noticed Carruthers with some of his Glasgow pals. Also at the bar was Ronnie Muir, Jim Swords' brother-in-law. Ronnie was a lovely man when sober but a nuisance in drink. The only way you could get him out of a place when he was pissed was to tell him you had phoned his wife. My pal and I were settling down to business over a drink when we heard a commotion. A couple of the Jock firm were setting about Ronnie. I jumped up and went to stop it but I did not have a chance; there were too many of them and they were led by Rab, one of the hardest men ever to come out of Glasgow.

'Stay out of it,' I was told, in no uncertain terms.

I looked around for support but my pal had gone through the slips and disappeared. I didn't blame him. Ronnie took a few whacks before he managed to escape. He had not been badly hurt but this could not be let go, so I walked around the corner to a phone box and dialled Jim Swords.

'Go back and keep an eye on them,' he said. 'I'll get the tools out and bring some of the firm over.'

I went back into the tense atmosphere of the pub and stuck it out for an hour, until the Jocks moved off. By the time the cavalry arrived, they were gone. Jimmy explained he had not been able to get access to guns any sooner. We toured the town looking for them, without success, so we all went back to Jimmy's car pitch to discuss what to do next.

'Right,' someone said, 'put the things in a bag for now, but check them first.'

I handed a gun to one of the boys to check. Why, I do not know, but he pulled the trigger. There was a loud bang and Jimmy flew off his feet. The bullet had hit him in the groin, just missing his bollocks. We were only a few hundred yards from Ancoats Hospital, so we got him there in short order. We told the receptionist that someone had driven past and taken a pot shot. Jimmy was bleeding heavily and it took a lot of stitches to close the wound. The problem with the Jocks would have to be put on hold.

Now JS is not known for his generosity. His favourite saying was, 'Some people like to spend, I like to keep mine.' He was fair but he was hard. So when one of the boys blew some dough that he owed to Jimmy, he knew he was in trouble. Eddie 'Jaws' Barber had been instructed to collect two cars from Oldham, the last part of a debt owed to JS and his profit on the deal. Eddie was to sell them to the trade, keep £200 for himself and hand over the remainder. Jaws being Jaws, he sold them, then decided he felt lucky, went to a casino and blew the lot. Now, there was no easy way to tell JS you had spent his money unless you could pay him back double, but here was a stroke of luck. With Jimmy in hospital, incapacitated and surrounded by well-wishers, what safer time to break bad news to him?

A few of us were at his bedside, discussing what to do about the Jock firm, when Eddie came in.

'Hi Jim, how are you?' he said, breezily.

'In fucking pain,' came the reply. 'Well, have you brought me my bit of change?'

'Er, no,' said Eddie, 'I have had a bit of a problem.'

'You mean you didn't get the cars and sell them?'

'Oh yes,' said Eddie. 'I sold the cars, no problem. But, er, I have done the money.'

Jimmy was sitting up in bed. Suddenly he reached forward, grabbed Eddie by the hair and gave him a swift left hook. Eddie yelped and broke free, then started down the ward at speed. Jimmy swung out of bed and hobbled after him, grimacing in pain, throwing apples and oranges from a fruit bowl at the fleeing figure of Jaws. The ward was in uproar.

A short while later, Rab Carruthers contacted JS to say he was sorry and had not known who Ronnie Muir was. The problem was smoothed over and it stayed that way. Rab would later come into my clubs and pubs and was always respectful. In fact one of his firm, a Glaswegian called John Shearer, became one of my closest friends. We went on to do a lot of work together and have a lot of laughs.

John once knocked on my door and asked me if I could find him any 'work'. I told him about a bakery chain that had a lot of outlets. They had a main safe and kept it in their shop window, so that it was always visible. John got hold of a couple of white coats and parked at the back of the shop. He did not need to break in, the yard gate was open and the back door was tied with string. There was even a handy trolley nearby that was used for carrying flour. They were in and out with the safe in minutes.

A pal and I went to meet them at a house. The safe was offloaded and we went to work on it, opening the keyhole and dropping in a condom stuffed with gelignite. Then we plastered the end down, put in the detonator, wired it up, retired to the kitchen and let it go.

After an almighty bang, we went out into the yard. The safe had gone: it had flown over the wall into next door's yard.

'Fuck me, Jimmy,' my pal said, 'how much did you put in?'

'All of it.'

'You should only have put in half!'

The guy who lived next door was okay about it; we told him the safe had come off a demolition site and we just wanted to see if anything was in it. He knew not to ask questions. But the door was now jammed shut so I told John to take it away. He later burned off the back – and incinerated the money inside.

Another time, I got a call from John to say he had gone through the wall of a shop in Ashton, on the outskirts of Manchester, with the son of a friend of mine and they had got away with a hundred sheepskin coats. John kept fifty while the other guy sold fifty to his brother, keeping two for himself. The police raided his house, found the two coats and charged him. He then made a statement that he had sold the coats to me, as John had told him that I was interested in buying his half. The police came round to my house but found nothing except some keys to a warehouse I had. They took me there and again failed to find any coats, but my bottle was going because I had four handguns taped on top of an exposed beam on the ceiling. I don't know how the Old Bill missed them but I suppose they were looking for bulky coats.

After showing me the statement that my friend's son had made against me, the police let me go, though they later charged John. He and I went to see the family of the grass. They asked us not to hurt him, and out of friendship for them we left him. But everybody that worked with him ended up getting nicked. I was lucky to get out of that one.

Rab Carruthers went on to become a major name in gangland circles. He remained in Manchester but, according to the *Daily Record* newspaper, would show up in Glasgow now and then 'to remind them he could take over whenever he wanted'. He later moved into the drugs trade, which proved to be his undoing, but he was always respected.

WHILE PEOPLE STILL tell tall tales about the time the Krays visited the city, a potentially far more serious case involved our pal Ricky Gore, and this time it really could have sparked a war between Manchester and London. Ricky was an enigma. One of the younger QSG, he was always his own man in that he was in the Army. He got involved in a bit of a robbery at one time, served a short sentence and did not like the nick, so instead he pursued a military career and ended up in the Special Forces: to all intents and purposes, he was on call to the SAS. He never spoke much about it, for obvious reasons, but would disappear for weeks or even months at a time.

'Chinatown' Bobby Dixey, a friend of ours and a face in London, came to visit for a few days and, as always, the troops turned out, including Honey Boy Zimba, the wrestler. We did the rounds before finishing up in Phyllis's, where everyone was larking about. We used to play a game, two onto Zimba, trying to put him on the floor. No-one ever managed it. He was immensely strong: I once saw him pick up Louis Schiavo and Ricky Gore by their belts and lift them both over his head at the same time. This time Bobby Dixey and Ricky got caught up in the horseplay. I think Ricky tried to pick up Zimba thinking Bobby was going to help him, Bobby instead turned bandit on Ricky and suddenly fists were flying. It was quickly stopped by the lads but egos were bruised on both sides. Bobby went back to his hotel and must have brooded about it, because he phoned London and told them to send up a team. Ricky Gore was going to get hit.

I got a phone call after lunch the next day to meet Bobby, and took him to a drinking club, the Queens. There he confessed what he had done. He looked mortified.

'Fucking hell, Jimmy, I have made a right rick. I phoned London and they are on the way up. I can't tell them it's off.'

I asked what he was talking about. He said he had two pals on the way to do Ricky and he could not stop them.

'I have made a fucking mug of myself,' he said. 'It must have been the booze. Ricky's a good man.'

We sent someone to Bobby's hotel to await the two hit men. In the meantime, Ricky got a phone call telling him to stay well out of the way.

The two Cockneys arrived by car and were brought to the Queens. I recognised them as soon as they walked in. One was a top face called Ted; the other was Nicky Gerrard, a professional killer and the son of Alfie Gerrard, one of Freddie Foreman's mob. It was widely known that Nicky had shot dead 'Italian Tony' Zomparelli in revenge for the murder of Ronnie Knight's brother David. He was once described by a senior police officer as 'one of the most feared men in the London underworld'. This was a delicate situation.

After a few minutes' explanation, Ted said, 'Fuck me, Bob, we thought you were in big trouble.' He then pulled out a handgun and Nicky did the same. For a second I wondered which way this was going to go, until they both started laughing. The tension deflated from the room like air from a tyre; we had averted a potentially lethal incident by a matter of minutes. With the ice broken, we went on to the Kensington pub for a drink. Ricky Gore looked shocked when we told him about the guns but he took it in his stride.

I guess Chinatown Bob had the 'Watford Gap' syndrome. When we were all in Spain, he would sometimes get drunk and be a bit lippy about northerners, calling us 'mugs'. Yet many of the most dangerous men in the London firms were Scotsmen or Mancunians. Nicky Gerrard continued on his violent path and was shot dead in London in 1982 by a gang wearing boiler suits and balaclavas. It seemed he had finally gone too far.

Such friction was rare, as we knew all the major Cockney villains by this time. The London underworld had found its feet again after the big police operations that took out the Richardsons and Krays in the late sixties. New gangs were making themselves busy and armed robberies were on the rise. The QSG as a group began to travel down there a lot to watch boxing shows and do a bit of business, while older Mancunian villains like Wally Downs and Terry Jeffreys had long had good contacts in the capital. It was inevitable that I would sometimes send a 'parcel' down there for sale or they would send one up to me.

Our favourite watering hole was the Log Cabin in Wardour Street, Soho, where Tommy McCarthy was mine host. Tommy was a great guy from the East End who had trained the heavyweight boxer Billy Walker. We would sometimes stay at his pub in Ascot, the Stag, where his wife Ann always made a fuss of us, and would return the hospitality when they came up to Manchester to stay at the Acton Court, a hotel Jack Trickett bought in the mid-seventies. Tommy was an ardent Man United fan. We also frequented the Latin Quarter in Wardour Street, where Ronnie Knight's brother was stabbed to death by Tony Zomparelli in 1970.

Ronnie Knight's A&R Club was always full of faces from both north and south of the Thames. Ronnie owned it with Micky Regan, an imposing man with grey hair who, I was told, was the real guv'nor. Micky was a gentleman. The few times I met him he never once tried to put me down with the Watford Gap syndrome. It was in the A&R Club that I was also introduced to the Reilly family. That was the start of a long and loyal friendship. The Reillys are a vast London-Irish clan. They were in the same business as me, with pubs and clubs, and could certainly look after themselves. Over the years, I was approached by other groups to join them and their company rather than the Reillys but always politely refused by saying, 'What would you think of me if I was with you and moved over to another firm?' The Reillys have made a few headlines over the years, and are men not to be messed with.

I also befriended Ronnie Baker, whose wife was a barmaid at

the Log Cabin. Ronnie had done a bit on the pavement, while his brother Kenny was a real grafter. Ronnie moved to Manchester and he and a pal of mine later opened a big club in Salford. After a while they split and Ronnie opened the Cottage Club in the Blackfriars area, then later he had the Railway pub in Newton Heath. He rang me one night to see if I could get my solicitor down to the nick, as his Kenny had been charged with trying to rob Salford Royal Hospital wage van, along with the old Manchester villain Wally Downs and Vodka John from London. Ronnie could not visit Kenny because he did not want the police to put them together as brothers. I went to see them with my solicitor and they were draped in blankets, having been stripped naked so their clothes could be forensically examined. Kenny's career later ended abruptly when the Metropolitan Police shot him dead during a robbery bid.

When the firm went to London for the fights or the football, we would stay at a good West End hotel, but if I was down for a bit of 'work' I would stay off the radar, sometimes in Bayswater with my friend Dave Barry, an ex-boxer who owned drinking clubs. I first met Dave in Manchester in the sixties when he knocked around with Alfie Osbiston, who was in the car game and worked for the firm for a while, and Brian London, the heavyweight boxing champion. We did lots of deals together. Dave knew all the firms and is respected by all. I can still vividly recall one memorable meal when I turned up at a restaurant to find him sitting with the film star Robert Mitchum and Jack O'Halloran, a heavyweight boxer turned actor who fought Muhammad Ali and appeared in the *Superman* movies – how many people can say that? Mitchum was staying in a flat in Bayswater while working on a film. I didn't want to pry into his life so I steered the conversation towards boxing, where I could hold my own, and we had a great time. Dave Barry seemed to know everyone, and that afternoon was something else.

HAVING NARROWLY AVOIDED conflict with the Glaswegians and the Cockneys, I completed the set when I almost had a war with some well known faces from Liverpol. I had gone along to the opening of my pal Bunny Westley's nightclub with a London friend, Paul Seabourne, when a handy-looking guy with a Scouse accent came over to us.

'Are you Jimmy the Weed?'

'I am.'

'You're with that fucking QSG mob and none of you are any good.'

He went on to call us 'grasses' and 'wrong 'uns', which was fighting talk in any language. I don't know where it came from: perhaps it was jealousy because we never seemed to get any serious charges. He was firm-handed but I was not going to back down. We had a bit of a stand-off until Bunny Westley intervened.

'You're wrong and out of order, Tony,' he told the Scouser.

'I don't know you,' I said to the man called Tony. 'I have never had any dealings with you. So why would you say what you said?'

His manner softened and he explained that one of his group, another Scouser called Tommy Lacey, had been slagging me off. Now this Lacey had previously been on my pitch trying to get a car on credit, so he had a bit of a grudge against me. The man said he was sorry and would sort out Lacey later. He introduced himself as Tony McMullen, one of a well-known and very tough family from the Scotland Road area of Liverpool; in fact I knew his brother Terry. We had a drink and straightened things out but I was miffed at Lacey.

The next day, Ronnie Baker phoned to tell me that Lacey and some Scousers were in his pub in Manchester. I asked Ronnie not to say a word, then told Paul Seabourne I was going tooled up and somebody might get hurt.

'No problem, Jimmy. I will make one with you.'

When I got there, the Liverpool lot were in the small area by the stairs. Tony McMullen was not with them. I waited until I saw Lacey go to the gents, then followed him. He was just about to piss when I hit him with a sawnoff shotgun on the back of the head and put him down, then stuck the gun in his face. He completely lost it.

'No, no, I got it wrong Jimmy, don't, don't.'

I told him how lucky he was and let him walk out. He had pissed himself. The men with him were okay, they were straight goers in town for a drink, so I left them alone. I became very friendly with the McMullens over the next few years, so it was just as well that a war between the two cities was averted. The thing was, in our world you could not back down from slights, so a small incident could blow up into something out of all proportion.

Paul Seabourne was an armed blagger who had helped to spring the train robber Ronnie Biggs from prison. They had been inside together, and when Paul was released he agreed to return to Wandsworth Prison and lob a rope ladder over the walls. He had a van waiting with a hydraulic platform, Biggs climbed the ladder, scaled the wall, jumped onto the raised platform and made off in a getaway car. Seabourne later served four-and-a-half years for aiding the escape, while Biggsy sunned himself in Brazil.

I had a lucky escape with Paul. He and another Londoner came to Manchester looking for work with my great pal Wally McNelly. I told them that I had a job but it was back in London. We went down there and I showed them a travelling jeweller. Wally was to steal a getaway car and the others were to wrap up the jeweller when he came out of his house in the morning, while I was to collect the 'parcel' and head back to Manchester with it. What we did not know was that they were under police observation. The cops watched Paul hide a bag containing two shotguns in a skip, and followed Wally as he tried to steal the car. They were both arrested before the job went down. Meanwhile I was on the early morning train to our rendezvous to pick up the package. When they did not show up, I made off. Wally eventually got just six months for trying to steal the car, while Paul pleaded guilty to conspiracy and other robberies, including the Sunblest Bakeries in Seven Sisters Road, and got a big sentence. If the police had followed them and let them do the work before nicking them, they would have got me too.

I could go on forever about Wally McNelly, who I first met in Strangeways in the early 1960s. He later got ten years for a bank robbery in Nottingham with Jimmy Hayes and Terry Duxbury, a master safecracker famous for blowing fifteen safes in one go at Timpsons Shoes. Duxbury hurt his leg getting over a fence and a security guard had him until Wally pulled out his Walther pistol, stuck it in the guard's face and told him to let go. They were arrested two weeks later when police surrounded two caravans in North Wales. Again both were armed but they gave up. Little did the others know it was a set-up and that Duxbury had rolled over, becoming Manchester's first supergrass.

After serving his time, Wally came home and worked closely with me. I could always rely on him, even though he was crackers. One night we had a run out to find a toerag named Rick, who owed me money on a deal. I had given Jimmy 'the Liar' McDonald some gear to sell and he had given it to this Rick, who said he had a punter for it. That was the last I saw of them or my gear. Jimmy the Liar should have known better; he had worked for the firm for years and ran a car pitch for me in the seventies. His big failing, as his name suggests, was that he was a terrible liar. I don't think he could help himself. He even came into Phyllis's one night and told us his mother had died, adding for good measure that the dog had been run over. Like mugs we bought him drinks to drown his sorrows, sent flowers and even paid for his new suit for the funeral. Shortly afterwards, his mother was seen in her local pub drinking half a mild.

Anyway, Wally and I went looking for him and Rick and found them in a pub in Chinatown. I walked over and gave Rick a smack on the head, then Wally and I dragged them out of the bar. We drove them to a hotel that I had bought and was renovating at the time, and took them through the backyard into the cavernous cellars. This Rick had pissed me off and I wanted to hurt him. Jimmy the Liar tried to talk his way out of it, saying he had been fucked over himself.

'What about the gold bracelet I gave you to sell?' I said.

'I lost it,' he claimed. 'I was showing it in a bar and it disappeared.'

A likely story. I had had enough of these two and their bullshit. I threw Rick onto a work bench. Wally grabbed his arms and pinned him down while I picked up a joiner's hammer. I took a couple of four-inch nails and put one in the centre of Rick's hand. With one hit, the nail went through his hand and into the work bench. I gave it another clout for luck. He let out a noise, not a scream, more like a gargling sound. Jimmy the Liar fainted in fright. When he came to, Rick was sobbing, with a cloth around his hand. I told them they had two days to get my money and pay Wally. Which they did.

The Liar was a good front man but just could not stop telling porkies. When he worked for me, he would even tell people my car pitch was his. I never said a word – let the taxman send him the bills – until one morning I walked onto the site and he was with a couple of customers.

'Where the fucking hell have you been?' he shouted at me. 'What time do you call this?'

He must have thought it would impress the punters. They looked distinctly unimpressed when I strode over, laid him out with one punch and said, 'I'm handing in my cards, good day.'

Off I went. At mid-afternoon, I got a call at the Theatre Club from the Liar.

'What do you want?'

'I have had a good day, Jimmy, I've sold three cars for cash.'

'Come to my house in the morning.'

When he got there and I counted the money, it was £70 light. Now I was raging.

'I'm sorry Jimmy, I went in the casino.'

I gave him a tenner and told him that, with the £70 he had nicked, that was his wages for the week. I found out later that he had used my money to pay a debt to Jim Swords.

The Liar became a bit of a celebrity, everybody knew him, he rarely had to buy a drink. He had been on Manchester City's books and played in their reserves until he got caught thieving, and he often used to stand at the bar with George Best and other City and United players. We stayed on good terms, but I don't think he and Rick ever forgot me.

I could not really blame the pair of them, as the motor trade was almost totally bent in those days. There were all sorts of scams being pulled and we were usually in the middle of them. My old mentor Ginger Davies had a car business in the Knott Mill area of Deansgate and called me out of the blue one day.

'Get some cash ready and come and see me. I have a move for you.'

I called in and he said he was selling up.

'But what about your silent partner,' I asked, 'the man that buys the cars for you to sell?'

'Fuck him,' Ginger said. 'All the bills are in my name.'

I counted twenty cars on his forecourt and made notes of the make, mileage, condition and colour of each. I told Ginger that because there was a bit of a story with them, I could only give him half the trade price.

'That's okay,' he said. 'I will ring you when I'm ready. It will have to be late at night.'

I collected some of my workers from the scrapyard and told them to stand by. Then I went to Jim Swords to see if he wanted to come in. I said he could buy the whole 'parcel' but I would keep an American Chevy for my corner.

On the Friday night, we emptied the showroom, driving the cars away somewhere safe. Then JS, Ginger and I went to my house. Jimmy went through everything and chipped off a lump of money for Ginger. The deal done, Ginger then left me and JS to reckon up between us. This was one I was not going to win! I did manage to finish up with the Chevy and a few quid.

JS always drove a terrible deal. On another occasion, I got a phone call from him with a proposition about a car.

'Why don't you come over to my house tonight and have a few drinks,' he said, smooth as silk. 'Bring your missus with you. I have something to show you.'

'Okay.'

Jimmy and Pam had divorced years before and he had since remarried, to a gorgeous girl called Lynn. She made us some snacks and we had a few drinks. I cannot say he overfilled your glass; instead you got a sermon about the demon drink. Then it was down to business. Knowing I was into American cars, he told me he had a Chevy Monte Carlo for sale that was the bollocks. I went out to his garage to see it and it was a stunning car. Back in the house, I asked what year it was, as I knew that when you registered a foreign car you got the current year's plate but the car could actually be two years older. You had to see the year of manufacture on the log book to be sure. He told me it was a 1978 and he wanted two grand for it. I asked him if he was sure about the year, as I had fallen for this move before.

'Show me the log book, Jim.'

'I have not got it yet,' he said.

With that, Lynn piped up, 'Jimmy, you have got it, it is upstairs, I have seen it.'

She helpfully went upstairs and brought it down. And there it was – a year older than he had said and than it showed on the plate.

Now money was his God and a little fib over a car was for him the order of the day, but Lynn was aghast.

'How can you do that to your best pal?' she said.

He shrugged. 'It's just part of the game.'

I bought the car after making a bid. 'That's the equivalent of a few expensive brandies you have had off me,' he said. We both laughed; that was JS all over.

Another time, I sold him a two-bedroom apartment in Puerto Banus. He got it cheap for seventy-five grand, then sold it on to a friend of ours, Ace, for eighty-five grand but with a condition attached. 'If you sell it,' he told Ace, 'I want half the profits because at that price you have nicked it off me.'

Fifteen years later, I was chatting to Ace and asked him if he still had the apartment.

'Fucking hell, Jimmy,' he said, 'it's worth three hundred grand now. How can I sell it? JS will want his whack out of it. I'll have to wait until he turns his toes up.'

It was all fun with us but not with JS, he always wanted his cut. It kept us on our toes and made for some good banter.

IN THE LATE seventies, a little firm was given the job of a revenge attack on a night club on the border of Manchester and Salford. The plan was to break into the premises above the club and set fire to it, so that the fire would spread down into the club. The team set to work and everything went to plan, with one critical exception: they did not give themselves sufficient time to escape. They poured an inflammable liquid and lit it, only for the building to explode before they could leave. One of the men was blown through the windows. He was lucky: he suffered little more than cuts and bruises and managed to get away. The other guy did not make it: he was burnt to a crisp.

My phone went late at night: could I fetch the pick-up truck from my breaker's yard and move a car parked in the street? I was not told about the fire, simply that the car, another American Chevy, was being repossessed. I later found out that it was the arsonists' getaway car and could have been traced back to them, so it had to go. The guys involved could not drive it away, as it was locked and the keys were with the dead man, but if left in the street it would attract police attention. I picked it up, took it to my yard and had it chopped up within hours.

The next day, two of my pals crept into the gutted building. The emergency services had not realised there had been somebody in the building and my pals found the remains of the dead guy. They scraped them up; what was left fitted into a shoe box. It was buried on the moors. To this day no-one knows for certain whether it was an attack on the club, which was owned by London Ronnie Baker, or an insurance claim, but Ronnie later told me he never got a penny because the fire had started in the neighbouring building, which was uninsured. Denis Crolla later told me he was on the work and had driven the car. He also told me the name of the dead guy.

Years later, Denis and I were nicked out of town: there was a warrant out on him for some unpaid fines. When the police asked our names, Denis gave the name of the kid that died in the fire. All hell broke loose.

'You have been missing for years,' this detective said. 'Where have you been?'

In the end Denis had to tell them his real name. Of course, now they wanted to know what he knew about the missing man. He did not give anything away but they gave him a very hard time before releasing us. I could not believe what he had done, bringing back a name that had disappeared twenty years before. For years after that, the firm nicknamed me and Denis 'Burke and Hare' after the notorious bodysnatchers. We did get up to a lot of naughty things but I thought that was a bit strong.

THROUGHOUT THE SEVENTIES, Manchester Police would, rightly or wrongly, have blamed certain of my friends or associates for many of the robberies on their patch. By the end of the decade, however, another mob was causing them even more headaches. The Crazy Face Gang were prolific blaggers. Led by Fred Scott and Lennie Pilot, they got their name from the scary Halloween masks they wore on jobs. Between 1979 and 1982, the use of guns in robberies in Greater Manchester nearly quadrupled and much of it was down to them.

Scott and Pilot had them well organized. Each member of the gang had a single job so that if caught, they couldn't implicate anyone else: only the bosses knew the full picture. They would drill holes in the rear number plates of cars right through to the boot, so that one of them could hide in the boot and watch a target. Then they would jump out to surprise their victims. They would pick up empty fag packets in pubs and leave them at the scene of their crimes, knowing that the cops would test them for fingerprints and end up looking for some unfortunate smoker. Pilot was particularly cunning. He once went into a police station to make a complaint, was told to get to the back of the queue, and while he was waiting his turn, dashed out, donned a mask, pulled off a robbery, then returned to the police station, providing himself with the perfect alibi.

I knew most of them, particularly Scott, Pilot, Kenny Connors and 'Tommo' Thompson. They would call in at my places for a drink now and then. We generally got on well but I had a bit of a row with Pilot when they were on the rise. He was not what I would call a hard man but he could be a pest in drink. He came into a pub I had acquired, the Kensington on Newton Street, had a few drinks and asked if he could leave his car keys behind the bar. The barmaid put them away. When Pilot came back for them, another girl was on the bar and could not find them. He started giving her a hard time, so she rang upstairs for me and I came down.

'What's up Lennie?'

He got a bit aggressive so I told him to get the fuck out of the bar. He came back after closing time and rang the doorbell. He was still going on with himself as I let him in and closed the door, and did not see the heavy end of a pool cue in my hand. I hit him over the head with it, gave him a whacking, then slung him into the street.

He came back a few days later and said he was sorry.

'Fucking hell, Jimmy, what the fuck did I say to you? I have

The classic 1970s interior of El Corrida, the swankiest massage parlour in Manchester. Its clients included alleged pillars of the community and more than a few famous people. It closed down after a mysterious fire.

The Kensington in the Piccadilly area, the first of many public houses I owned. Manchester was a mecca for drinking dens and clubs, though many were destroyed to make way for the Arndale Centre in the seventies.

Thin Lizzy lead singer Phil Lynott at his wedding to Caroline, the daughter of TV presenter Leslie Crowther, on St Valentine's Day, 1980. Phil wrote 'The Boys Are Back In Town' about the QSG and 'Johnny The Fox Meets Jimmy The Weed' about me.

Rita with Bob Geldof, then the lead singer of the Boomtown Rats, at the same wedding reception that evening. Geldof was one of many musicians that Phil Lynott helped out over the years.

Denis Crolla and I on one of our early trips to Spain. We worked together on some dodgy things, so much so that someone nicknamed us 'Burke and Hare' after the notorious bodysnatchers.

Jim Swords with Billy Creswell, whose daughter married my son Tony, and Big Frank Platt. Frank was one of the original Market Mob and went on to work as doorman for me for many years.

Sharing a joke with Jack Trickett and Roy Gardner, a multi-millionaire who sponsored our boxing night at Belle Vue. Jack and I later fell out when he cut me out of the boxing and made a statement about me to the Board of Trade. We did not speak for ten years.

The exterior of the landmark Brown Bull Hotel, once the favourite haunt of George Best and other footballers, on the Manchester-Salford border.

The grand reopening of the Brown Bull and a large Hereford bull stands at the bar drinking pints of ale for a publicity stunt. Rita and I revived the pub.

Me and Rita with the top Irish comedian Dave Allen, a regular in my clubs when he was performing in Manchester and a wonderful storyteller.

The QSG on tour: sitting near ringside to watch boxing in Las Vegas. Jim Swords is in the foreground in the white shirt, then Jack Trickett, Vinnie Schiavo, an unknown guy who was on our trip, me in shades and Joe Swords. In the foreground you can make out the hair of actor Robert Redford, who moved seats after a tongue-lashing from Jimmy.

Congratulating a bruised but happy Alan Minter the day he took the world middleweight title from Vito Antuofermo in Vegas.

With heavyweight champ Larry Holmes, who referred to me as 'the Little Englishman'.

Larking around with the great boxing trainer Angelo Dundee at his Miami office while wearing Muhammad Ali's robe.

In front of Angelo's wall of fame, with photos of all his world champs. We had a wonderful time with him and his wife, and have remained friends to this day.

Kevin and Beryl Taylor on their yacht *Diogenes* in Miami. Several of the QSG were entertained on Kevin's boat, as was Deputy Chief Contable John Stalker, something that was later brought up to discredit him during the so-called Stalker Affair.

Tommy Burke with his close friend Cassius Clay, later Muhammad Ali. Tommy, one of Manchester's great characters, became part of Ali's entourage and was with him for many of his biggest fights.

On a trip to San Francisco, I just had to visit the cell of Robert Stroud, the famous Birdman of Alcatraz. He spent most of his life in prison, whereas I 'walked' from all of my numerous court trials.

The launch of our own promotional venture (*from left*): trainer Brian Robinson, Les Simms, who owned the Belle Vue arena, Jack Trickett and me. I loved boxing but circumstances and rivalries conspired against me.

PROFESSIONAL BOXING
BELLE VUE MANCHESTER
ONDAY, MARCH 28,

The boys in Spain: Ricky Gore, Vinnie Schiavo and Joe Leach at the back, Jim Swords and Louis Schiavo in front. We invested in properties out there and it was also a bolthole for any of the boys when they were on their toes.

Bo Hogberg, the hell-raising ex-boxer from Sweden who I knocked unconscious with a box of tiles.

Enjoying a drink with Londoner Clifford Saxe in the Queen Vic in Spain. The 1983 Security Express robbery, which lifted £6 million, was planned in Cliff's pub, but they never nailed him for it. He also famously gave the TV reporter Roger Cook a black eye.

been in bed for two days. I have got lumps on top of lumps on my head.'

'You have got to behave yourself in my gaffs, Lennie.'

We had a bit of lunch and that was the end of it. I actually liked Lennie. He was flash and full of himself but was good company, always having a joke, a good-looking guy who liked to be out and about. Fred Scott, who was ten years older, was the opposite. A taciturn man, he kept to himself, rarely ventured into town and was all business. At one time he offered his services to us but was told that we did our own work. He was also in the porno trade and had girlie magazine and video shops.

Kenny Connors was a witty person, always up for a laugh, but another nuisance when pissed. One night when my doorman, Gilly 'Concrete Face' Grundy, would not let him into the Senator Club, Kenny refused to take no for an answer and went on and on. I heard the noise and went to the door. Kenny was trying to push past Gilly, giving plenty of verbal. I told him to fuck off, as he was upsetting other people coming in. He called me a cunt. I gave him another warning.

'Fuck you,' he replied.

I hit him with a right-hander and he went over the bonnet of a parked car and lay in the street, out cold. Gilly picked him up and sat him in a doorway until he came round, when he finally pissed off. I didn't have any hard feelings against him, he was a likeable pest.

I had not seen him again for twenty-five years when he walked into a bar owned by my sons. His daughter worked there.

'Hello Jimmy,' he said. 'How are you?'

I bought him a drink and he sat there for a while, but after a few rounds, the same old Kenny surfaced.

'You took a fucking liberty beating me up twenty-five years ago.'

'Kenny, you never came back for a return and if you had I would have hurt you properly. And now after all this time you are bringing it up? We are old men.'

His daughter finally got hold of him and took him out. That was Kenny in beer.

The Crazy Face Gang were unstoppable in their heyday. They hit factories and mills, a hat company, a dairy, a bank and even the Oldham Council's direct works department. They were so rampant on the cobbles that Jim Anderton, the publicity-mad Chief Constable, put armed officers on the streets to combat them, the first time this had ever happened on the UK mainland. Eventually, Scott and Pilot were caught and were locked up on remand to await trial. The cops went to see Scott and conned him into believing that Lennie Pilot had rolled over. It was untrue, but Scott fell for it and admitted everything. The cops then went to Lennie and said Scott had coughed. Lenny told the cops to sod off, until they brought Scott into the room and he admitted it. At that point Lennie, disgusted, started talking too. I could not believe it when I heard the pair of them had caved in.

Scott claimed in one of his statements that he did some work for the QSG but that was not true. He and Pilot did grass up my pal Wally McNelly for supplying shotguns to them. Wally, who was just finishing a five-stretch, got a gate arrest as he was being released and finished up with me on the remand wing at Strangeways, when I was there for an airline ticket fraud. Wally had actually been minding the guns in question for me but was offered good money, so he sold them on. I had a few words with him but he told me he could replace them for less than he had sold them. He finally got a deal put to him: plead guilty and you will get three years. With his form he could have got ten, so he took it.

Scott and Pilot were sentenced in June 1983. A string of other arrests and convictions followed, based on their evidence. A lot of their associates pleaded guilty but I believe if they had gone not guilty they could have got away with it. They failed to challenge the supergrass system, which was later abandoned because it was unsound. Tommo Thompson kept his mouth shut and got the most bird out of all of them, twelve years. We were on the same landing in Strangeways and used to walk the exercise yard together. He was the heavyweight on the firm. I liked him a lot.

It was later alleged in court that Jim Swords had put out a £50,000 contract on Scott, Pilot and the cop who had turned them, a Manchester detective called Exton, but this was garbage. The truth is that they only grassed up each other. They had nothing on the QSG. Although the Crazy Face Gang were a threat to the public, they were not and never could be to us.

By the late seventies, in fact, many of the QSG had legitimate money. Jim and Joe Swords had the car pitch and barrows, the Schiavos had various businesses, Jimmy Riley was making fortunes in scrap metal and Jack Trickett owned a successful hotel. Even those of us who had dabbled in crime were virtually straight. They had pretty much stopped 'working' and were now pulling the strings instead. It was time to enjoy life.

9

STARS AND BARS

N 1979, I BOUGHT the Senator Club off an ex-policeman called Jimmy Rowe, in partnership with Joe Swords and Vinnie Schiavo. Originally called the Stage and Radio, the club, in Newton Street, had a history going back to the forties. Jack London, the former British heavyweight champion, had worked the door there, and Bobby Critchley and his henchman Harry 'the Savage' Hilton once chopped up someone inside. When I took it over, the Senator featured live music and attracted a nice crowd. The Irish comedian Dave Allen would often come in after performing at the Palace Theatre and tell tall stories, footballers like Paddy Crerand and Sammy McIlroy were regulars, while the actor Bill Tarmey brought in the *Coronation Street* crowd. My compere, Tony Hulme, was known as 'Mr Manchester' and could fill the club on his own.

Anyone who has ever worked in clubland knows it is full of characters. On one memorable occasion, I booked the singer P.J. Proby, famous for splitting his pants on stage. He was staying at a hotel I had bought and could not pay his bill, so I asked him to do a few spots at the Senator. His opening night was great, but the next night he was pissed and messed up the show, telling the customers they were cunts. I had to drag him off the stage and throw him out. He came back to my hotel later that night, legless, with a bottle of vodka in his hand. I let that go, got him up to his room but slung him out the next day. What a talent the man had, but when he worked for my pal Tom Robinson at his Talk of the North club he did the same thing. I hear today he is still going strong and has straightened himself out.

On another night, Tom Robinson had the comedian Bob Monkhouse topping the bill, and after the show we all went on to the Piccadilly Hotel for breakfast. As we were eating, the singer Dusty Springfield came in with a dark-skinned girl and joined us. Bob started cracking filthy stories – his club act was very blue and if you had not seen it you got a shock – and we had a hilarious time. It was the first time I had realized that Dusty was gay and that her friend, a popular soul singer of the day, was her lover. The Piccadilly Hotel had a breakfast bar called the Horseshoe and was the 'in' place for club owners and actors. You could get breakfast and champagne from four in the morning onwards and it became the final meeting place after we had been out all night. I had breakfast with Andy Williams, Jack Jones, Matt Munroe and many other stars there.

In 1980, I expanded into Chinatown, an area that had become increasingly popular as night-time trade shifted across the city centre during the construction of the Arndale Centre. Ted O'Neill, a big pal and a big man who had worked the doors for years, had a private members' club there called Salimis. It was a good earner, but one day at a funeral he told me he wanted out and did I know anyone who would buy it.

'I'll have it, Ted,' I said. 'How much?'

We did the deal there and then and I added it to my growing portfolio of licensed premises, which included the Senator Club and the Kensington pub in Piccadilly. I renamed it JR's, after me and my wife, put in Ronnie Earl to run it and it did well. It was an afternoon drinker at a time when it was hard to get a legal drink after 3 p.m. The police were hard on any pubs selling after time, so I thought it would be a good move. It was.

JR's was next door to the restaurant of my Chinese pal Charlie Chan, who pretty much ran Chinatown. Charlie would come in my club every day and always drank double Martell, which was my tipple too. He spoke broken English but you could have a deal with him; he certainly knew how to chip you down in a bit of business. As his sons, Alan and Raymond, grew up they took over from him. There was plenty of aggro with business rivals and Alan was chopped up with machetes by some Triads, but went back and did them in return. They opened restaurants and video clubs all over Chinatown and one of the first lap dancing clubs, Long Legs, and went from strength to strength, a great family. My sons and old Charlie's sons are pals and still have the odd night out together.

Some of the names that would work for me in Manchester and Spain over the next decade went on to be big stars: Syd and Eddie, who became Little and Large, Freddie Starr, who was originally with the Delmonts, Bernard Manning, the Grumbleweeds, George Roper, Mick Miller, Ivor Davis, Jerry Harris, Jackie Carlton, Foo Foo Lammar, Jack Smethurst of *Love Thy Neighbour* fame and the impressionist Franklyn James, who to me was better than Freddie Starr but not as crude. Tony Christie performed for me, as did a good band called Sweet Chariot and Angie Gold, a great singer who never made it as big as she should have in the UK. I brought the Detroit Emeralds over from America. Bobby Ball was a regular in my Senator Club and was always good for a laugh, and then there was Manchester's own singer-compere, the great Tony Hulme, with my regular house band the Clive Allen Sound. Another great act was the reggae singer Gary Nash, while the best Elvis-style voice belonged to big Jim White.

Foo Foo Lammar deserves a special mention. Real name Frank Pearson, he was another Ancoats lad who became the most famous drag artist of his day and a wealthy club owner in his own right. As far as we were concerned he was one of us. He might have been gay and worn women's clothes but, believe me, he could fight; we called him the 'rough, tough puff'. He used to fill my Senator Club on a Monday night and enjoyed huge success with his own venue, Foo Foo's Palace, a favourite with hen and stag parties.

Karl Denver was another great lad. His Karl Denver Trio hit the big time when their song 'Wimaway' finally knocked Acker Bilk's longstanding number one 'Strangers on the Shore' off the top of the pop charts. I had known Karl for a few years by then, having first met him in a pub in Hulme with Johnny Davis, a guy who would not back down from anybody. I saw Johnny have a few fights, including one with the legendary Scotch Dave. Karl stayed the same even when his career took off, always happy to have a drink with the lads. He was not just a great singer but also a fantastic storyteller and mimic. He could throw his voice and had a trick of talking to his wristwatch so that you would think the watch was talking back to you: you could not see his lips move, even close up. When he ordered drinks off waitresses he would drive them crazy by throwing his voice: they would not know who was talking to them. Karl went on to play many gigs for me at my pubs and clubs and had a good life, travelling the world. In between, he would always be wheeling and dealing.

The QSG knew pretty much every celebrity, entertainer or sports star in Manchester in this period. Anybody who had anything at all to do with the club scene would mix in our company. The snooker ace Alex 'Hurricane' Higgins came from Northern

Ireland but lived in Manchester for much of his adult life. I got to know him very well after first having a run-in with him not long after he had won the world title. I was in the Press Club with Ronnie Earl to see Alex take on three guys who had won the right to play him in a local club competition. They were just ordinary lads but Alex did not give them a chance: the first one potted only two balls.

'That did not take long,' Ronnie said to him at the bar.

'I'm not here to teach them,' said Alex.

He may have been the world champion but he could be a bastard. We finished up late in the Showbiz and arranged to meet the next day in the Theatre Club, Les Simms's afternoon drinker. By the time Alex came in, we'd already had a few. I got up to buy him a drink and asked him what he wanted. He didn't answer, just looked at me as if I had two heads. I asked him again.

'Who are you?' he said, in that obnoxious manner he had.

'I'll show you who I am,' I said.

I grabbed hold of his cue case, leant it on the bar and jumped on it, smashing his cue in two. He let out a scream and Ronnie came over.

Alex was crying: 'My favourite cue!'

'You had better go,' Ronnie told him. 'The Weed is only in first gear.'

Later on we did become pals, to my cost. Every time we met he was in my ribs for money or favours, more so in later years. I once found him asleep in a doorway in Didsbury, an upmarket suburb of Manchester where I had bought a flat with a lady friend. We ended up taking him home with us. He stayed a few days, borrowed a few pounds and was off. Give him his due, when he was on top he did come in my bars, which was good for attracting the punters. He never spent a penny but that was Alex. What I do not understand was why people did not help him years before his decline, the same with George Best. They only want to name places after you when you are dead.

IN MARCH 1980, a little mob of us flew to Las Vegas to see the middleweight title fight between Alan Minter and Vito Antuofermo. Jim and Joe Swords, Jack Trickett, Vinnie Schiavo and I booked rooms at Caesars Palace and bought some of the best seats in the house. After checking in, we went on the town. I met a girl at the bar at Caesars and took her to the Sands to see Paul Anka in concert, a great show.

The following day we were sitting around the pool, sunbathing and chatting to the promoter Mickey Duff, when this lovely girl asked if the sunbed next to me was free. Then she sat down and began talking. I had just ordered drinks and asked if she would like one. 'Gin fizz,' she said. We spent the next couple of hours in conversation. She was full of curiosity about England and where I lived. Somehow her face seemed familiar.

At about four o'clock, one of the lads said, 'We're hiring a helicopter to take us to San Francisco for the night. Are you coming?'

'Are you mad?' I said. 'What for? I have a beautiful bird here chatting me up.'

The lads left to go to Frisco while I ordered us some food and champagne. She told me she was an actress and then it hit me: she was Susan St James, from the TV series *McMillan and Wife*. She was waiting for friends to arrive for the fight. I spent a lovely evening with her. We sat there till late that night: moonlight, soft music, champagne and a beautiful actress for company. It was magic.

I saw her the next day having lunch by the pool and she thanked me for dinner. Sadly we never met again. When the boys came back and asked what I had done the night before, I casually told them I had spent a very pleasant evening with a beautiful Hollywood star. They had a hard time believing me.

The venue was packed with celebrities on fight night. Muhammad Ali was there, along with a whole list of other great fighters and film stars. I noticed Joe Louis, the great old Brown Bomber, at ringside in a wheelchair and went over to ask how he was. He couldn't talk well by that stage but he nodded back. We were just settling into our seats when Robert Redford and another guy sat down on the row in front of us.

In one of the intervals between fights, a few English fans of Minter came over to Redford and asked for his autograph. He refused and his pal said, 'Write to his fan club.'

Jim Swords, who was sitting behind him, tapped Redford on the head.

'Sign the programme for them,' he said. 'Who the fuck do you think you are?'

Redford didn't like that at all. A few minutes later, he and his pal got up and did not come back. They must have found new seats.

We were now in our pomp. Most of the guys were making plenty from various businesses and were looking to invest it. Around this time, I went to Spain with the same guys – Jim, Joe, Vinnie and Jack – with a view to buying property as a consortium. JS had owned a villa out there since the early seventies and knew the area but did not speak the language, so we took Les Grey, a car salesman friend of ours. Les was a flash type but good at his job and, crucially, spoke Spanish, so he could conduct the negotiations. In the end, Jim Swords bought five small houses on his own. He pretty much nicked them off the builder: they had not been yet fitted out with kitchens or bathrooms and the builder was in financial trouble, so JS got them for a song. Spain became a second home to the QSG for the rest of the decade.

We had been travelling there for holidays for years. Les Simms had a boat in Puerto Banus when it was just taking off with the jetset; Sean Connery was two boats down in the harbour. Vinnie Schiavo and I discovered Benalmadena when we rented a couple of little villas though another great character, Frank Evans, a Salford lad who trained in Spain as a bullfighter. They called him *El Inglés* – the Englishman – and he later wrote a book called *The Last English Bullfighter*. In between killing cattle, he got into all sorts of deals. I told him that I was going over to Spain with Vin and our respective partners and sons, and we were looking to rent for a month. He said he would speak to a Spanish pal. A week later, he told me he had just the right place: two small, new villas in Benalmadena. We were to meet his pal in Torremolinos to pick up the keys and pay him.

We arrived, collected the keys from a young woman and got directions to what turned out to be two sparsely equipped properties. Somebody had dumped bedding, knives and forks inside and that was it: no TV, little furniture and basic amenities. The whole site was only half-finished.

After a week, a Spanish guy came round and said he was Manolo Hidalgo, Frank's friend. He was looking for payment. I told him we would settle the bill later. Once he had gone, I told Vinnie, 'Fuck him, he has had us over.'

A few days later, a coach pulled up and offloaded a group of people, who began walking around our villas. One young couple come over to us and asked what we were doing. They were Portuguese but spoke English. We said we were staying at the villas for a month. They told us they had bought the villa I was in and it was not for rent. Manolo must have pulled some sort of stunt. We told them we were staying and to contact the builders. They left.

The next time we saw Manolo was the day before we were due to leave.

'What do you think we should do?' said Vinnie.

'Leave it to me,' I said.

I had found an old cheque book in my case for the District Bank, which no longer existed. I told Manolo that we had run out of cash and I would have to give him a cheque.

'No problem,' he said. 'I will give it to Frank to cash for me.'

With that we were off back to Blighty. A few weeks later, Frank Evans came to see me.

'What have you done, Jimmy? Manolo's got a cheque for a bank that does not exist.'

We told Frank the story. He said he could not understand it.

A few weeks after that, I was outside the car pitch in Ancoats with Vinnie when this bloke walked towards us.

'Fuck me, Vin, this guy looks like Manolo.'

It was. 'I have come to see you,' he said. 'You never pay me. You bad lads.'

I was on him straight away. 'No Manolo, after you go I paid the Portuguese people, they came back with the builder.'

It was all bullshit but he just laughed and that was it. Never con a con artist. We still joke about Manolo Hidalgo.

THE BROWN BULL was a three-storey, twenty-two-bed hotel and pub on the corner of Chapel Street and New Bailey Street, on the Salford-Manchester border. A distinctive curved building with a brownstone frontage, it had a colorful history. A bloke called Billy Barr had run it as a hotel for commercial travellers, until one day in 1967, George Best walked into the public bar for a quiet drink. He liked its homely, anonymous feel, and became a regular. Within weeks, many footballers and faces of the day were drinking in there. 'The Brown Bull was a home for those who didn't belong anywhere else,' wrote an ex-United player, Eamon Dunphy, in his book about Matt Busby, *A Strange Kind of Glory*. 'Actors from the nearby Granada Studios joined villains, dodgy bank-managers, gamblers, journalists and other refugees from suburban conventions.' Bestie practically lived there for a while, as did his pals like the City player Mike Summerbee. It was never the most glamorous of venues but it attracted crowds of hangers-on.

Those days had largely gone when, in 1980, I took it over on a twenty-eight-year lease. It had been neglected for some time and was in a bad state both upstairs and down, but the rent was only £50 a week and I knew it had potential. I paid ten grand cash for the lease and another hundred grand doing it up. It was an awful lot of money in those days but the Brown Bull was almost on the doorstep of Granada TV and I knew I could attract their business. At the grand reopening I had the Manchester United team there, actors including Mark McManus, later of *Taggart* fame, and a big, brown Hereford bull with an advertising sign strapped to its side that stood in the bar drinking pints of bitter. I had heard that a farmer used to take it down the pub with him, so I contacted him and he agreed to bring it to Salford for the publicity.

The Brown Bull was revived and was soon filled once again with sports and TV personalities. Every day after training, United players would call in for lunch. The local office workers could not believe it: lunch, a pint for £1.10 and a famous footballer standing at the bar. From the old school, Paddy Crerand was a regular, while the heavyweight boxer Brian London drove in every Monday from Blackpool for lunch and to see friends. My instincts were right and soon I was getting a lot of bookings from Granada as well, accommodating visitors while they were filming at the studios.

Some of the actors and actresses proved to be a pain. They wanted five-star treatment and thought they were superstars. Pat Phoenix, who played Elsie Tanner in *Coronation Street*, was one of the worst. Granada rang one Sunday afternoon, after the public bar was closed, wanting to know if I could give the *Corrie* cast tea, coffee and sandwiches. I agreed but told them I had no staff as such, as the bar closed at 2 p.m. on a Sunday and the staff went home. The actors duly arrived by bus, came in and sat about reading their lines. We put out the tea and coffee and plates of ham and cheese sandwiches.

Then Pat Phoenix lurched over to the bar, going on with herself and waving a plate of sandwiches. Rita asked what was wrong.

'You do not cut those in half,' she snapped, 'you cut them in quarters and cut the crust off.'

My wife told her we had only had half an hour's notice from Granada and that we had no staff on duty. She carried on complaining until her husband, Alan Browning, told her to shut up.

Liz Dawn, the *Corrie* stalwart who played Vera Duckworth, created a massive scene when she booked into a double room with some guy. They had a few drinks at the bar, then disappeared to the room. The following day, same sketch. On the third day, she was coming downstairs with this feller at lunchtime when a man sitting at the bar jumped up and confronted them. Dawn went white: it was her husband. He punched the bloke she was with and then attacked her. It transpired that she had been having a fling with a wine salesman she had met in the Film Exchange. The salesman legged it out of the bar and she ran upstairs, while I calmed down her husband and got him to leave. The following morning she came down for breakfast with a black eye.

The biggest prat of all was the actor George Sewell, who often played villains and had been in *Get Carter*, the Michael Caine gangland flick. Sewell stayed with us for a good while and after closing time would often eat with us in the hotel kitchen. We treated him like one of the family. Then one day I was over at another hotel in the gay quarter of Manchester and spotted George at the bar. I went over to say hello and ask if he had checked in at the Brown Bull. He did not reply, he just looked right through me. Maybe I had found out that despite his tough, East London image, he was just a little puffy. I met him a couple more times over the years, once at Charlie Kray's funeral, when I said hello again but he slithered round the buffet table.

I discovered that a lot of actors do not live in the real world. Vinnie Schiavo and I were once having a meal at a beach bar in Fuengirola when Tommy Boyle, who had done a bit on *Coronation Street*, walked in with a girlfriend and a guy called Peter from James and Peter's, a top hairdressing shop in Manchester where my wife went. Also with them was the well-known actor Donald Pleasence, who had a girl in tow. I knew her from around Manchester; she had a very loud mouth. Tommy spotted me and came over to say hello, while the hairdresser said hello to my wife. With that, the waiter said, 'Can I put you all together?' It seemed like a good idea. Tommy introduced us to Donald Pleasence and he was good company, unlike his girlfriend who was insulting bar staff, effing and blinding every other word.

After a salad and some wine, they really got stuck into the booze. Tommy was telling me about the films Pleasence had done with the likes of Steve McQueen, Richard Burton and Sean Connery: he played Blofeld in the Bond movie *You Only Live Twice* and had been in *The Great Escape*. But as the drink went down, Pleasence also became very vulgar. Eventually we all went on to the beach to get some sun and sleep off the booze.

We had been there about an hour. Pleasence was lying next to me. All of a sudden he sat up and started screaming that his gold Rolex watch had been stolen.

'I had it here on my wrist when I fell asleep,' he yelped.

Then he turned to me and Vinnie and said, 'You have got it.'

A crowd was gathering.

'Listen, you fucking faggot,' I said. 'I have taken nothing and if you say it again I will fucking batter you.'

Just then his loudmouthed girlfriend returned from the toilet.

'What's going on?' she said to the superstar.

He told her he had lost his Rolex, looking at me. With that, she opened her bag and brought out the watch. She laid into him with a further torrent of abuse. Vinnie, my wife and I picked up our belongings. We had had enough.

'The next time I see you, where it is quiet,' I told him, 'I am going to stick that watch up your arse.'

A few days later, we bumped into them again. Mr Superstar was all over me, saying how sorry he was, that it was all the beer's fault. But you could not stay in their company for long, they were too much trouble. Tommy and Peter eventually moved out of the villa Pleasence owned and came to Marbella to stay on the boat with us for a few days. Tommy told me the story. Superstar had met the girlfriend in the Film Exchange, a private club in Manchester, a few years before and they spent a lot of time together. He liked her foul mouth and being tied up and whipped. They ended up being barred from most of the bars. I saw Pleasence on and off afterwards but I could never take to him after the watch incident. I told him that Vinnie and I would never do that sort of thing, we would sooner give you a watch than take one. These people had never heard of the pride and honour of a good villain.

With some people, fame or authority goes to their head. Malcolm Allison was not the only football manager who got on the wrong side of Jimmy Swords. Another was Ron Atkinson, who took over at Manchester United in 1981. Bavadage, an upmarket club owned by a pal of ours, had a copy of the FA Cup on display and we were in there one night with some United players, having fun. We had filled the cup with champagne when in walked Ron. He got the needle right away and said something to the midfielder Sammy McIlroy, who a lot of people did not know was Jim Swords' brother-in-law: they married sisters. Ron made a grab at the cup but Jimmy beat him to it and tipped it upside down on Ron's head. He was soaked, and fucked off out of the club. Some people say that was the real reason Sammy McIlroy moved on from United: he was sold to Stoke City in 1982 when he was only twenty-seven and at his peak as a player.

One great little spot where a lot of footballers of Irish descent mixed with us was the Circus Tavern on Portland Street, reputed to be one of the smallest public houses in the world. You were sure to find a face from Ireland in there, if you could get in. My great friends Terry and Kath Corless ran it for thirty years, and their customers included George Best, Liam Brady, Kevin Moran, Ray Tracey and Shay Brennan, as well as bands like the Furey Brothers, the Wolfe Tones, the Dubliners and Paddy Reilly, who made that great hit record 'The Fields of Athenry'. I also befriended a group of young Manchester United supporters from Tramore, County Waterford, who stayed at the Brown Bull. I looked after them, introduced them to players and took them to visit Paddy Crerand's pub in Altrincham. One of them, Joe O'Shea, invited Rita and me over to Tramore, where they had a hotel just off the beach. We fell for the place and made many friends there. Shay Brennan even retired there after he left Manchester United and later died there, on the golf course.

IN MARCH 1981, Rita and I returned to Las Vegas with one of Manchester's great characters, Tommy Burke, and his wife. Tommy was a naturally funny man who had been on the stage in his younger days in a double act called the Star Brothers. During the day he drove a hackney cab, and one day he picked up a fare and recognised him as Angelo Dundee, the renowned American boxing trainer, who was in Manchester with his light-heavyweight champion, Willie Pastrano. Tommy was a boxing nut and immediately struck up a conversation. They ended up sitting in the cab at the side of the road for an hour, talking boxing. Angelo told Tommy he would call him if he ever needed him. And he did, later asking Tommy to join him at his famous Fifth Street Gym in Miami Beach. There he met a young man called Cassius Clay, who changed his name to Muhammad Ali. Tommy went on to be assistant cornerman at more than a dozen of Ali's fights. His job was to stay down by the ringside, timing the rounds and looking after the equipment. He was there when Ali won the title from Sonny Liston, when Henry Cooper knocked him down at Wembley, and at the legendary Rumble in the Jungle against George Foreman. Over the years I have met a lot of famous people, but Tommy knew everyone.

Tommy was now running the Cumberland Club in Salford for Dougie Flood, who the QSG did not get on with. But everyone liked Tommy, his jokes and stories. I jumped at the chance to go Stateside with him and meet some of his boxing cronies. We stayed again at Caesars Palace, where I found out that heavyweight champion Larry Holmes was preparing for a title defence. I went to the arena at the back of the hotel and there was the great man himself, training to fight Trevor Berbick. After watching his sessions for a couple of days, I introduced myself and asked if he minded my being there, as no-one else was about. He said it was okay and after a few days we were friends. He called me 'the Little Englishman'. Eight or nine year later, I was back in Vegas and stepped into a lift at the Sands Hotel to see the huge figure of Larry Holmes standing there. He took one look at me and didn't miss a beat. 'The Little Englishman!' he said. 'How are you?' A top man, Larry, and very shrewd – he made a fortune from real estate investments outside the ring.

After our stay in Vegas, Tommy and I and our wives flew to Miami, where Angelo Dundee had booked us into a hotel near his house. I could not wait to meet 'Mister Boxing', the trainer of the great Ali and many other world champions. Tommy and I were having a beer in the hotel bar when a call came for him at reception. I had to do a double-take when, standing there, was the comedian Mike Winters, of Mike and Bernie Winters fame. He had come to drive us to see Angelo at the gym. It was surreal. On the way, he explained that after he had split from his brother, he had been living in Miami and was now ghostwriting Angelo's autobiography. He was very likeable.

At the gym, Angelo instantly made a fuss of Tommy and warmly shook my hand. He told me that he had trained nine world champions and I asked him about Carmen Basilio, one of his greats. He took me into his office and showed me his wall of fame, with photos of all his fighters, and took pictures of me sat at his desk and in front of his wall. I even put on Ali's robe. From there we went to his house for drinks and lunch. We sat and talked for hours. He was impressed that I knew so much about boxing.

Angelo said our timing was just right, as his brother Chris had a show on and he had left ringside seat tickets for us. Over beers, he told me that his family came to America via Ellis Island and that their real name was Dundini.

We had a fabulous few days. Angelo and his wife Helen could not have looked after us better. One night he brought some friends, a guy named J.B. Goth and his girl, and the eight of us went to an Italian restaurant. After a great meal, J.B. suggested we go back to his place for a drink. We drove into a garage, parked the cars and got into an underground lift. When the doors opened we were in this luxury office. He then opened some double doors to this massive private bar. The drinks were put out and I started to look around the bar. The walls were studded with photos of film and TV stars. J.B. came over.

'Those are all the people I have done work on,' he said.

'What do you mean?'

He told me he was a plastic surgeon and this was his clinic. His celebrity patients could not meet at just any place so the offices, bar and lounge were above the clinic. Pointing to one I recognised as Eddie Fisher, the crooner who married Debbie Reynolds and Elizabeth Taylor, he said he had done about five jobs on him. I also recognised Shirley Bassey.

Rita loved the glamour of it all, and I have to admit it was fascinating for someone of our background to meet the rich and famous and watch how they lived. I have never been one for celebrity bullshit but I do like to observe outrageous people, and Miami in the eighties was a great place to do that. One evening, we were having a cocktail at the bar of our hotel on the Strip when a striking blonde came in wheeling a bicycle. She ordered a drink, sat down and started talking to the girls, asking where they were from. She looked in her early fifties but was still very attractive and you could tell she had been a stunner in her day. She said she cycled to the hotel bar every night for the happy hour – it kept her fit!

'She was a nice person,' I said to the barman after she left.

'Do you know who that is?' he said. 'That's Vikki LaMotta, the Raging Bull's ex-wife.'

The movie *Raging Bull*, with Robert DeNiro playing the boxer Jake LaMotta, had come out the year before and made Vikki famous. When I told Angelo, he said, 'Yes, that would be her, she lives near the beach off Collins Avenue.' We left the next day, so I had no chance to talk to her again. I would have liked to have asked her about Jake.

We had been in Miami for a few days when a pal of mine, Kevin Taylor, turned up on an ocean-going yacht, *Diogenes*, that he had just bought. He took us all out for a day in Biscayne Bay. The weather was warm, the water calm, and we had a very pleasant time. Little did I know that that short trip, and another Kevin made on the same vessel with a few of the QSG, would later be raked up during the so-called Stalker Affair in an attempt to discredit Kevin, us and a senior Manchester police officer.

Our week in Florida went all too quickly. We visited Angelo's house every day, sat in his garden talking boxing into the evening before dining at his favourite restaurants. When we left, he gave me a pair of Ali's boxing boots. I gave Helen Dundee a Waterford Crystal decanter as a thank you gift. She loved it and showed us her collection of crystal. For a few years afterwards, I would send her Waterford; every time someone was going to Miami I would say, 'Take this with you, here's a telephone number, ring it.' They always got a shock when Angelo Dundee answered.

Three months after my visit to Florida, a few more of the firm went out there and took a five-day cruise around the Bahamas on Kevin's yacht: Mick Brown, Joe Leach, Vinnie Schiavo and Jack

Trickett, together with my security man, Dessie O'Connor. As Kevin later pointed out in his autobiography, 'These were no more than social visits and I was happy to entertain the boys by way of a thank you for the help they had given me in the Vanland days, when I was often struggling to make ends meet.' The trip was innocent enough, though that was not how it was later portrayed.

Kevin had a wide circle of friends. Another of his many pals was a police officer called John Stalker, who he first met in 1971 when their children were at the same school. As Stalker rose to become Deputy Chief Constable of Greater Manchester, he and Kevin remained close. In December 1981, Stalker and his wife went out on the *Diogenes* with Taylor, though apparently Stalker spent most of the week throwing up with a stomach bug. The fact that Stalker had been on the same boat used to entertain the QSG six months earlier would later be one of a tissue of innuendoes used in an attempt to discredit Stalker and persecute Kevin Taylor.

In January, 1982, Kevin threw a fiftieth birthday party at his mansion at the little village of Summerseat, near Bury, north of Manchester. Kevin by then had joined the Tory Party and in fact became chairman of Manchester Conservative Association. He invited Rita and me and asked if I would supply drinks glasses, as I was in the pub trade. I duly did so. There must have been around 100 people there, including the Conservative MP Cecil Franks. I was introduced to this slim guy in spectacles and told him I ran the Brown Bull. He said, 'Oh, I'm just up the road from you, I'm the boss at the Crescent. I will have to come and see you and have a beer.'

I thought he meant a pub and was a fellow landlord, but he explained he meant the Crescent police station on Chapel Street. It was John Stalker. I didn't know him from Adam. I remember he wore a black shirt and black trousers and looked a bit like a musician; in fact he had played in a band in his youth. He got on the piano and started to play and the little actress out of *Coronation Street*, Lynn Perrie, started singing. They performed a duet. Someone produced a camera and I was photographed in a small group with Stalker's wife, though I did not know who she was.

Stalker would later say he had no recollection of meeting me. That is quite possible – there were scores of guests and, as one of Manchester's top cops, he must have shaken the hands of thousands of strangers at social functions over the years, so there was no reason why he should have remembered me. But that brief, forgettable encounter would come back to haunt both of us.

THE SUMMER OF 1982 saw us back in Spain. The World Cup was being played there, and the Scotland team lodged in a hotel about a mile from Puerto Banus. Despite having a strong squad, they were knocked out in the early stages. Some of the players stayed on for a few days to soak up the sun and drown their sorrows and I met up with two of my pals from Manchester United, Joe Jordan and Gordon McQueen. They came in Patrick's Bar in the port, along with Frank Gray, Kenny Dalglish and a couple of others. We had a good day watching games on the TV and later moved onto the patio. The players were still sick about getting knocked out and everyone was getting pissed.

At about six o'clock in the evening, Kenny Dalglish's wife arrived. She was in a shocking mood and screamed at Kenny about drinking. He told her he would be home later. With that she picked up a drink and threw it over him. They had a stand-up row and in the end Kenny walked off, with his wife following, still giving him verbal. Later Gordon McQueen told me that Kenny was a non-drinker but had broken out and started drinking a few months earlier. The rest of us carried on and I ended up having a good few days with my Man United pals in the port and on the *Sherama*, a yacht bought by Jack Trickett.

Living in the port on the boat was great, we could have a night out and then invite people back for a few drinks. We met the film actor Ronald Fraser and he spent a bit of time with us on board in Puerto Banus. He was a wise man, and told nonstop jokes. He had stopped drinking on doctor's orders and liked to smoke a spliff instead. 'I am going into the galley, Jimmy, for a herbal Woodbine,' he would say. He would not smoke in front of others but told me that it helped him after years of being alcoholic. The entertainer Des O'Connor was another regular in the port bars. When he got up to sing in Duke's Bar, everybody would pile in to hear him. It was electric at times.

But you know what they say about all good things.

WE HAD NOTICED around this time that we were being watched. Certain police officers were starting to wonder where we were getting the cash to open all these businesses and buy big houses and other properties. It had to have come from somewhere.

This was the era of the supergrass, when many firms were brought down by a Judas in the camp. Yet nobody ever grassed on us. Partly this was because we were ultra careful. We did not take unnecessary risks and we kept everything on a need-to-know basis. There were many times when I did not know what even my best pal was doing because I was not included in that bit of work. Regional police forces were not geared up like today for surveillance and intelligence. There was poor cooperation across force borders, so if a post office was knocked off in Yorkshire and they thought a Manchester crew was responsible, they were not interested. We were pretty much a step ahead of the police as regards intelligence. The only time we had a problem was when the leaders of the Crazy Face Gang made statements, and later with a grass called Burton, but otherwise it was rare for anyone to break our defences.

Old Carmen Schiavo had a yard in Ancoats where he stored the family ice cream vans. His sons, Louis and Vinnie, also used it as a breaker's yard and scrap metal site. One day, Louis and I were in the yard when we noticed a van parked thirty yards down the street.

'Why is that there?' I asked.

'I don't know,' he said. 'It has been there hours now and funnily enough it was there last week.'

On the roof there was a kind of ventilation shaft that would spin when you were driving. As I watched, this thing rose like a periscope.

'That's the Old Bill!' I said. 'We're on camera!'

'You're joking.'

Louis grabbed a petrol can and we went out to the van.

'Throw that petrol on it and set alight to it,' I said, loudly enough for anyone inside the van to hear. 'It's only an old scrapper.'

The doors burst open and out jumped several red-faced plain clothes police. They gave us furious looks before driving off as quickly as they could.

Shortly afterwards, we got word that police were also watching us from the tower of Ancoats Hospital. We knew the chef there – we would sometimes get an early breakfast from him on our way home from the clubs – and he told us. From the tower they could look all over my scrapyard and the car pitches. We bought binoculars and started watching them back. In a chapter about the QSG in his book *Stalker: The Search for the Truth*, the journalist Peter Taylor wrote: 'Detectives grew suspicious when their cover was blown on more than one occasion. Once, when a particular car pitch was being watched from the top floor of an old mill that overlooked the site, men were said to have come out with air rifles and blown the windows out of the observation point.' He also quotes a senior detective as saying, 'If we were watching them from a room across the road, they wouldn't make themselves scarce; they'd walk right across and put a brick through the window. They'd let us know they knew. There were lots of stories about how they got their information out, but nobody cut put their finger on it.'

We later found out that the Regional Crime Squad were so frustrated by our discoveries of their surveillance that they were convinced we had corrupted senior officers and were being fed information. The truth was, we knew everybody in Manchester: cab drivers, bellhops, doormen, cleaners, barmaids and waiters. We very rarely had to go looking for information. It came to us.

However, it is true that we did know bent cops. There were a few of them about in those days. The worst – or best from my point of view – was a guy I first met when he was a sergeant in the Moss Side area. He is dead now, but I won't name him to spare his family's blushes. I was with Ginger Davies, who was wanted for a driving offence. He gave this sergeant a £5 bung and the offence disappeared. The next time I met him, he was an inspector at another station. He came down to the scrapyard and said there had been a complaint by one of my neighbours that a fellow seen at my yard was out to kill him. It turned out that this neighbour had given prosecution evidence in a trial at Leeds, and had been moved to Manchester for protection. By chance he recognised Wally McNelly, who had just left prison after ten years, and mistakenly thought he had come after him. This fellow shat himself and ran to the nick. The inspector told me the story, which was very helpful of him, so I bunged him a few quid. From then on I often went to him with problems such as people's speeding or traffic offences and he would get them written off, for a price. He was on the payroll not just from me but from everybody. We would meet him in the sauna bath at a local leisure centre to pay him.

He then moved to another patch in north Manchester, where he was the head man. There he excelled himself by putting us onto a local bookmaker and marking our card when the bookie went to the airport to pick up his daughter. The bookie's empty house was robbed of a safe and briefcases with the cash float for each shop. The cop also sold me some MoT books that the police had confiscated from thieves. When the books were found to have gone missing from his station, along with some cash, he fell under suspicion and promptly retired. Another sergeant we knew was rumoured to have had his daughter's teeth fixed with the backhanders he had received for tipping off club owners that they were going to be raided.

The other thing that bothered the cops was how often I was acquitted in court cases. They liked to think this was because I was getting inside information, but often it was a combination of police incompetence, my own street smarts, and great lawyers. One of the best was my brief Tom Burke. He represented me when I went on trial for police assault, a fucking liberty. I was nearly run over while standing on a street corner in Chinatown when a coach swung round the corner and its cab mounted the pavement. The wing mirror swept over my head; if I had been two inches taller it would have killed me. Naturally, I banged on the side and shouted abuse at the driver. I had not seen a policeman standing in a doorway behind me. He grabbed me and said he was arresting me for being drunk. I struggled with him, while trying to tell him what had happened, which he must have seen. He was having none of it and called for help. That was when I lost my head and gave him a few cracks. The heavy mob pulled up in a riot van and worked me over with sticks, then drove me to the nick and charged me.

Tom got me bail the next day, but the prognosis was bad.

'You have got a problem this time, Jim,' he said. 'There are too many witnesses going against you. If we could only show what really happened, we would have a chance.'

Then it hit me: I *would* show them what had happened. I hired a coach and driver, got a guy dressed up as a policeman and others to act as bystanders, and a pal of mine professionally filmed a staged re-enactment of the incident. When all the paperwork came to Tom Burke, he also noticed that the photo of the officer with a mark under his left eye had been taken with a Polaroid camera, which apparently was not admissible as evidence. The case went to crown court, where the prosecution produced three police witnesses plus the officer who was hurt. They said I was fighting everybody. However the judge blocked the photo showing the injury, as we had hoped, then gave permission to play my video to the jury, to save me from having to explain it all verbally. It made everything clear, and killed the case. We also proved that one officer was not there; he admitted he was reading another officer's notes. I was found not guilty and awarded £5,000 personal damages, plus costs.

Another case I won was a civil one. A finance company repossessed one of my vehicles illegally, a mobile stores van for taking expensive tools and parts to building sites. They would not release it, knowing it was not on H.P. but on a personal loan, but once in their hands they could see value in keeping it. So I set to work to fight them. Tom Burke was my brief and, after writing to them, we decided to sue for the van and loss of work.

I got a phone call one day to say the van had been seen in the Bury area. A week later, a strange thing happened. Jack Trickett rang to tell me that he had found my van burnt out on a farm. I let Tom know and he then added some other tools and things to our claim, legitimately of course.

The case took several years to come to court. On the first day, the finance company's lawyers tried to say I was responsible for the fire. We had a meeting with the judge and told him the van was my property and if I had wanted to fire it legally I could have, but it was worth more to me intact. On the second day, the other side threw in the towel and we settled. I was so pleased with Tom and the amount he negotiated for me that I gave him a nice drink on top. Another case won.

In total, I have faced eleven crown court or high court cases and have won them all, in the sense that I never served a day's custodial sentence: I was released at the end of every trial, even when I was convicted, sometimes because of time already served on remand. Not all my pals outside the firm were prepared to put in the hard work and have the right brief to advise them, and would lose out as a consequence. And that's how much of my life of crime went.

The police saw it differently. In the game of cat and mouse between us, they were convinced I had some kind of secret advantage, some source of information that thwarted their best efforts. They became determined to find out who it was.

10

TOP OF THE WORLD

BY 1983, I WAS sitting on top of the world. My portfolio of licensed premises now encompassed half a dozen pubs, including the revived Brown Bull Hotel. I had got rid of Nitos but acquired the Senator Club and JR's, then bought the Theatre Club off Les Simms, although I lost the licence after a few months in a police crackdown on private members' clubs. Money was pouring in. Not content, however, I began to explore a host of different ventures.

I had already begun to establish myself as the biggest ticket agent in the north-west. I first saw how the ticket game worked when I was a barrow boy and Bobby McDermott was the big dealer. 'Mac' also ran the street traders back in the day. I was in his Cellar Club paying in for my barrow when I saw an apple box stuffed full of cup final tickets. With a mate, Micky Martin, I started to buy tickets myself and resell them at a profit. As I became better known, I bought tickets off players, managers and ground staff.

Football in those days was bent. Managers took bungs, sold tickets for big games and basically made money any way they could. In my view they had to, as the wages were nothing like today. Why do you think Brian Clough never got the England job? As for players, I have spoken to many over forty years, some of them personal friends, and I do not think there was one who did not sell tickets. I could blow up the whole thing, but why? They were my friends and helped me make a lot of money. My word is my bond and I would not be me if I revealed their identities.

Cup finals were the jackpot games. Each player was allowed 115 tickets for family and friends and many found their way onto the black market: I bought them, so I know. In fact I gave one manager, who shall remain nameless, £19,000 for tickets in one hit. Their clubs would deny it but I dealt with players and managers across the country. Manchester United manager Tommy Docherty was one of the fair ones. The older players had been taking tickets off the juniors, selling them and giving them the short end of the deal. Doc put a stop to that. He would pool the tickets and then divvy up the funds fairly between the players. Doc didn't take a penny but he was in the middle, the same as most managers in those days. He will tell you it was part of the job.

I met the Doc through following the Reds and always found him easy to talk to. I have been a lifetime supporter of the club and would go to all the home games with Jack Trickett and Vinnie Schiavo. We had seats in the executive suite and would often have a bit of a chat with the Doc. When he was sacked in 1977, for having an affair with the wife of club physio Laurie Brown, I got in touch with him and asked if he would do a deal to call in my pubs and say hello to people. I had five pubs at the time. He agreed to do it, so I laid on a driver, picked him up and took him round all the bars. We had a drink in each and it was a great success, every bar was packed out.

I went on to do a few more things with Tommy Doc. He was guest of honour at an amateur boxing dinner show I put on at Belle Vue that raised £4,000 for Sale A.B.C., where a young Ricky

Hatton boxed. Tommy presented the prizes and the cheque to the trainer. He and I also opened a school fete, of all things, in Glossop, in which my sister was involved. The whole town turned out.

The best was when I got a call from a pal, 'Fat' Rab Shearer. He was running a young amateur football team in Runcorn. They had won everything but had no-one to present the cup to the kids and he wanted to know if I could get the Doc for 2 p.m. on a Sunday. I rang Tommy and told him.

'Fuck me, Jimmy,' he said, 'I am at a christening at twelve-thirty. How long will it take?'

I told him one hour there, one hour back and half an hour at the presentation.

'Okay,' he said, 'I will sneak off and go back to the christening later.'

I picked him up at Jack Trickett's hotel in Stockport at 1 p.m. and off we went. We arrived at this little pub, had a quick drink in the bar, then went upstairs for the presentation. It was packed with kids and their families. Tommy got straight into his stride, shaking hands with parents. After presenting the kids with their medals, we got sucked in. The drink flowed and the half an hour turned into four hours. Tommy would not leave. That was the kind of man he was.

I just said, 'This is what football is all about!'

'You had better believe it,' said Tom.

We did a few more things together before I had to leave Manchester: I was involved in a massive investigation and it was better I was not there (see Chapter 12). I didn't see Tommy Doc again for a few years but I still think about what a great man he was for football. The game misses people like him.

Plenty of other managers were flogging tickets out of the back door: I went to visit one at his house on the south coast and he actually gave me a suitcase-full. So I decided to open a proper agency working out of offices at the Brown Bull. I called it Sporting and Entertainments Box Office Limited (motto: 'The impossible we can do') and it became a vehicle not just for football tickets but for boxing, tennis, snooker, golf and rugby, as well as theatre seats and pop concerts.

Inevitably all this activity attracted attention from the press. I was in my office when some guys came in wanting FA Cup tickets. I had Manchester United letterheaded notepaper on my desk. I was showing them the tickets when out came the cameras and bang, bang, bang, they snatched some photos and legged it out the door. They had already got a bit of info out of me. The next thing, I was in the Cheshire Cheese pub in Ancoats, which I owned by then and which was used by a lot of the Manchester-based press, when someone came in with a fresh copy of the *Mirror*. I was on the first, second and third pages, exposed as a 'big ticket dealer'. It showed pictures of handfuls of tickets and of my desk with the United notepaper and the names of Arthur Albiston and Gordon McQueen.

Before another Cup game, a manager rang me and asked me how many tickets I wanted. I told him 500. He said the only way he could get me that many was if I became a sponsor for the club. So I sponsored a ladies' night and got my tickets.

On another occasion, a United player phoned me on the eve of their FA Cup final against Brighton & Hove Albion.

'Jimmy, I have got two hundred standing tickets in my hand, do you want them?'

'Fuck me, it's Friday night,' I said. 'I could have got big money for them a couple of days ago but all the grafters will have gone down to London by now.'

The player, who was a big star, said, 'Look, I can't do anything with them. Why don't you come and get them and just sell what you can?'

We had been getting up to eight times face value, so I knew there would still be demand if I moved quickly. I told the player I would get my sons to drive down and meet him at the team hotel. They duly arrived, picked up an envelope with the tickets and drove straight to Wembley, where they slept in the car for a few hours. At nine o'clock they were ready for the arrival of the first touts. They did not wait for punters, instead they served the touts at three times face value, sold up in an hour and were back in Manchester in time to watch the game on TV. I gave the player face value for each ticket plus a drink. It did not end there. The game was drawn and went to a replay. This time a briefcase was delivered to me full of replay tickets, which I sold for twice what I paid. The tickets came from club officials.

For another Wembley game, I booked a train from British Rail on a private basis direct to Wembley Station, and filled it. Everyone on board had a ticket for the game and a free lunch with wine provided by my own catering staff on board. There were different compartments depending on what price ticket you had at the game. If you had a top seat you were in the champagne coach; a cheap ticket got you half a bottle of wine. On another occasion I sent sixteen coaches from the Brown Bull Hotel and Granada TV even filmed it. That's 800 tickets. Where did people think they were coming from? I am not into exposing names but you could find someone at every club in those days who would sell tickets for big games, and that includes some directors.

Eventually it did bring some unwanted publicity. I got a phone call at the Brown Bull to say Bob Greaves, the longstanding presenter for *Granada Tonight*, wanted to speak to me. He said he was fronting a show about business people helping the underprivileged and asked if I could get twelve tickets for a Liverpool–Manchester United cup final: six for Liverpool kids and six for Manchester. It was already widely known that I had tickets for both sides and was running coaches from both the Brown Bull and the Adelphi Hotel in Liverpool. I agreed to supply some tickets with free coach travel and he asked me to go on the show to present them. I could have sold the trips plus tickets for £150 each, or £1,800 in total, so I was doing my bit. Nevertheless I had a funny feeling about appearing. At the last minute I decided instead to send a singer who worked for me, John Bowie, to the Granada studio in Liverpool with the tickets. Nobody queried him when he arrived, he was just called in front of the cameras.

'Welcome Jim Donnelly,' said Bob Greaves, 'or should I say, Jimmy the Weed? Thank you for the tickets, they will go to a deserving cause. But tell me Jimmy, where did you get these tickets from? Did the players sell them to you?'

You should have seen his face when my pal said, 'I'm not Jimmy, I'm John, his driver.' I only wish I had gone, I would have told him to fuck off and kept the tickets. He rang me from the show but I would not talk to him, he had tried to set me up. So much for doing a good turn.

Greaves was the main face of Granada for many years and was very well known to viewers in the north-west. He came into a bar one night when I was there with some of the firm. There was a bowl of fruit on the bar and somebody picked up an apple and threw it at him. It was not meant to hurt him, just embarrass him, but it hit him on the head and flattened him. I bumped into him a few times after that but he kept well away.

I also started to act as an agent for several United players. I was a bit of a pioneer: football agenting was in its infancy then, largely because there was not much money in it. The highest paid player at United in the seventies was Lou Macari and he was on £800 a week, good money but hardly a fortune. I got Gordon McQueen, the Scottish defender, a nice little payday for letting balloons off the roof of the CIS building to celebrate their anniversary, and picked up appearance money for a few other players. I also looked after properties in Spain for some of them.

I must have been the first person in Manchester to do sporting dinners and brought a friend, Micky Martin, in with me. With hindsight it had the potential to grow big and I should have stuck with it, but the money was not there at the time. I put on cabaret dinner shows at Belle Vue, brought the Detroit Emeralds from the States, and had the comedian Bernard Manning on a few times. Bernard was always a good draw but used to give me merciless stick. 'I see the Weed's in tonight,' he would tell the audience. 'Thank fuck for that. At least I know my safe's okay at home.' Sporting and Entertainments Ltd also had a security arm, run for me by an ex-boxer, Dessie O'Connor. We provided personal security, bodyguards and doormen.

I also started a company called Northern Leisure, with a fellow called Ged Ford as the general manager, selling holiday packages. I had access to 300 apartments on the Costa del Sol through management companies over there and people I knew. I would charge by the head, they would pay a deposit and book their airline tickets and I put my percentage on top, so out of every family that went to an apartment or villa I had my wages and then settled my bill in Spain.

Even all of that was not enough for me. As a lifelong lover of boxing, I harboured ambitions to promote fights. British boxing had been in the doldrums for a decade, but in the late seventies and early eighties a new wave of world champions arrived, the likes of John Conteh, John Stracey, Alan Minter and Maurice Hope, to give the sport a big boost. Jack Trickett was also a huge boxing fan and was dabbling in promotion. Funnily enough he and I had boxed on the same bill years before as amateurs, when he was a senior and I was a junior. So we got together with Les Simms, who had Belle Vue, the region's biggest boxing arena, and formed a conglomerate to promote shows in Manchester. A Moroccan lad called Najib Daho, who was the city's best prospect at the time, signed up for us on a six-fight deal, £600 per fight. We launched the venture as co-promoters with a picture in the *Manchester Evening News* of us all wearing boxing gloves.

I got a call from a pal who said Frank Warren, the young London promoter who was then shaking up the fight game, wanted to see me and Jack Trickett regarding TV for our shows at Belle Vue. I had met Frank's uncle Bobby years earlier, a man I had ultimate respect for. I arranged to meet Frank in the Britannia Hotel in Manchester and phoned Jack to tell him. He had broken his leg and was in hospital, so I went to meet Warren on my own. We had just started talking when who hobbles in but Jack. He was clearly in pain but did not want to miss a thing and had caught a taxi ten miles to be there.

Warren cut to the chase.

'We want to bring television to Manchester,' he said. 'We will give you one third of the money for the TV rights, I will have a third and my partner will have a third.'

'Thanks for doing us a favour,' I said sarcastically, 'but we don't need you. You think you are going to give me a third of my own home city?'

'That's right,' he said. 'And I have heard about you. Keep your hands out of the till and we will all do okay.' He smiled that cold smile of his.

I was fuming. Jack Trickett tried to talk me round but I told Warren to fuck off, this was my city and I didn't need him or his TV money. The meeting collapsed and Warren left.

Najib went on to win five fights in a row at Belle Vue and put himself in contention for a title shot. He later won British and Commonwealth titles and even had a crack at the IBF world title, but by then I was out of the picture.

WITH ALL OF my interests, I was now taking £50-60,000 a week. I sailed on the Med in the summer, jetted to Vegas for title fights and gambling, dined at the best restaurants five or six nights a week and drove a Rolls-Royce. My brothers were also doing well, and for a giggle we drove around to our parents' house in Wythenshawe, each in his own Roller, just to show the neighbours who had said we would never amount to anything. I bought a big house on the edge of the countryside with plenty of land. I even owned a racehorse, part of a deal with my friend Tommy Brennan, who was in the horsey fraternity. It was called Springtime Double and was stabled at Ascot with Jocelyn Reeve, the trainer. It cost an arm and a leg to keep and never won a race. The worst thing that happened, my nephew Terry, who had registered the horse with the Jockey Club, got nicked with four kilos of cannabis. He was found guilty and when the police read out the fact that he was a racehorse owner and drove a Mercedes, which was in fact twenty years old, the judge gave him five years. I couldn't get rid of that nag quick enough; the thing was cursed.

Looking back, I don't know how I did it all, but I was a whirlwind of ideas and schemes. On the criminal side, I now had links with major villains across the UK, Ireland and Spain. Such was my reputation that many of them came to me with deals. I bought anything: gold, diamonds, fur coats, booze, furniture. Everybody knew they could come to the Weed. In one deal alone I bought a parcel of gold rings, chains and bracelets with over £1 million on the tickets. I gave half of scrap weight for it, split it up and sold the lot in twenty-four hours, making £100,000 profit.

In another nice deal, I bought and sold a smallholding in north Wales. A fellow called Mick Skinkiss came to see me in the Senator Club. He had this beautiful place in Mona, Anglesey, but he had shot an intruder there and wanted out. He gave me an aerial photo. The place had five bedrooms, planning permission for more rooms, a static caravan on site and a pond. He wanted £16,000. I told him to come back in a couple of hours. I had just bought Vinnie Schiavo and Joe Swords out of their share of the Senator Club and was a bit short of cash, but I knew they would go for the deal. I soon had their share of the money, that's how we were, and bought the place. Two weeks later, I advertised it in the *Manchester Evening News* at £35,000 and sold it to the first punter who called. It made a nice little earn for the firm but for a long time Mick Skinkiss swore I fucked him over, the idiot. He asked me for a price and I gave it to him. I never even saw the place, only a picture.

Then came a much bigger score, one of the best earners I ever latched on to. I was having a nice brandy in the private bar of the Senator when a half-drunk Post Office security man came in with a young bird. The Senator was across the road from the main sorting office and I often let the management use my private bar upstairs. I knew this particular security guy, we called him Champagne Charlie because he loved the high life. I used to stick birds into him from my massage parlour. On this particular night, he asked to speak to me privately, so I took him into the kitchen. He wanted to know if he could run a bar tab for champagne. He produced a diamond ring and said he would leave it with me as collateral. I looked at it.

'Don't you know the difference between diamonds and marcasite?' I said, throwing the ring on the floor. 'It's shit.'

He did not even pick it up: he clearly did not have a clue whether it was real or not. I now knew I had found the keys to a treasure trove. He told me the ring had belonged the female impersonator Danny LaRue. I later picked it up. It was genuine.

Champagne Charlie had stolen the ring. He worked security on the mail coming into Piccadilly railway station. If any mailbags had been tampered with, he would dip in his own hand and then report it or nick another employee, and that was what he had done to get this ring. I gave him a couple of bottles of champers to make him look good to the brass he was with and told him that he had extended credit, but in future he was to come to me, and only me, with anything he took from the mail. I told my manager, Frank Platt, to give him the VIP treatment.

Champagne Charlie turned out to be a goldmine. In those days, if you were going abroad you had to place an order for travellers' cheques at the bank, and they would be posted out on an overnight mail train. They were ripe for plucking. Over the next few months I must have made two or three hundred grand out of Charlie. Then one night he came in the club while I was in London. Frank Platt looked after him with the usual champagne and told him I was away for a day or two. He confided in Frank that he was in trouble and needed some cash, and handed him a bag. Frank took it upstairs to have a look and found it was full of emeralds and rubies. He did not know what to do, so he called in the firm. I got back just in time to prevent the gems from disappearing into greedy hands, but my pals now knew about Aladdin's Cave, and they wanted in.

I met Charlie the next day. He told me he had a stash of

£250,000-worth of travellers' cheques and wanted twenty pence in the pound for them. By now I suspected that his mouth was too loose. The whole thing was getting too big, too many people knew about it and somebody was going to get nicked. So I set him up. I arranged to meet him at a pub to buy the cheques, then watched as his car pulled up and he entered. He had nothing in his hands, so I knew the cheques had to be in the car boot. I went in to meet him, while my accomplice emptied his boot.

After a short meeting, Charlie and I went back out to his car. A look of horror crossed his face when he opened the trunk.

'Fuck me, Charlie.' I said. 'Someone must have known you were coming and screwed your car. Who else have you told?'

He started frantically rummaging through the boot, swearing he had told no-one.

'I'm out, Charlie,' I said. 'This is no good. Don't ever contact me again. You've been dealing with others.'

I knew it was time to walk away from Charlie, and I was right. The next time I saw him he was on reception at Strangeways. He had gone on to deal with another firm, had inevitably been caught and was serving a four-stretch. His partner in crime had a warehouse full of vintage cars he had bought from the proceeds but Charlie had nothing, having blown all his money on 'brass'. Give him his due, he could have landed a lot of people in it if he had told all, but he did not. He also knew he had had ten times what he was charged with. I felt no remorse because he was a dog anyway, nicking his fellow workers for pilfering while doing the same himself. If you are going to be a thief, be a thief, but don't play both sides of the fence.

ONE WELL-KNOWN villain I worked with a lot around this time was Eric Mason. Eric was a Londoner, from Paddington, but when

I first met him, in the mid-sixties, he was on the door of a club in Nottingham owned by a big man called Tommy Brennan. My construction company had a contract to supply steel erectors to work on a power station, so I was staying there at the Silver Mirror, a small hotel by the railway station. I was getting paid a day-rate for each man plus out-of-town allowance, and every night I went to Tommy's club with my foreman, Brendan Withers, to gamble my profits. One night, I did my brains in on the blackjack table. Tommy sent Eric over to tell me my credit was good at the table as well as at the bar. We became friends.

Eric Mason and I hooked up again when he moved north and came to live in my hotel around 1981, and that was when I really got to know him. He'd had a chequered past. Eric was close to the Krays and had been involved in their trip to Manchester with the boxer Joe Louis. He had also made enemies of their rivals, the Richardson gang, who ended up putting an axe in his head in a fight in central London. It left Eric in a very bad way but he was as strong as an ox and recovered. He had since done quite a bit of bird and had also moved around the country doing this and that, before pitching up in Manchester. I found him as good as gold; you could not want for a better pal. He was tough, could fight and never backed down. He was ideal for me with all my bars: I was running six pubs and two nightclubs at the same time and Eric would go round them all every day and keep an eye on things.

Despite his gangland credentials, Eric was actually a professional shoplifter. He worked a few hours every day and you would not believe the amount of gear he could steal. He could go out in the morning and come back with £2,000-worth of crystal decanters, Waterford glasses, Lladro china and other top brands. I suppose he had decided there was no big porridge if he got caught and he was comfortably earning £3-400 for a couple of hours graft. He also wanted to come in with me on some of my work, and that was when things started to go wrong. He was making pals with other firms, some of whom I had had problems with. Eric did not seem to understand loyatlty, or that in Manchester we helped out each other.

One case was a sad incident involving Les Grey, the Spanish-speaking car salesman who had translated for us when we first went to the Costa del Sol to look at properties in the early eighties. Les had moved back to Manchester, I put a few pounds in with him in various deals and we did okay. Mason and I were having a drink one afternoon in a Piccadilly pub when Les walked in. I had been out delivering Manchester United tickets and had a briefcase with me containing about 100, all differently priced and worth a lot of money. Les said hello and we got into a bit of a drinking session.

I went to the toilet. When I came back, Les was on the floor covered in blood. His face was twisted to one side, his jaw was obviously broken and his nose was bust open.

Eric was shouting, 'He tried to nick the Weed's case.'

Some guys took Les to hospital. Eric told me that he saw Les move my case and throw a coat over it, as though to steal it. I left it at that and went on my way.

A couple of weeks later, Les came to see me and mumbled that it was all bollocks. He and Mason had been working together: Eric was going around the country shoplifting with Les as his driver, but had not paid him. That day, Les had asked for his money. Beating him up had nothing to do with my briefcase, Eric just did not want to pay him. I told Les I knew he would not do such a thing to me and we went on to do business together for many years.

I was a true pal to Eric but it seemed that he could not keep up.

He would go off on his travels, then turn up with somebody influential from another city and ask for me to vouch for him. You had to give him a gee and tell them Eric was okay. I would later get phone calls from people saying Eric owed money and reminding me I had given him a good name. I soon realised he had been the same in London all those years ago, never with one firm, always moving. I also saw that every time he got a tickle, he would be off to another city flashing his money and impressing a new group of cronies. So as much as I liked Eric, I would eventually cut my ties with him.

Another good money-getter was Ricky Edmund. Ricky was a bit loud in drink and fancied himself at the fisticuffs game, but lacked the steel of someone like Eric. He rubbed up one of the firm one night and got a smack on the chin for his troubles. To patch things up, he bought a yellow Rolls-Royce from Jim Swords. Ricky used to swan around Manchester in his Rolls and loved to be seen in the swankiest places. To his credit, he was a very good thief.

One day I had been out shopping and pulled up at the Brown Bull to see the yellow Rolls parked outside. Well you could hardly miss it. Ricky was at the bar.

'Hello Ricky, how are you?'

'I have a parcel for sale,' he said, all business. 'Do you want to have a look?'

He had been following a jewellery salesman for weeks and had done the boot of his car. I said if it was okay I would make a bid. He went out to the car, came back with a briefcase and we climbed up to my office on the first floor. He opened the case to reveal trays of rings holding diamonds of all sizes. The smallest was half a carat, up to two carat. There were no prices on them, only code numbers and the size. I told Ricky that I would have to hold on to them to get a true value. He pulled a face but agreed to give me a couple of hours.

I phoned a pal who was a working jeweller. He had a look and vouched that they were good quality with no flaws, so when Ricky came back I offered him twenty grand. He pulled his face again but did not want to go around getting bids, so we did the deal. I told Ricky to come back later and I would have the money for him. I broke up the parcel and sold it off piecemeal for over fifty grand. When the story hit the papers a couple of days later it said the haul was worth three hundred grand! I later spoke to a pal called Tommy who said he had been working with Ricky and that Ricky had only given him seven grand for his share of the diamonds. He thought he had been shortchanged. I said nothing but that's what you got with Ricky. He would even have over working partners.

After that deal, I bought another parcel of gold chains, bracelets and rings from him. The lot weighed four pounds. I gave him £1.50 a gram and sold it on at £2 a gram. Good money. He thought he was back in favour with the QSG when he bought the Roller and kept offering gear very cheap but everyone was careful with him.

Having said that, he did pull off some jobs. I was reminded of one of them one Easter when I was walking along Market Street with a pal and he said, 'Let's go in Thorntons and get some chocolate eggs for the kids.'

'Thorntons take some dough over Easter,' I said.

He looked at me quizzically, so I told him what Ricky Edmund had done one Easter weekend in the early eighties. He and his partner, a Liverpudlian called John, had the idea to rob Thorntons. They found out that every shop had a floor safe, and John was very good when it came to safes. They knew that when the shops closed on Easter Saturday, they would be shut until Tuesday because of the Bank Holiday. That meant the takings up to the Saturday night would be left there ready for banking on the Tuesday. They hit every branch with a duplicate master key that fitted the lock on every store. In twenty-four hours, they had done eight shops, and by the time they opened on the Tuesday and discovered the theft, Ricky and John were in Spain.

A couple of days after telling my pal that story, I turned on the TV to hear of an even more outrageous robbery. Masked bandits had stormed the Security Express headquarters in east London, tied up and blindfolded the guards, poured petrol over one to make him reveal the combination to a safe, and made off with more than £6 million. Soon after, the mob the police believed to be responsible turned up in southern Spain, which no longer had an extradition agreement with the UK. Ronnie Knight, Clifford Saxe, John Mason, Ronnie Everett and Freddie Foreman would become known to the press as the Famous Five, and the Costa del Crime was born.

11

COSTA DEL CRIME

THE LONG-FIRM fraud, or 'LF', involves opening a business, obtaining goods from suppliers on credit, trading for a while to build up stock, then having a back-door clearout and disappearing with the profit. It requires a front man with a clean credit rating who can order goods on tick, and will sometimes be run legitimately for months, even years, to forge a relationship with suppliers so that you can place huge final orders before going bump. LF-ing was something a lot of villains dabbled in. The best made a lot of money.

Our pal Mark Klapish was one of the top long-firm fraudsters in the game. By the late 1970s, he had opened up – and closed down – all over the place. One of his locations was Belfast, where he had a shop called Pricerite, selling wholesale jewellery and fancy goods. His wife would drop him off every day in a Rolls-Royce at the airport, he would fly to Belfast to be picked up in another Rolls, do what he had to do, then fly back again in the evening. Mark knew how to live; he had a personal table at the Piccadilly Hotel.

In the mid-seventies the IRA bombed his Belfast premises, apparently destroying the stock. However, the police would later allege that Mark had done a deal with the IRA and had removed the stock before the bombing, then claimed insurance for it, a new twist on the traditional LF. When Mark sent gear over there it would go in the front door, out the back, be reloaded, the place would burn down and the furniture would come back to England for resale: a double shuffle. I met some of the Belfast guys with Mark when they sent furniture vans over to Manchester, and even bought some stuff off them. I guess you could call them half terrorists, half criminals.

Unfortunately for Mark, there was a judas in his camp. He employed a fellow called David Bertelstein, who often went by the surname Burton. Burton was a fantasist: he claimed to have worked as a driver for the Krays twins, which was bollocks. He was also a snitch, giving the police snippets of information in return for money or leniency. This included telling them about Mark's schemes, including the firing of a warehouse in Kent Street, Belfast.

In January 1983, Burton was arrested for cheque fraud. He obtained bail by claiming he had evidence of police corruption in Manchester, naming an officer who was already under suspicion and who later retired from the force. That August, Burton also made a lengthy statement associating the businessman Kevin Taylor with the Quality Street Gang. He was trying to save his own skin, because he was suspected of colluding with Klapish and the IRA to defraud the Northern Ireland Office through their LF scam, but in the event, they were both charged with conspiracy to obtain property by deception to the tune of £500,000.

The pair of them had been hawking washing machines about, and some of the lads had bought them. Hence Joe Swords was implicated, and for allegedly receiving a stolen washing machine he was remanded as a Category A prisoner, which was unheard of for such a minor charge. Vinnie Schiavo and Jack Trickett were also charged around the same time in relation to alleged receiving of goods: in Vinnie's case, a car, and in Jack's, I think, a fridge. It was coming on top. Jack pleaded guilty but Vinnie fled to Spain after Jim Swords posted bail for him. That meant that Jim ended up in court too, under his real name of Monaghan, as the *Manchester Evening News* reported:

> The stipendiary magistrate ruled that Jim Monaghan of Railway Rd, Urmston, will have to pay bail of £25,000 for the disappearing Schiavo, described as his lifelong pal. Schiavo, 41, disappeared the day before detectives tried to execute a warrant on him for his alleged part in a £500,000 fraud. Monaghan, also 41, said, 'I'm shattered. I will have to sell my house.'
>
> Monaghan denied having business interests in Spain and Blackpool, that he owned a warehouse, three Rolls-Royces and had an interest in a city club. He said his house was valued at £50,000 and he earned £250 a week selling cars.

Of course, JS had no intention of selling his house or anything else, he was simply laying it on for the court.

None of us knew it at the time, but Burton's claims about bent coppers had opened Pandora's Box. Between 1982 and 1984, there had already been a concerted attempt to nail the QSG by the Regional Crime Squad. They saw us buying pubs and clubs, owning properties in Spain, driving Rollers and spending all day lounging outside car showrooms drinking tea, and they could not understand where the money was coming from. So the investigations started. They did not get far. They even tried to tie the Crazy Face Gang to us but that did not work. Frustrated, they began to suspect that we had inside information.

Corruption had become a burning issue within Greater Manchester Police. The Chief Constable, James Anderton, went so far as to disband his vice squad after a raid on the Lord Nelson pub caught officers drinking illegally after hours. The pub was in Newton Street, as was a police station, and officers were always in there, boozing in a room upstairs. My own pub, the Kensington, was nearby and my little Senator Club was around the corner, so I was also used to the habits of the cops.

When the Senator first opened, it was a private club and was obliged to have a committee and minuted meetings. You had to be a member to drink in there, allegedly.

I came in one night when Frank Platt was on the door.

'We have got the Old Bill in here, Jim,' he said.

'What do they want?'

'They are all right, they are just having a drink.'

'Are they really. We'll see about that.'

Three of them were standing at the bar.

'Hello,' I said. 'How can I help you?'

'We are just calling to see everything is all right.'

'Can I see your ID?'

They pulled their warrant cards out.

'You are not from licensing?' I asked.

'No, we're not.'

I turned to my barmaid.

'Maureen, how long have they been in?'

'About two hours,' she said.

'Lock the doors,' I told Frank Platt. Then I turned to the cops. 'Go and sign the book. I am dialling 999 for your colleagues. You are not members and you are not legally entitled to be in here. Oh, and you are not paying for those drinks.'

I got them to sign in, pronto. I don't think they were out to get me for serving them illegally, I think they just wanted to blag a few drinks. I slung them out anyway.

It was the norm for the licensing department to get free drinks. Some of them would phone to tip you off before a raid, then call in for a free drink or with the wife for a free meal as payback. It seemed to be a perk of the job to them. If you did not play ball they would raid you at all hours, or stick a girl in your club, claim she was hustling in there and get you closed down for keeping a brothel.

Many a time the cops would say to me, you have got pubs and clubs, you know what's going on, why don't you help us out with a bit of information, we can make it easier for you, you won't get raided – all that bollocks. Any of the other lads nicked over the years heard the same. We just ignored them. When you have been beaten up or stitched up by them as many times as I have, you have no time for them, but I accept they have a job to do. Some of the old-time sergeants who gave you a whack if you were out of line were all right, but the younger ones always wanted to prove themselves. It was a game: they were on one side and we were on the other.

As the police tried to tighten the screw on us, even our solicitors came under the spotlight. Over the years, the QSG had used the best lawyers in Manchester, and David Middleweek was the best of the best. He defended many of us at one time or another and it got to the stage where the Old Bill were ill with all the not-guilty verdicts he won. Then they nicked David himself. In a meeting, David was alleged to have asked an officer if he would ever accept money to reveal the contents of a police file on one of his clients – Mick Brown, if memory serves me right. They later secretly taped another meeting with David and his office was mysteriously burgled. He was arrested and charged with trying to pervert the course of justice. David denied the charge and said he had been merely trying to ascertain if the officer was bent or not, so he could inform his client. His first trial ended with a hung jury, as did a second trial, after which he was formally declared not guilty. The police gave up on him, but then he was the best.

WITH VINNIE, JOE SWORDS and Jack Trickett all feeling the squeeze from the law, it was my turn next. It began when burglars cracked a safe in the offices of a London travel agency and made off with thousands of open airline tickets, along with official stamps to authorise them. You could travel around the world first-class on them. Basically you rang an airline, said you had an open ticket, and if they had the seat availability you could fly anywhere. Word quickly went out and a 'parcel' was bought, with Wally McNelly going to London to collect it from a leading villain down there. Then the tickets went for sale, through former travel agents who knew how to move them. We even had our own stamps made, with joke names like 'ATC', short for 'Arsehole Travel Company'. No-one seemed to notice.

I sold some of the tickets to people in the racing game, including a tic-tac man from York Races called Sirs. He was travelling with his family to Australia when they were was stopped at the airport. Then they nicked a pal of mine, Jimmy Kennedy, a barrow boy who I had put in as the middle man. Unfortunately he mentioned my name to the police. I forgave him, as I should never have put him in that position; he wasn't a tough boy. The upshot was that I was charged with what the police said was a £10 million fraud, which was a bit of an exaggeration. I was released on bail.

Jimmy Kennedy was the only person who could directly implicate me, so I bought him a ticket to Spain to get him out of the way. I knew they would put a warrant out for him, but by the time he turned up, my trial would be over. Foolishly I bought his plane ticket on my own credit card, not thinking the police would go to the extent of looking into it. Well, they did look into it and I was promptly rearrested and charged with perverting the course of justice as well. They banged me up in Strangeways over Christmas. So now I was in custody, Joe Swords was on remand, Vinnie Schiavo was on the run, Jack Trickett was facing a charge, Mark Klapish was up for long-firm fraud and Jim Swords, Joe Leach and the rest were being watched constantly. That was most of the QSG in trouble, one way or another.

I spent about four months on remand. By coincidence I was allocated the same cell I had been in with Jim Swords way back in 1962. All the Crazy Face mob were in there, and in the cell next door was Barry Pollard. Born in Salford, Barry was a generation younger than me but a very tough man, built like a brick shithouse. He was charged with an armed robbery and other stuff. He eventually was found not guilty after two-and-a-half years on remand but was convicted of receiving a fur coat. The judge gave him three years for the coat but he had been on remand for so long that he was released for time served.

I was not in long before I nearly caused a riot. My son Dominic had been arrested for burgling a jeweller's and was on the young prisoners' wing. As a remand prisoner, I was entitled to visit with him. If we had exercise in the morning and the YPs had it in the afternoon, I could go to see him then, so I was getting two exercises a day. On this particular Sunday, we went to the pictures and Dominic sneaked over to sit with me and Wally McNelly. The screws spotted him, piled over, grabbed him by his ear and tried to drag him out. I gave one screw a dig and the whole place stood up. There were only half a dozen screws on duty and it looked like it would really go off. They pulled my son upstairs back to his wing.

Then we were all lined up and marched back to our various wings. The duty PO took me out of line to the office.

I told him straight. 'You don't want a riot on your hands. Don't treat YPs like that. That is all you have to do. But don't ever grab my son like that in front of me again.'

I went back to my cell. Then the heavy mob came in. They didn't attack me, they just stood there. I told them their cards were marked and if anything more happened there would be a riot. They knew to take it seriously. For several days after that, they let out only three people at a time from each landing to collect their food at meal times and take it back to their cells, rather than whole landings at once. They did not want a lot of prisoners gathering together for fear it would kick off.

I had another row not long afterwards. My wife had to open one of my pubs every day at noon. This meant she could only make morning visiting times, not afternoons. First visits began at 10.20 a.m. and I could not understand why I had not been called out for her visit. Then, at 11.55 a.m., I got the call: 'Donnelly, you've got a visit.'

Rita was waiting in a strop.

'What the fuck is going on,' she said. 'I have been here for an hour and a half. They have only just let me in.'

The next minute, 'Time's up Donnelly.'

'What do you mean?'

'No visit after twelve.'

When Rita left, I went to the PO's box and had a go at them but they acted ignorant.

By the time I got back to my landing, everyone else had been served lunch.

'What about my food?'

'Too late, Donnelly. You have missed it. You weren't in line.'

I was near the hot plate, so I picked up a plate and threw it at the screw. They grabbed me and bundled me up to my cell. A couple of days, later the PO came to see me and asked me to calm it. I decided to play it straight and palled up a couple of screws, giving them show tickets.

The way it was looking, even if I was acquitted over the airline fraud – and my barrister said he did not think the case stood up – I would still go to jail for perverting justice by helping a witness leave the country. So I did a deal with the prosecution. They dropped the charges on Sirs, who I said did not know the flight tickets were bent, while I agreed to plead to one charge of fraud. They brought it down from £10 million to a specimen charge because they couldn't prove anyone else was involved. It wasn't worthwhile to have a massive investigation pursuing every suspect – which was just as well, from my point of view, as loads of tickets had been used. More significantly, a very important person in legal authority in Manchester had travelled on the tickets, and I threatened to expose him if they did not compromise. It worked: I had them by the balls. They agreed to leave the perverting justice charge on file, and as I had done time on remand already, it meant a non-custodial sentence. The deal was done before I went into court and, after a bit of a hearing, I was out. The prosecution were just happy to get me on a guilty.

I FOLLOWED THE others to Puerto Banus, where we lived on the *Sherama*, a beautiful, eighty-three-foot yacht that had once belonged to Lady Astor. Jack Trickett had bought it from Terry Dignam, one of a wealthy family from Stockport. It had fittings in oak and teak, Cartier clocks giving the time in different countries, and bedrooms with full-size baths. The lounge was a lovely long

room with a fixed dining table. One slight downside was that you
had to walk though each other's cabins to get to yours. The vessel
could sleep ten comfortably. I stayed there even though Jack and I
were not on the best of terms. While I had been in Strangeways,
my friend and partner had decided to offload me from the boxing
promotion to go on his own, and had put on a show without me.
It would prove to be the thin end of the wedge. Jack, I would discover, was avaricious and wanted everything for himself, but at
that stage I did not know the extent of his ambitions. Jack was
always charming.

Spain was full of Cockney villains on the run from the police.
The Security Express crowd were there, as well as some of the
mob suspected of the massive Brinks Mat gold heist in late 1983.
I met Freddie Foreman, Ronnie Everett, John Mason, Jimmy
Jeffries, Micky Riley and many more 'chaps'. Some, like Neil
Robertson and Micky Green, had made a small fortune operating
a big VAT fraud on gold. Micky, a former member of the
Wembley Mob of armed robbers, went on to make more money
than anyone. The cops and the press have him down as Britain's
biggest drug baron, and the truth is the cannabis trade was a great
temptation out in Spain. Morocco, where most of the stuff is
grown, was just a short distance away. Once a villain, you are
always looking at the financial potential of any opportunity. Some
people were doers and some were investors and that was how it
worked. A few of the lads also got into property and timeshare. It
was the next move on if you had money.

We spent a lot of time drinking together, and we all got on, but
inevitably the police came sniffing around. In May 1984, two
Flying Squad detectives arrived from London to investigate the
Security Express robbery. They were observing when, that June,
Vinnie Schiavo and Jack Trickett took a day trip on the *Sherama*

to Gibraltar with Freddie Foreman and his crowd. I had been due to go but cried off because I did not trust the engines on the *Sherama*. The English police had no jurisdiction out there, so there was little they could do except gather intelligence. It was later said in a court case that the boat 'should have been flying the Jolly Roger' on this trip, which I thought was a bit strong.

Another guy on the run in Spain was Larry Dunne. He was one of the Dunne brothers, who were said to be the men who introduced heroin to Ireland. They were one of the two big firms in the Dublin underworld at that time, the other being the gang of Martin 'the General' Cahill, which specialised in high-value burglaries and robberies. I had first met a couple of the Dunnes in Spain in the late seventies. They were big lads, rough and ready but not particularly sophisticated. Larry was eventually recaptured and was jailed for fourteen years for supplying drugs.

Jim Swords had bought five houses and an apartment complex, with two full-sized pools, about five minutes from Puerto Banus. The complex was predominantly Swedish and most people there were very friendly. One night, we had a BBQ at the poolside and invited everyone around. A tough-looking Swede with a flattened nose turned up with his wife and introduced himself as Bo Hogberg. He had been a very good boxer in the same era as Jim Swords and had won a European title. He had also served some prison time and apparently had a reputation as a hellraiser. As the night wore on and the booze flowed, he became a pest, pushing a couple of the wives into the pool. That would have been okay if they had been in swimsuits but not when the girls had spent time getting ready and had nice dresses on. He finally got the warning and left.

Hogberg became a problem every time he arrived at the complex drunk, until one night when I was on the patio with a pal and our wives. Hogberg came into the garden, picked up a drink and started slagging the girls. I told him to leave. With that, he flicked a drink on one of the women, then threw a punch at my pal. Boxer or no boxer, he was getting it. I grabbed a sweeping brush leaning against a wall and hit him over the head with the heavy end. He fell over and I was on him. We had a stack of tiles boxed up ready for some tiling to be done and I hit him over the head with three or four boxes, knocking him unconscious. His head split open and spewed blood.

We left him where he was and he lay there for a while without moving. When his family came looking for him, we told them he had been fighting with some strangers and had fallen in the garden. They carried him away. The next day, we found out he had collapsed again and was in hospital with suspected brain damage. The police came round to see me and I told them the story. They seemed pleased. 'He very bad man,' one of them said. 'We have lot of problem with him.' Nevertheless, I was on the next flight home in case he died.

I next saw Bo Hogberg a year later, when I was at a villa I had bought. I was in the pool with Joe Jordan, the Manchester United player, when Hogberg walked past with his wife. I could see her pointing towards me but he just carried on. Thank God, I would have hated to take him on in a fist fight. Hogberg died in 2007. Recently I heard the Swedes are making a feature film about his life. I wonder if they will tell the story of when he met the Weed, the last man to knock him out.

Ricky Edmund, the thief, came to see me in Fuengirola. He told me he was staying with Curly Lowe, one of the old faces, who had a small holiday apartment in Los Boliches. I had many a deal with Curly over the years. He was as hard as nails but you knew once you had done the deal that was it, there were no comebacks.

About a week after I had met Ricky, Curly found me in my local bar, the Rovers in Los Boliches. He was worried about Ricky. He had left Curly's apartment in a Jaguar car, saying he was going to meet some pals, and had not returned. He had been gone for days, leaving his money, clothes and passport in Curly's place. Curly could not report it to the local police because you never knew with Ricky, he might be up to anything, or he could have been nicked and did not want the police to get his money or passport or to know where he was living.

After weeks, he was finally reported missing. Then the police revealed they had found a Jaguar crashed into a tree but with nobody in the car, only some blood. So everybody assumed that he had crashed his car, done a runner to avoid the police and was hiding out somewhere with pals. He never returned to Curly's apartment and eventually Curly went back to England after his holiday.

Months passed. After pressure from Ricky's family, a new search found his body 500 yards inland from the crash. The autopsy found that Ricky appeared to have been shot in the head in his car and must have staggered off the road. A lot of names were thrown about as to who could or would have done it. Ricky had made a lot of enemies. Some even said that he had not been shot but had simply crashed the car and then wandered off and collapsed. To this day his demise is a mystery.

I RETURNED TO England that autumn to offload one of the most lucrative parcels of tickets I had ever bought. Frank Sinatra was booked to play six nights at the Royal Albert Hall in September 1984 and every night was guaranteed to sell out. I was on it early and snapped up as many tickets as I could. The opening, or gala, night was to be a black tie affair packed with guest celebrities. I obtained a seating plan and factored it into my prices: if you sat beside a star, you paid more. I organised coaches from the Brown Bull, a ticket plus two nights in a London hotel, and for the gala night I sent down three coaches with 150 people. Champagne was served on the coaches and a number of celebrities travelled with me, including Colin Crompton, compere of the popular *Wheeltappers and Shunters Social Club* TV show. After costs, I was making £100 a head. It reached the stage where people were queuing for tickets, so I contacted the London tout Stan Flashman and bought a few hundred off him. I must have sent over 1,000 people to see Ol' Blue Eyes and made about £25,000; not bad for a couple of weeks' work. With the football tickets still going strong, it helped to establish me as probably the biggest ticket dealer in the north-west.

I was a bit surprised when Jack Trickett came to my house with a proposition. When I was in Strangeways, Jack had continued to promote boxing without me, even though we were supposed to be partners. He also got our star fighter, Najib Daho, to box just for him, despite the deal we had to co-manage him. Some pal. Jack said he did it because he thought I was going away for a long while. Now he said, 'Look, I have done one promotion on my own and I have another at the Granada TV studios. Give me some help with this, then we can get back together.' Well, I put everything to one side and helped him, the big fuck.

The show was at Stage One at Granada and featured Errol Christie, the hottest prospect in British boxing. I went along on the night with Eric Mason and John Shearer. Who should I spot near the ringside but John McVicar, the armed robber whose life was made into a successful film, and Eddie Richardson. Now Eric had been badly chopped up by the Richardson firm in an attack many years earlier. In his autobiography, Eric claims Richardson and McVicar made a sharp exit when they heard he was at the boxing show, implying that they were scared to face him. That's not how I remember it: in fact Eric said he was going for a piss and didn't come back. In fairness that was not like him, he was usually dead game, but I guess he didn't fancy it that night.

I put myself about all evening, shaking hands and filling in for Jack when he wasn't around, but I could see the writing on the wall. I felt like a flunkey. It was clear he had his own ambitions. Eventually I knocked it on the head and took Eddie Richardson and friends back to the Brown Bull for a drink into the early hours.

I decided to promote on my own. First, I contacted a pal who was in business on oil rigs and asked if he would sponsor me.

'No problem, Jim,' said Tony Millward. 'How about ten grand?'

I was bowled over; it was much more than I expected. Next I phoned a couple of guys in Glasgow to see if I could book their fighter. 'Get hold of Ian McLeod,' I said. 'There is £1,800 if he will come to Manchester to fight Najib Daho in an eliminator for the British title.' Then I phoned Trickett and put the deal to him. I still needed him because he had Najib and also the credentials with the Boxing Board. He went for it, with a few provisos: he wanted the same money for Najib, £1800, conveniently forgetting the £600 per fight deal we had previously agreed. I went along with it, knowing I had the sponsorship cash to back me up, and put the undercard together to include Eddie Smith, a very good local middleweight I was managing who was number three in the ratings. The bill was set up for 24 January 1985, at the King's Hall, Belle Vue.

In the middle of this, Les Simms phoned me and said Muhammad Ali was coming to Manchester. Les had rented space out at Belle Vue for the Ideal Home Exhibition and Ali was booked to open it. Les wanted me to get some more boxers there for the media, and to take care of Ali. I set one of the large rooms out for Ali to relax in before he walked round all the stalls of more than 100 furniture exhibitors. After he had done his thing, we got him back to the room for the press. I introduced myself and the local fighters and had my video people filming us all. I have known a lot of famous sportsmen and celebrities over the years and it takes a lot to impress me, but I don't mind admitting that meeting Muhammad Ali, the Greatest, was a personal highlight.

Then it was back to my show. Contracts signed, I got a phone call from Trickett. He had just taken a call from Frank Warren. Warren was stuck with a TV slot but no main event or venue. Could the two of them come in with me on the promotion side, a third each? Warren would bring in TV and pay £4,000. I told Jack no way, I did not need TV as I had a £10,000 sponsor and was confident the show would sell out.

About a week later, Jack came on again.

'Listen,' he said, 'Warren has been back on, he is desperate, why don't we split fifty-fifty? The TV exposure will do you good.'

I fell for it. Jack never lifted his hands: he sat on the phone while my sons and I did the donkey work. We drew up the seating plan, rented and set out the chairs, hired the ring from my pal Jack Dillon, an ex-wrestler, found doormen and cashiers for the walk-up on the night and sorted out the VIP bar. Jack held the purse strings: I did not want any accusation from the Boxing Board about missing money. The whole bill cost £12,000, whiel coming in we had £10,000 sponsor money, £4,000 TV money, seating for 2,000 people and most tickets sold; the walk-up took £1,900. I duly handed it all to Jack, no fingers in the till here. As far as I was concerned, we were on for a healthy profit.

My first inkling of trouble came on the day of the fight. Eddie Smith rang me from the weigh-in to tell me his opponent had not shown. I was gutted but was so busy with last minute things that there was nothing I could do. Then came the first bout of the evening. 'My lords, ladies and gentlemen,' said announcer Nat Basso, 'this is a Frank Warren-Jack Trickett promotion.' There was no mention of me, even though the fight programme read, 'Promoter, Jim Donnelly.' Jack had had me over.

When the dust had settled, I never saw a penny. Trickett said the show lost money. We finished up after the promotion in the Thirty Nine Steps restaurant in Deansgate, where I was told there was nothing in the pot. I was furious with Jack, not so much about the money but about being kept out of the loop and sidelined at my own event, after I had done all the work. Even Jim Swords said, 'Why don't you crack him?' Perhaps it would have cleared the air if I had, but I could not do that to someone I had been through so much with. A couple of days later, JS fell out with him too. He said it was because of me, but really it was over a Rolls-Royce he had given Jack to sell. Jimmy said Jack short-changed him.

Najib Daho went on to win the British title and fought for a world title, but by then he was not my fighter. Jack and I never worked together again. I learned that Jack Trickett was for Jack Trickett. The thing was, you had to like him, he had a way with people. Everybody fell under his spell. But he hurt me deeply, and Jim Swords and I did not speak to him for ten years after that.

AS IF ALL THAT was not bad enough, I came under surveillance from the Irish police as well. In the early eighties, the Dublin Gardai set up a team to investigate links between Irish gangsters and international criminals. They were especially concerned with three things: stolen goods being shipped abroad, armed gangs travelling between different countries to commit robberies, and drugs flowing into Ireland. For example, in July 1983, Martin Cahill and his gang pulled off the O'Connors heist, taking £2 million in gold and diamonds from a jewellery manufacturing plant in Dublin. Some of the gold was offered for sale in Manchester and London. I ended up with a large parcel of tom that Wally McNelly flew back with.

The Irish mob began to come to Manchester regularly, on the pretext of attending football matches, and would often stay at my hotel, returning home with various 'wages'. No doubt they were up to all sorts, and there were plenty of opportunities for me as well. One gang was suspected of commuting between Dublin and England to rob over £1 million from banks and security vans in a three-year period up to 1984. Sometimes they flew in, did a heist and flew out again all on the same day. Another person of interest to the police was Michael Gilson, known to us as Dublin Mick. He was a regular guest at the Brown Bull and spent a lot of time with Mick Brown of the QSG. They often went missing together. I would wonder what they were up to, but what they did was their business.

One night I was at the bar of my Senator Club with Eric Mason when the ex-footballer Paddy Crerand came in with his wife. We exchanged greetings and they sat down with a drink. After a short while, Paddy came over.

'Jimmy, do you know you have police in here?'

I usually have a good radar for detecting the Old Bill but not on this occasion.

'What makes you say that?' I asked.

'I was at an after-dinner show at the Britannia Hotel last night,' he said. 'It was a police do and there was a large group of Irish cops over from Dublin, staying at the hotel. Now two of them are standing at the end of the bar.'

'Are you sure Paddy?' I said. 'Those two are staying at *my* hotel and I invited them to my club to watch the show tonight.'

'I'm certain, Jimmy. I had a drink with one of them.'

'Well blow me.'

'Look Jimmy, I'm just letting you know. Don't say anything to them that will embarrass me.'

'Of course not, Paddy. Don't worry. And thanks, pal.'

Paddy was concerned that I might get pulled for serving drinks after time, but I knew this was more serious. I rang the Brown Bull and told Rita to check the room these men were in. They had claimed they were on a golfing trip and had even brought clubs with them, but sure enough Rita found invitation cards and other material relating to the Britannia Hotel seminar. I left the club and went back to the Brown Bull. After double-checking it was true, I waited for the two policemen to come back, then challenged them.

'Evening, lads. How come you're not staying with police mates at the Britannia?'

They looked shocked. One of them blurted out that it was orders from Dublin and that they had been booked in at my place by their boss. They said they had enjoyed the hospitality and my club. I still threw them out, telling them to fuck off and take their golf clubs with them. But I now knew I was under obs by the Gardai as well as by GMP.

Not long afterwards, Dublin Mick was nicked in Ireland with a parcel of heroin. Unbeknown to me, he must have been doing deals in Manchester and taking back drugs. They even subpoenaed one of my barmaids to testify at his trial that he had been booked into my hotel. Mick got fourteen years. I knew it was bang

on me and it was time to get away again. I began to make arrange-
ments to sell the Brown Bull and return to Spain.

Then one morning, I awoke with a gun to my head. Armed
police were all over my house. Spain would have to wait.

'What do you want?' I asked.

'We are looking for guns and money,' one of them said. 'And
we're looking for the Kelly brothers.'

The Kelly brothers were two Irish lads I knew who worked in
the double-glazing business in Manchester. The police had them
down as blaggers. They searched the house but found nothing, so
they took me to the Brown Bull and searched that, waking up my
residents, a liberty. In my residents' book, they found the names of
Don and Tony Kelly, who had stayed the night there a couple of
weeks earlier after a christening. The cops were delighted. They
arrested me and drove me across the Pennines to a police station
in Leeds. There I found out how serious it was. A Tony Kelly was
wanted for armed robberies in Yorkshire and for questioning
about the murder of a police sergeant, John Speed, in October
1984. Sgt Speed had gone to the aid of a colleague who had been
wounded while questioning two men acting suspiciously. In the
chase that followed, Speed was shot dead.

'As far as I know, they are window-fixers and not into anything like that,' I protested.

Of course, they didn't listen. Instead they dumped a large
amount of Irish punts on the table and said that they had another
of the firm in custody.

'We found this money in Mick Brown's house,' one of them
said. 'It's marked.'

Mick had bought a parcel of about £10,000-worth of punts at
half-price. The police had found it in his loft and tested it. It
turned out the money was part of a ransom payment made in

Ireland after a postmaster was kidnapped, and was traceable. Mick said he had bought the punts innocently, believing them to be legal.

After twenty-four hours, they bailed me. My charge sheet read, 'Suspicion of the murder of Sergeant Speed,' which sounded fucking awful. Nothing came of it, thankfully, and Mick Brown was eventually acquitted of money laundering. Neither of the Kelly brothers was ever tried for the murder of Sgt Speed, and it later emerged that another criminal, since dead, had done the deed. It also turned out that they had been after the wrong men anyway. In November 1986, a different Tony Kelly, from Dublin, was jailed for fourteen years for his part in the kidnapping of Jennifer Guinness, of the famous brewing family, in Ireland. The cops had been after the wrong men all along.

My Irish connections may have caused me some grief but they also came in handy, particularly if I needed to get someone out of the way for a while. One night I got a phone call from a pal's wife in Glasgow. She said her husband, Robbie McCann, was in a lot of trouble and could I help. 'Don't worry,' I said, 'I'll look after him.' Robbie was a good man, one of many firm friends I had developed in Glasgow since my construction company had worked there years earlier. I had even lived for a while opposite the Kelvin Hall, and got to know all the key gangsters, men like old Arthur Thompson, who ran the market area, and Bobby Dempster, a partner of Rab Carruthers. I would often attend boxing matches with them and inevitably the odd parcel would sometimes go up there or come down from them to Manchester.

Robbie arrived at my hotel at midnight, looking like he had not slept for a couple of days. He told me he was wanted for a gangland murder. We discussed things and I decided to get him out of the country. I asked Eric Mason, who was living at my hotel, to come with me. I would pay all the expenses. We drove to Holyhead, left the car and took the sea ferry as foot passengers over to Dublin. Then we took Robbie down to Tramore in County Waterford and left him there with my friends. He asked Eric to stick with him for company and said he would pay him a few bob. I advised Eric to stay as he was getting nowhere in Manchester.

Six months later, Robbie was arrested in Dublin, extradited and stood trial for murder. The verdict was not proven. I was happy to have helped a friend.

All this time, the QSG was getting wealthier. I personally was a walking money machine. If I ever wanted extra capital to expand, I went to the firm. We did not need to go looking for deals; they came to us. I had a security agency, a travel agency, after-dinner events, boxing promotion, ticket scalping and my licensed premises. The list of pubs and clubs I had at one time or another in Manchester, Salford and Stockport would include the Egerton, the Bank of England, the Kensington, the Brown Bull, JR's, Nitos, the Theatre Club, the Senator Club, the Cotton Club, the Cheshire Cheese, the Ram, the Manhattan, the Angel and the Oxford. I would also own a hotel in Blackpool for a while. Joe Swords was my silent partner in some of them, while my wife was often down as the licensee or manager. Many of these I ran simultaneously and by 1984 I was taking fifty or sixty grand a week. It was too good to last.

12

THE STALKER AFFAIR

THE EARLY EIGHTIES was a bloody period in Northern Ireland. The Troubles were at their height, bombings and shootings were commonplace and every week seemed to bring a fresh atrocity. People became hardened to it. So when three Royal Ulster Constabulary constables were blown apart by a bomb in October 1982, I cannot say I gave it much heed. I was busy building my business empire and had other things on my mind. Little did I know that the bombing would set in train a sequence of events that would envelop me and many others for years to come.

What seems to have happened is that some members of the RUC, outraged by the slaughter of the three constables, decided to take a more aggressive approach to the two main Republican terrorist groups, the IRA and the INLA. On November 11, members of an RUC anti-terrorist unit shot dead three unarmed members of the IRA at a roadblock outside Lurgan, firing 109 bullets into their car. Less than two weeks later, a seventeen-year-old boy was shot dead and another was badly injured in a hayshed, also near Lurgan. Three weeks after that, two more unarmed men died in a hail of police gunfire on the outskirts of Armagh.

These extra-judicial killings raised grave suspicions that the RUC was operating a secret 'shoot-to-kill' policy against terrorist suspects in the province, executing them without recourse to the law. The killings were investigated by the RUC itself and some officers were prosecuted but acquitted. During the trial of one constable, it emerged that many of the original police accounts of the shootings were untrue: the constable said he had been instructed by senior officers to tell lies in his statements. His claims caused uproar and led to demands for an outside investigation.

In May 1984, the Government gave in to these demands and selected a senior officer from an outside force to conduct an independent inquiry. It chose John Stalker, the Deputy Chief Constable of Greater Manchester. Stalker had a long and unblemished track record as a detective and appeared to be the Establishment's man, having been recommended by his own Chief Constable, Jim Anderton, and by Her Majesty's Inspector of Constabulary. Stalker set about his investigation with vigour and seemed to be making headway, but in doing so he rattled cages at the RUC, some of whose officers did not want a serious examination of their methods and who put a series of obstacles in his way.

What did any of this have to do with me or the Quality Street Gang? Nothing, as it happens, but that was not how it played out. Instead we became embroiled in the most sensational police corruption investigation of the era, with far-reaching consequences for all involved.

JOHN STALKER WAS born and raised in Failsworth, east Manchester, and joined the police as a cadet when I was a bike boy at Smithfield Market. He rose through the ranks, working in the CID, drugs squad, Special Branch and the complaints and discipline department, and in 1978 was appointed head of Warwickshire CID at thirty-eight, making him the youngest detective chief superintendent in the country. He later returned to Manchester as deputy chief constable, the number two to James Anderton. In short, he had enjoyed an exemplary career as a police officer.

Stalker had worked the city centre in the sixties and probably locked up people I knew, but I do not recall ever meeting him. He did, however, become a close friend of my pal Kevin Taylor. Their friendship began in the early seventies when their daughters went to the same school. I believe they actually met at a school PTA meeting: that's how these sinister conspiracies always start! Kevin at that time was running a secondhand commercial vehicle pitch in Ancoats, which was how we knew him.

Their career paths could hardly have been more different. Kevin, a Salford lad, left school at fourteen and became a professional gambler. He was an expert in kalooki, a version of thirteen-card contract rummy, and travelled the country to play. The world of pro gambling is as straight as a corkscrew and Kevin knew all the twists: marked cards, copy cards, signs and signals, whatever it took to win. In his autobiography, *The Poisoned Tree*, he tells how one night in London he was approached by some heavies who fronted him £20,000 to play in a high-stakes poker game at the Grosvenor House Hotel. He protested that poker was not his game but they assured him everything would be fine and, sure enough, it was. 'That night I won £180,000,' he recounted. 'The croupier was magic. I couldn't see what he was doing. All I know was that every time I got a good hand, somebody had a hand nearly as good.' He was paid £27,000 for his 'work' that night. Kevin was no villain but nor was he quite the straight man people thought: he was a good card player and could win as much by playing straight as by cheating, but he did like to cheat.

I got to know Kevin well when he moved next door to Jim Swords' car lot on Great Ancoats Street in the mid-sixties and opened Vanland. His first stock was an old van he bought for £15 and sold for £80. He invested his profits in more vehicles and expanded. It was Kevin who taught me about fencing off derelict land. Ancoats was dotted with old plots, many of them bombsites from the War. No-one had reclaimed much of this land; some of the occupants had died in the Blitz and no-one knew who it legally belonged to. Kevin would go the Land Registry, find out if anyone was registered as the owner, check with the council to see if the rates had been paid, and if they were in lengthy arrears or if there was no listed owner he would simply start paying the rates, fence off the land and assume ownership. Then he would apply for planning permission. Believe it or not, it worked. Nobody else seemed to want the land and at the time it was not regarded as being worth much, even though it was right beside the city centre.

Kevin moved into property investment more heavily in the seventies. He had a gambler's instincts and was not afraid to bite off what seemed to be more than he could chew. With his constant gambling and the cost of erecting units on his parcels of land, he often ran short of cash and would borrow money from some of the QSG. 'They helped me out in lots of ways and even lent me money without quibbling,' he later wrote. 'I knew about their reputation but to me they were just good neighbours. Nothing was too much trouble for them if you asked. I dismiss the idea they were organized big-time crooks and I'd rather spend the time of day with the likes of them than many of the people I met when I later went into politics.'

As the years rolled on, Kevin became rich, buying a big mansion and yacht. He still played cards but in nicer places. He also involved himself in politics and became a bigwig in the local

Conservative association. He had a wide circle of friends, and I knew he had a pal who was a senior police officer. Their friendship was no secret: Kevin had even been for mess dinners at police HQ. It did not bother me.

It was also no secret that Kevin was friendly with us, given that he had run a showroom next to us for years. His driver and minder when he went out gambling was Colin 'Tiny' Brown, who had been part of the firm for years. I first met Tiny in Rose Hill remand centre in 1956. He was six foot four and built like a brick shithouse. He later went to Portland borstal and was the daddy there until Jimmy Monaghan arrived. Tiny was from Salford, one of the few 'outsiders' on the firm, and was a great person with a sense of humour. As well as driving Kevin, he worked on the doors of some clubs owned by a pal of ours. So Kevin was close to the QSG but he knew little about my shadier activities. And he never said anything to us about Stalker.

None of this would have mattered had it not been for two things. Firstly, there was a longstanding suspicion that the QSG had a mole, or moles, within Greater Manchester Police and that we were able to get hold of intelligence about us. Secondly, John Stalker's Northern Ireland investigation, which was still at this time secret, began to throw up evidence that could have been very embarrassing to the authorities. So began what became known as the Stalker Affair, with myself, Jim Swords and several other QSG members in the thick of it.

IN MAY 1984, soon after Stalker had set to work in Northern Ireland, the officer in charge of internal complaints at GMP, a guy called Peter Topping, was told of allegations that Stalker had been 'corruptly associating with a number of people who were involved in organized crime in Manchester'. These allegations came from David Burton, the over-imaginative informant who worked with our pal Mark Klapish on long-firm frauds. Burton had actually told his police handlers a year earlier about an unnamed senior officer being 'on a pension' from the QSG. He also said that Kevin Taylor associated with us. Now, within two months of Stalker being given the controversial RUC investigation, Burton started making specific claims about him. Coincidence?

Having been involved with Klapish, Burton would have picked up gossip about the QSG, but no more so than dozens of other no-marks around Manchester. He was also a liar, pure and simple. Even his main police handler called him 'a dangerous informant' and said he would pick up tips from one officer and then pass them on to another to appear knowledgeable and, no doubt, to get paid. Working with Klapish, he would have known that Kevin Taylor was next door to us at Vanland, and everybody knew Kevin was pally with Stalker. So he put two and two together – we knew Taylor, Taylor knew Stalker – to make five. Kevin Taylor later called it 'infantile logic'. Yet some officers took Burton seriously, apparently because he had given good information in the past, including telling of a planned IRA attack on Klapish's premises in Belfast. Personally I think the police believed him because they wanted to. They saw us poncing about the town in our Rollers and Bentleys, owning clubs, sitting around our car pitches in the sun drinking tea and gossiping, and it was an affront to them. They hated it.

I barely knew Burton. I remember meeting him briefly at Klapish's warehouse. The next time I saw him was in the exercise yard at Strangeways, when I was on remand for airline fraud and he was up for long-firm fraud. We were walking around the yard and he said hello and I said hello back and that was the only time

I spoke to him. He was a smarmy bastard and for two pins I would have given him a smack. In the end, Klapish was jailed for four years for conspiring to obtain property by deception, while Burton got only two-and-a-half years after a senior officer visited the judge in chambers and gave him a list of occasions when Burton had helped the police. Charges against Joe Swords, who denied any involvement, were dropped when Burton refused to testify against him. He was happy to feed the cops bullshit behind the scenes but not prepared to stand up and be cross-examined in the dock.

Burton's innuendos about Stalker would probably have gone nowhere had it not then been for another remarkable 'coincidence'. In June 1984, one of his police handlers, a superintendent called McGourlay, played a round of golf with a businessman he had not met before called Gerry Wareing. Wareing was a friend of Kevin Taylor's and, during their round, he apparently told a few stories about villains taking trips on Kevin's yacht in Spain and described parties at Kevin's house. He said the guests included John Stalker and members of the QSG. He also dropped a few names, including Jim Swords, Jack Trickett and me. McGourlay was troubled by what he heard and, two days later, went to see the internal complaints boss, Topping, to pass it on. He later said that he thought Stalker should have been warned about this gossip, but Stalker was not warned. Instead, about ten days later, Topping personally interviewed the snitch Burton, who allegedly 'reiterated his accusations against Stalker'. Topping then made some inquires about Kevin Taylor and ascertained that he was indeed a friend of Stalker's and had been entertained by him in the police mess. This was not news to anyone except Topping.

On July 17, Topping submitted a four-page report to Assistant Chief Constable Ralph Lees detailing allegations about Kevin

Taylor, the QSG and Stalker. This was passed further up the chain of command to James Anderton, and would impel the launching of a secret investigation into John Stalker. The contents of this report would not become public until more than a decade later, when it was revealed that, among other things, Topping said, 'What is particularly disturbing about the activities of the Quality Street gang is their ever-increasing involvement in drugs, and there is now a strong indication the IRA is associating with them in this most lucrative criminal area.' He went on to say the QSG had 'contacts in Africa' and 'access to their own shipping facilities'. Presumably by shipping facilities he meant a couple of holiday yachts. Stalker himself would later describe this report as 'histrionic and self-justifying'. However, on the basis of it, officers were authorised to start making discreet enquiries about Kevin Taylor and his associates, and eventually a momentous decision was made to launch a full-blown investigation.

In February 1985, GMP set up a top secret operation called the Drugs Intelligence Unit (DIU). John Stalker was not told about it, even though he was second-in-command of the force. It employed around ten officers and would operate for three years, until February 1988. There is much dispute about whether the DIU was really a drugs unit or whether that was just a cover name. Many people, including me, believe its priority was to investigate the alleged links between Taylor, Stalker and the QSG. The officer in direct control of it was the same Chief Superintendent Peter Topping who had started the ball rolling with his memo the previous summer.

The DIU set up what it called Operation Kalooki, the name of the card game that Kevin specialized in. Between 1985 and 1986, its officers secretly watched Kevin's office in St John Street for a total 114 days. They trained cameras on his home, tailed his car, tapped his phones and opened his mail. Detectives even approached his sister and asked about his days at Vanland in the sixties. Eventually his solicitor wrote to the police to ask what it was all about. They refused to say. They also trained cameras on our car pitches from the top of the CIS building; the window cleaners and security staff there told us. DIU detectives also visited David Burton several times in Preston Prison, where he was serving his sentence. Apparently he further embroidered his yarn about Stalker being 'on a pension' and how the QSG could get things 'straightened' through the police. I was supposed to have bumped into Burton one day in Bridge Street and had a conversation in which I referred to Stalker as a 'Kevin's man' and a 'top jolly', or bent copper. It was utter bollocks. Obviously Burton was pumping the cops with all sorts of hearsay and gossip.

Then something strange happened. In March 1985, David Burton suffered a suspected heart attack in prison and died. The police said his death was not suspicious, but two old lags who were in the same prison later told me he had been 'taken care of'. I suppose that is how powdered glass goes down.

AFTER MY SPLIT with Jack Trickett, I ploughed on alone in boxing. I still loved the game, even though there was no money in it. You could not dream then of ringside seats at £200 or more: we were lucky if we could charge £15. I did it for the prestige and the hope that we would find a champion. In March 1985, I was granted my own promoter's licence, over the objections of Nat Basso, who was up Jack's arse. Basso headed the Central Area Council of the British Boxing Board of Control, even though he was also a manager, trainer and MC: no conflict of interest there, then. My obtaining a licence only made things worse between me and Jack.

That April, Marvin Hagler was due to defend his world middleweight title in a mega-fight against Thomas 'Hit Man' Hearns in America. Frank Warren had the closed-circuit TV rights to show the fight at cinemas and theatres across the UK and sold franchises to various people in different towns and cities. A guy I knew, who managed the singer Paul Young, bought the rights for Manchester and was going to screen the bout at the Apollo Theatre. He phoned up Jack Trickett and gave him tickets on approval to sell. Then he phoned me and did the same. The tickets did not sell well and Jack, unbeknown to me, sent his back, complaining that we were selling to the same people. He later said he did not want anything to do with the tickets because I was involved, implying that I was crooked.

I handed all the monies and any unsold tickets into the box office on the night, but Paul Young's manager went to the police and said that I owed them £5,000: they claimed not to have received the money I handed in. Well, I did hand it in and even took a receipt for it but foolishly threw it away. For once in my life I was straight. With what happened later – I was charged with theft – I wish I *had* nicked the money. I later discovered that, when the Board of Trade investigated the Hagler-Hearns ticket sales, Jack Trickett decided to add a little spice by giving them a statement saying that as soon as he knew I had tickets, he sent his back and wanted nothing to do with it. I had been making my way back into boxing and this was his way of getting back at me. A lot of mysterious things were going on at the time over the Stalker Affair. I think the powers-that-be were putting the frighteners on people and I was the fall guy.

I still had to use Nat Basso to MC my shows because there was nobody else. He and Tommy Miller, the matchmaker, were on wages from me, but even then Basso would advertise Trickett's next promotion from inside the ring at my show. And on the afternoon of a promotion, I had to pay all the fighters' wages up front, plus the doctors and officials, the implication being that I could not be trusted. 'We do not want villains in the game,' Basso used to say, but this was one time in my life that I played by the rules. In the end, I walked away. I was getting nowhere and they had killed my love of the game.

In June 1985, I went with my London pal Dave Barry to watch Barry McGuigan win the world title against Eusebio Pedroza. It was a good evening and I won a bet on the result with the former champ Terry Downes, but all the time I had an uneasy feeling. It went back to a chance encounter with Kevin Taylor in the Piccadilly Hotel one afternoon. I had gone there to meet the area committee of the British Boxing Board of Control to discuss my application for a promoter's licence. Kevin was in the restaurant having Sunday lunch with a senior police officer. He came out and walked over to me.

'Jimmy,' he said, 'you had better be on your toes, because you do know you are under observation, don't you?'

I never asked him why or what it was about.

'Fair warning,' he added. 'Just watch yourself.'

To this day I have never found out how he knew, but it added to the general air of paranoia.

Not long after, Vinnie Schiavo returned from his long sojourn in Spain to face the music. In October 1985, he was sentenced to nine months, suspended for two years, for handling a stolen Escort XR3. The following month, he was jailed for nine months for passport offences and six months for failing to surrender to bail. I had a feeling I might be next in line, and decided to get ready for the off myself. I accepted an offer of £165,000 for the Brown Bull, though I still kept my hand in by taking over the Egerton, a pub around the corner. At about the same time, the Inland Revenue came after Rita, saying they wanted £200,000 in unpaid tax. Someone had it in for us.

THAT CHRISTMAS, WE heard more bad news. Phil Lynott had collapsed at his home in Kew and been taken to a drug clinic. His mum, Phyllis, later rang me and said he had been moved to a hospital. His organs had been ravaged by abuse. Phil had for some time been hopelessly hooked on drugs and booze but, like many addicts, he was clever and hid it well. I had been in many situations with him but never saw him out of it. My last recollections of him were at my brother-in-law's wedding and at Jack Trickett's Acton Court Hotel, and he had seemed in control. Thin Lizzy had split up but Phil had been pursuing a solo career and still had plans. Certainly his talent never left him.

I had often made the trip to Howth, near Dublin, to see Phyllis, the Godmother, and would stay at a small hotel at the golf club. If Philip was around he would drive over to pick me up and take me to the house. There were always people there, with drink flowing. Phil could relax at home in a way he couldn't anywhere else. He had no edge on him, and it was always fun. He told everyone about the QSG, about the inspiration for 'The Boys Are Back in Town' and about 'Johnny the Fox Meets Jimmy the Weed'. Phyllis used to blag his American guests that I was a film producer and I would have birds swarming over me. As they say in Dublin, the *craic* was good.

This time there was no way back for Phil. He was diagnosed with septiceamia, and his vital organs began to pack up. A few

Entertaining the Costa del Crime at a cabaret show I staged in Spain. (*From left*) Neil Robertson, who died after an unexplained fall from a tower block; gangster Ronnie Knight; Tony 'Is This The Way To Amarillo' Christie; Londoner Micky Riley; the lovely singer Angie Gold, a close friend; and me.

With the comedian Mick Miller and Davie Moore. Mick refused to take any payment for a New Year's Eve gig he did for me. Davie, a big man on the Costa del Sol, later had to do a quick body swerve to avoid the attentions of the Spanish police.

Louis Schiavo and Jim Swords tussle over a £20 note.
There can only be one winner, and it ain't going to be Louis!

Former Manchester United manager Tommy Docherty raising a glass at my
Egerton Arms pub. The Doc was a great help in bringing in the customers.
Standing at the bar are United players Arthur Albiston and Kevin Moran.

The 'Quality Street connection' of tycoon in secret police report

Mystery of Jimmy the Weed

Club boss sought by police in gun quiz

Gangland shooting in city street

Manchester Evening News

BRITAIN'S BIGGEST REGIONAL NEWSPAPER

TUESDAY, AUGUST 11, 1987

Bid to kill man in city street

Gangland shooting

Quality Street Gang are named in court drama

The Quality Street gang 'just a myth'

I made a few headlines over the years, not least over the Stalker Affair and also after the shooting of John Stones, which the police tried to pin on me.

Talking with Eric Mason, the London heavy who was once chopped up by the Richardson gang. Eric was good company and we became close, but in the end he caused so many problems that I decided to do away with him. He doesn't know how lucky he was.

Getting the treatment from drag artist Frank 'Foo-Foo' Lammar at my sixtieth birthday party. We called Frank 'the rough, tough puff': he had a heart of gold, but he could fight for fun when called upon.

Marvelous Marvin Hagler was the guest at an event promoted by my one-time partner Mickey Martin (*left*), who has brought many top performers, celebrities and sports stars to Manchester over the past twenty-five years.

Karl 'Fat Neck' Power (*left*) and my son Tony (*right*) with former boxing champion Dave 'Boy' Green, a great guy. Fat Neck is world famous for gate-crashing top sporting events by dressing up as a competitor.

My Tony at a dinner with Wayne Rooney and Mike Tyson. Tony has never walked away from a scrap, and still boxes now.

Dominic and his lovely wife Natalie on their wedding day in Cancun, Mexico. Lots of the chaps were there.

With Eric Mason, Mixie Walsh and Deaf Paul at Mixie's birthday party in his home town of Blackpool. Mixie is a bit of a legend in the seaside resort and one very tough, staunch man. I also moved to Blackpool and made it my base in the early nineties.

My Scottish pal John Shearer, with whom I worked closely. We got into – and out of – a few scrapes together.

Gilly 'Concrete Face' Grundy (*left*), my right-hand man and loyal doorman for twenty-three years, and Bob 'the Jeweller' Spanner, another of the old QSG who settled in Blackpool.

Organising Ricky Hatton at a charity function. Ricky is a good lad with a great heart. He has battled through depression and drink problems and come out on top.

Barry Pollard (*left*) from Salford with his pal Tony Boyd. Salford has produced more hard men per square mile than just about anywhere, and Barry is one of hardest.

With John (*left*) and Arthur at a family wedding. The lads both served a bit of porridge but put it behind them and are now wealthy men. And Arthur's sons have one of the most successful street clothing companies in the UK.

With Jim Swords, who is still in fighting trim, and my youngest son, Raefe. JS will always be the guv'nor.

In Thailand with my friend Nancy. I discovered the country a decade ago and fell in love with it. It's a lovely place to spend my retirement.

I still like to keep my hand in and helped out at an event in Manchester for Mad Frankie Fraser. It was nice to do a favour for an old mate. Frank is fast approaching ninety but looks well. Our mutual friend Micky Cohen is in the middle.

days after being moved to hospital, on 4 January 1986, he died. He was thirty-six years of age. What a loss.

The funeral, in Dublin, was extraordinary. I took my Rolls-Royce over on the car ferry. Everybody was there: there were thousands in the cortege from the service at the Church of Assumption and so many cars that they could not all get in to see the burial at St Fintan's cemetery. Phyllis tried to jump into the grave with him. I got her back in the Rolls with my son Tony driving and took her home. We then looked after the security at the house to stop people getting into the grounds – they were coming over the walls. The reception was at a hotel in Howth. I remember talking to Bono there, and Mick Rossi from Status Quo. Everybody was gutted. Phil was such a generous guy and had helped so many musicians over the years. I'd had so many good times at the house in Dublin, but this was a very sad one.

I still listen to Phil's stuff to this day. To me, he made the Rolling Stones sound second-rate. Don't tell me Mick Jagger could sing, he could shout but Phil could sing. And some call Keith Richards the greatest riff player but to me Gary Moore was the greatest lead guitarist in the world. They were a unique band and Phil was a unique man. He will always be missed.

THE POLICE PROBE into John Stalker and Kevin Taylor eventually built up files on more than 5,000 people. Many of them had absolutely nothing to do with crime, Stalker or the QSG. Even Kevin Taylor did not have a criminal record. He was simply a gambler, and he took that attitude into his business dealings. He took big financial risks and if they paid off he benefited handsomely.

Through his company Rangelark, Kevin had bought a number of derelict properties in Trafford Park. He had a vision that this moribund area of Manchester might became a thriving business centre, and time would show that he was right. He bought another site in Cheshire and obtained planning permission to turn it into a tip, and on a third site, near Bury, he got permission for a housing development, funded partly by the sale of his yacht, *Diogenes*. Kevin had a deal with the Co-op Bank to put up much of the money to buy these sites. He had several companies and some of his inter-company dealings were complex. Ultimately he and his companies owed the bank £996,000. The assets they had purchased, however, grew in value to well in excess of that: the Trafford site alone was worth around £1.5 million.

The police made themselves busy. Whenever Kevin found a potential buyer for one of his sites, detectives approached them, asked questions and let it be known they were investigating Kevin; sometimes it slipped out that they were from a 'drugs unit'. This was enough to scare off any buyers. Kevin was caught between a rock and a hard place: he could not sell and reap the big profit that was there, yet the longer he kept the land, the more the interest accrued on his bank loans, putting him under massive cash-flow pressure. All three sites eventually went in a firesale and the bank more than got its money back, although the sale values were far lower than they should have been. In July 1986, in 'receivership', the land at Trafford Park was sold to Trafford Development Corporation for £1.2 million. Today it would be worth many times that. Kevin was basically asset-stripped.

Meanwhile, John Stalker had been making slow but steady headway in his shoot-to-kill inquiry. In September 1985, he produced a highly critical interim report recommending the prosecution of eleven RUC officers. Not surprisingly, his relationship with the

RUC deteriorated. Stalker had uncovered the existence of a secret MI5 audiotape of one of the killings, in a hayshed in Lurgan, and had been exerting pressure to obtain a copy. The head of the RUC, Sir John Hermon, had promised to hand it over, then refused. Stalker made it clear that he was unhappy with this. He made an appointment to interview Hermon on 30 April 1986. Hermon failed to keep the appointment.

Ten days later, Greater Manchester Police declared their hand when they raided Kevin Taylor's mansion in Summerseat at eight o'clock in the morning. According to Kevin's account, they seemed mainly interested in his old photographs, particularly any that might feature John Stalker, and took away three albums, including one that contained a soon-infamous photo of me with Mrs Stalker at a party. They also searched a number of offices, including his accountants' and his solicitors'. The search warrants had been issued after police claimed Kevin had defrauded the Co-op Bank of £240,000, even though the bank itself had not complained. Even stranger, the matter was being investigated by the Drugs Intelligence Unit, even though it was an alleged fraud that had nothing to do with drugs. Kevin was not at that stage charged, nor would he be for another sixteen months. It was all very mysterious.

The seized photos were taken, along with a report by Peter Topping, to a secret meeting on May 19 of senior law officers, including James Anderton, in Scarborough. They decided Stalker would have to be investigated by an outside force and would be taken off the shoot-to-kill inquiry. Nine days later, Stalker, who suspected nothing, received a shock phone call from the police authority. He was curtly told he was being removed from duty. Later he was placed on extended leave pending the investigation of alleged disciplinary offences. The police authority had received a top secret report, compiled by Topping and approved by Anderton, that outlandishly implied Stalker might be sympathetic to the IRA, so it really had little choice. Stalker later called the report 'a smear campaign of the worst sort'.

With the raid on Kevin's home and Stalker's suspension, the shit really hit the fan. Reporters from the newspapers and from heavyweight TV documentary teams were suddenly flocking around and there were selective leaks to the press. *Panorama* quickly aired a programme called 'Conspiracy or Coincidence?' Suddenly the Quality Street Gang, who had been little heard of in public before, became national news.

Colin Sampson, the Chief Constable of West Yorkshire, took over Stalker's shoot-to-kill inquiry. The timing could not have been more fortuitous for some: Stalker was removed just as he believed he was about to obtain the MI5 tape of one of the shootings. Sampson was also tasked with conducting a separate inquiry into the allegation that, between 1971 and 1985, Stalker 'associated with Kevin Taylor and known criminals in a manner likely to bring discredit upon the Greater Manchester Police'. Now bear in mind that Kevin did not even have a criminal record, so how you could bring discredit upon the force by associating with him was anybody's guess, but this was the nonsense that the secret unit within GMP had been sniffing around for two years.

Sampson and a team of eleven officers and two typists set about interviewing numerous people. They took 169 statements and questioned a large number of other witnesses who refused to make statements. They even asked the drag artist Foo Foo Lammar if Taylor and Stalker had ever been seen in gay bars or dancing with other men. It was ridiculous. On Sunday, June 15, I was interviewed at length by a chief superintendent and an inspector. For once I had nothing to hide – I knew John Stalker about as well as I knew Elvis Presley – but I refused to make a written statement.

The tabloids were hot onto the QSG and tried to contact Jim Swords and a few others. JS phoned me to discuss what we should do.

'Have you had the press round?' he asked.

'Yeah.'

'Well I'm not saying anything but we could do with you saying something because we are not having them nicking us on trumped up drugs charges.'

It would be a safety net in case anyone was minded to fit us up. So I arranged to meet the *News of the World* in the presence of my solicitor and gave them a few tidbits. 'We are terrified at the moment because of what the police are up to,' I told them. 'Look at my car outside. Anyone could come in the night, put a kilo of coke in the boot and then nick me.' That Sunday, they ran a big story based on an exclusive interview with me. Unfortunately they said I had been convicted of credit card fraud, which was untrue. They also said guests were 'in a state of undress' in a swimming pool at Kevin Taylor's house, but how else do you go swimming? They ran the story to suit themselves but I suppose that was no surprise.

Life still had its funny side. A large crowd of us took a trip to Royal Ascot that summer, run by my pal Terry Corless from his pub, the Circus Tavern. We had a great day in the sunshine at the races, though nobody won a penny. After we had gorged on lobster and champagne from tables at the side of the coach, one of the lads said, 'I have got a surprise for you. We are all going to Windsor Great Park to see the polo.'

It was fascinating to see how the toffs enjoyed themselves. I spoke to the club captain when we arrived and he said we had just missed Prince Charles, who had been playing. I had a bit of fun with him.

'I bet you could build a lot of terraced houses on that pitch,' I said.

'My dear James,' he replied, 'that is a polo *field*, not a pitch.'

I felt a right cunt.

Then I went to the toilets and looked at the noticeboard, which had the club rules and various messages. There was a note pinned to it that read, 'Will the person who took the ring out of the gents' toilets please bring it back.' So they do have royal tea leaves.

The following Sunday, my name was in the newspapers over the Stalker Affair. The club captain rang his pal in Manchester and said, 'Was that the same Jimmy that bought me the champagne that's in the *News of the World*? Oh my God.' We had a good laugh at that.

The cops also saw my spread in the newspaper and came back to interview me again. This time I agreed to make a written statement basically reprising what I had told the *News of the World*: I had been to Kevin's birthday party, had met Stalker briefly and that was it. Joe Leach and Dessie O'Connor also made statements and Vinnie Schiavo gave an interview, all saying quite truthfully that they had never met Stalker. Joe Swords spoke to them but gave them nothing and JS fucked off to Puerto Banus to avoid them, making it quite clear he would not be saying a word.

I decided that Kevin Taylor had been right with his warning and that it was time to join JS, even though it came at a bad time financially. I had bought the freehold of a pub called the Red Bull and obtained planning permission to demolish it and build a new pub and two townhouses. I was also in the middle of building a massive nightclub in Chinatown. I had put eighty grand into it, and a major brewery had agreed to stump up £600,000 for a share of all my projects. Then the police went to see them, and they got cold feet. The nightclub was scuppered. I sold some assets, including the land beside my big house in Alkrington for £100,000, and moved back to Spain in the summer of 1986, buying a villa there.

I had to leave my company Northern Leisure, which rented out Spanish apartments and had an office on Princess Street, in the hands of Eric Mason, and gave him instructions to basically do an LF with it. Money that came in went into his pocket and no bills got paid, so it collapsed. But Eric messed it up, then got himself beaten up. We had brought in John Lynn, a dangerous Glaswegian who later got seventeen years for attempted murder for shooting an Irishman in a Blackpool hotel. Eric and John set up this thing in Blackpool. A parcel of jeans arrived. John wanted to sell them, pay the people and order double again. Mason, as usual, wanted money straight away. That's the only thing that spoils the LF job, you have to sit on it, get respectful with suppliers. The next day John travelled down to see Mason. The gear had gone. John had put in £5,000 for expenses and so had I before I left the country. I heard later that John and his pal Willie had captured Mason and smashed his hand.

THE SO-CALLED Sampson Report was completed that August and was circulated on a strictly need-to-know basis, stamped 'Confidential'. However its contents soon leaked to newspaper and television reporters. It had this to say about the QSG:

> The Quality Street Gang is the name given to a group of Manchester criminals who are regarded by a number of senior police officers as being the organisers of incidents of major crime in the city. The membership of the gang appears to be ever changing and many criminals claim membership or asso-

ciation because it enhances their reputation amongst their fellows. Historically the group has its origins in the late 1960s and early 1970s and appears to have emanated amongst barrow boys, market traders, and used car dealers. Of those people identified as belonging to this group in its early years only a few continue to associate and are suspected of currently being active, they include James Patrick MONAGHAN alias Jimmy Swords, Joseph Kevin MONAGHAN, Michael Roy BROWN, Vincent SCHIAVO, Louis SCHIAVO, Jack TRICK-ETT and James Anthony DONNELLY.

Not one of these men had ever been convicted of anything that could be called 'major crime'. The document went on to say:

> As a group the Quality Street gang acquired a considerable reputation with fellow criminals, the public and the police, for although individually they were dealt with by the courts for relatively minor offences, by reputation at least, they were making a good living from crime and were not getting caught.

The key phrase there was 'by reputation at least'. This was typical of the report. There was remarkably little fact in it: instead it was crammed with unsourced innuendo. It even said that Stalker should have been aware of who I was when we met briefly at Kevin's party.

> Donnelly's association and involvement with criminals and Taylor goes back to the 1960s and has been maintained ever since. The Brown Bull public house of which Donnelly was part owner was regarded as a meeting place and clearing house for stolen property and was the subject of close police interest.

But by the time I had acquired the Brown Bull, Stalker was in a very high administrative position in a major police force, and would have had little knowledge of who was running which pub in Salford. It was ridiculous.

In fact, in 145 pages, the report came up with nothing substantive at all. Sampson ultimately recommended that John Stalker should be disciplined for infringing minor rules about the use of police staff cars for private journeys. He also suggested he was guilty of 'discreditable conduct' by associating with Kevin Taylor, even though Kevin had no criminal record and was friendly with many politicians and others in public life. The police authority disagreed: they effectively rejected the thrust of Sampson's hurried report, gave Stalker a minor reprimand and reinstated him as deputy chief constable.

Stalker returned to his office but soon concluded that working with Jim Anderton would be impossible. In March 1987, he retired from the force to work in the media and write a memoir, *Stalker*. 'I cannot impute mischief or malevolence to anyone,' he wrote, 'but nevertheless I believe, as do many members of the public, that I was hurriedly removed because I was on the threshold of causing a major police scandal and political row that would have resulted in several resignations and general mayhem.'

The Government later acknowledged that there was *prima facie* evidence of a conspiracy to pervert the course of justice by RUC policemen but ruled out criminal proceedings against them. They then appointed yet another Chief Constable, from Staffordshire, to investigate the RUC. Eventually, the only punishments handed out to any Northern Irish officers were reprimands. The full truth has never come out and probably never will. It was the biggest waste of time and money you ever saw.

Incredibly, Manchester Police pressed on with their investigation of poor Kevin Taylor. In September 1987, he was charged with trying to defraud the Co-op Bank. Given that he had been investigated by what was supposed to be a drugs unit, this was a very strange charge: there was no mention of drugs. By then, Kevin had been impoverished. No banks would lend him money for his business ventures, as being told by the police that a prospective borrower is being investigated for drugs trafficking and organized crime is about as damaging as you can get. Kevin was forced to go back to gambling, backed by his old friend Sid Otty, but with the stress of everything he was no longer able to pull it off and soon gave up. His health deteriorated, he was forced to sign on the dole, was unable to keep up his mortgage payments and lost his beloved family home in Summerseat. They ruined Kevin's life.

Somehow he kept going. He would come to see me at the Brown Bull, usually with lunch wrapped in newspaper from his favourite fish-and-chip shop in Hanging Ditch. Loans from friends and his positive nature kept him afloat. His case came to trial in October 1989 and, over the next few weeks, under strong cross-examination, the truth finally began to emerge: the police had lied and bullied and their case came crashing down. In January 1990, the prosecution withdrew and Kevin was officially declared not guilty. By then he was bankrupt. He took the only course left to him and sued the police. He would have to wait another five years for his day in court.

My final word on Stalker is what I told the cops when they asked me directly about him: I did not know the man and never had any connection with him. As far as I know he was a straight policeman. His boss, however, was an utter buffoon.

13

ON THE RUN

LIFE WAS GOOD in Spain in the autumn of 1986, away from the pressures of police investigations. Jim Swords and other members of the firm were there, along with faces from London, Liverpool, Tyneside and Scotland. We all stuck together, no arguments, and could take over an entire pub on a night out. Every Sunday we would find a nice beach bar, perhaps fifty of us with wives, girlfriends and kids, and would order up a load of seafood and salads and listen to live music. Strange, it was never 'them from up north' when we were all together in one place.

I have mentioned how Jim Swords liked a penny. One of the crowd out there was Davie Moore, who came originally from Chester. He had arrived in Spain a beach bum but became involved with speedboats and made a fortune. Davie said he was looking to sell his sixty-foot cruiser, which slept eight people plus crew. I told JS, who at the time was looking to offload a villa and four small houses. He was interested, so I sat them down and they did the deal.

'Right,' said Jimmy afterwards. 'I am taking you to the Valparaiso restaurant. Everything is on me. Then we'll go to the boat. I have bought a vintage Hennessy brandy for you and we'll have a good drink, as I am staying on the boat tonight.'

Good as his word, we had a great night but I did not stay long on the boat afterwards and only drank a small amount of the top-notch brandy he had bought for me.

We met up again the next day and I was choking for a drink.

'Give me a large brandy,' I said to Jim.

He pulled out a bottle of cheap Spanish piss, not the vintage Hennessy. Seeing me look at it in disgust, he said, 'I've cocked on that deal with Dave Moore. You cannot get this fucking boat insured.'

So now I knew, no vintage brandy for me. I started laughing.

'What's so fucking funny?'

'You have rung the brandy from last night, you tight fucker.'

Lynn, his lovely wife, told him, 'It's a wonder you have not asked him to pay for what you had last night.'

That was Jimmy all over.

He undid the deal with Dave, a stand-up gent who agreed to reimburse him for his out-of-pocket expenses. I don't know what Jimmy did with the Hennessy but I never got to finish it.

Another good pal, Maurice 'Mo' O'Connor, was also doing well out there. Mo came from Dublin but had been brought up in Manchester, and I had helped him out a fair bit over the years. He once came to my car pitch and asked if he could have a car, promising to pay me back a bit each week. 'Okay,' I said, 'but don't let me down.' I gave him a one-owner MG 1100 and off he went. I didn't see him again for four years! He got nicked in Sheffield for kiting cheques and credit card fraud and got a six-year sentence. It sounds implausible, six years for credit cards.

The next time I saw him was when the doorbell rang at my Senator Club. Gilly, my doorman, went to the door and there was Mo, asking for me.

'Fuck me, Mo,' I said, 'where's my car money?'

We both laughed. I cracked open a bottle of champagne, stuck a bird into him and gave him some running around money.

Mo moved to Spain and became a wealthy man. Now he was looking after me. 'Jimmy, I owe you,' he said. 'For years you have been good to me. I am going to take you out for the day and everything is on me: champagne, whatever you want.'

Denis Crolla and I took him up on it and did the rounds with him until seven in the evening. Then he announced, 'I am taking you somewhere special.' It turned out to be the biggest brothel in the world, based in a hotel in Los Boliches. The ground floor was one massive bar area with running fountains and over 100 girls of every colour and nationality, all in various states of undress.

Mo threw two grand on the bar.

'We're staying until that's gone,' he told the barman. 'Send some girls over.'

I finished up with two, Mo with two and Denis with one. We got in the lift and went to the rooms we had been allocated, taking bottles of champagne with us. We did not know that the girls cost about £75 each for twenty minutes. I was in the room drinking and playing games with the two girls for a while and eventually must have crashed out. When I woke up, they were still there and had ordered more drinks.

I went down to the bar. No sign of Denis and Mo. I sat there with the girls for a while, then got the barman to ring the lads. They came down and said they had fallen asleep as well.

We were presented with the bill. It came to over five grand.

'Fucking hell, Mo, what's going on?'

He told me the clock had been running at £150 an hour each girl, times five girls, £750 an hour for about five hours, plus the champagne and tips. Mo also said he had no more money. There was murders. In the end the security gorillas let Mo out to get more money. While he was out, one doorman made himself busy and threatened what he would do if we didn't pay. Mo came back with the money and settled the bill. Our one consolation was that we had earlier stuck some snide £20 notes into them at the bar and they had changed them.

As we were leaving, the main bouncer, with a smirk on his face, said, 'See you again, bring plenty of money.'

'Fuck off,' said Denis. 'You have had us over.'

The bouncer hit him square in the face with a knuckleduster and knocked him down. I moved towards the lump but Mo got hold of me.

'Leave it, Jimmy, there's too many of them, we'll get murdered.'

We carried Denis away and took him to hospital. His jaw was bust.

A few days later, we returned and put both barrels of a shotgun through the door. They got the message. I went back a few weeks after that and the head doorman was all over me, apologizing and saying he had thought we were tourists. He had made some inquiries and found out that we were firmed up and that the Cockneys had said they would make one with us. I was now on free drinks and it was all, 'Bring your pals in.' So Mo had paid off a bit of the lifetime debt.

Mo owned a bar and Ronnie Knight became our regular drinking partner there, or else we would go to Ronnie's house for barbecues. One night I was in a bar with Ronnie and his new girlfriend, Sue Haylock, when his ex-wife, the actress Barbara Windsor, stormed in and confronted them. Sue did a runner and left Ronnie to it. Sue was crackers but in a nice way, and good company. She had no edge on her. Ronnie was the same, he never tried to put northern people down. I would go in his restaurant, the Mumtaz in Fuengirola, and he would sit with you and have a drink. It was sad later on when he lost the lot. Clifford Saxe was another nice fellow. Cliff had run the Fox pub in Hackney, where the infamous Security Express robbery was planned. In Spain he went his own way and never got involved in any nonsense. I went on the piss many a time with him. They eventually tried to extradite him for trial. Sadly he died a few years ago.

Problems from home occasionally intruded on my pleasant idyll. I was in a bar with Ronnie Knight and a few Cockneys when a taxi pulled up and out got Eric Mason with a feller called Ted. I could not believe it. This Ted had given me £100,000 to invest in new projects, but the deals had collapsed before I had left for Spain and his money had gone. He had been trying to sue me – and now Mason had landed him on my doorstep.

'What the fuck do you think you are doing?' I asked Mason. 'You have brought a creditor to me.'

There was nothing Ted could do anyway but he had given Mason two grand and paid his expenses out there to find me. I sat down with Ted and explained the facts of life. He felt so guilty he gave me another five grand. Wiped his mouth, that was it.

Eric also came across his arch-enemies again, the Richardsons, out there. We were drinking in Patsy's Bar when this woman came in, saw him and started screaming, 'That horror's here! That horror's here!' Meaning Eric. She ran outside to tell her companions, who turned out to be Eddie and Charlie Richardson. Eric went through the back exit and disappeared, just as he had that time at the boxing in Manchester.

He stayed in Span for a while and talked Ronnie Knight into doing a book about his life, called *The Black Knight*. The money was to go into a Jersey bank. A few months later, Ronnie was trying to get hold of Eric. He said fifty grand had gone missing. Sue Haylock told me that Mason had had him over. I never found out the end of that one, but they never spoke again.

Ronnie and Sue married in June 1987. A few of the firm were invited to the reception at El Oceano, a big place right on the beach. It was a bit of a turnout, the booze flowing, Sue dancing in a £3,000 wedding dress and a pair of gloves, the Flying Squad observing from unmarked cars and journalists hanging out of a helicopter overhead.

I would also regularly go to Marbella to see Freddie Foreman, often driving up to his country club for Sunday lunch. Freddie even asked me if I would run the club, which was good of him as I was on my toes. I told him I would have under different circumstances. Freddie also put on an amateur boxing show at Marbella football ground and asked my son Tony to help train the Spanish team. Life was easy but there was always something going on to keep me busy.

Eventually, however, I decided to go back home and put the store in order. I had bought a new nightspot in Manchester, the Cotton Club, and had other interests that needed looking after. Plus Big Frank Platt had left the chip pan on at my house in Alkrington and caused a fire that damaged the kitchen, so I had to sort it out. Rita and I flew back. We had not been home long when we got the terrible news that she had cancer. It was a bombshell: she was only forty-two. The taxman was still after her for £200,000, as our business interests were in her name. Yet Rita was undaunted. She carried on working at the Cotton Club at weekends, despite her illness. She loved it there and everybody loved her. It was good to see her happy even if she was sicker than we thought.

The Cotton Club was just off Piccadilly, in Stevenson Square. It was great, like a Manchester version of Ronnie Scott's in Soho. I had my old band, the Clive Allen Sound, playing every night and all the stars used to call in. It gave me little trouble. Lionel McAffrey, who had worked for me for years, was on the door with a guy called Smokey Joe, who liked a spliff, and they ran things very smoothly. The only incident that stood out came when a couple of troublesome Irish guys turned up on Lionel's night off, and because they looked smart the stand-in doorman let them in. They started playing up inside the club and I knew there was going to be a row. At 2 a.m., the band finished and I told the two guys to drink up. One of them told me to fuck off. I thought I had better end this before it got out of hand, so I went to the kitchen for a steak knife. Then I walked over to where these two sat and said, 'For the last time, drink up and get your feet off the chair.' Before the nearest guy could open his mouth, I hit him in the neck with the knife. It went through the flesh and pinned his head to the back of the seat. He screamed.

Just then, my Tony came in with his pals. They ran over.

'Fucking hell, Dad, you could have killed him.'

I pulled the knife out. It had only gone through the skin but the blood was flowing. The lads put a towel round him and slung the two of them out. They turned out to be from a travelling family. They never came back but did send their apologies. The one I stabbed later got twelve years for shooting somebody in a club across the road.

Eric Mason appeared on the scene again. I did not want to bother with him but I had a bit of work on and he was available. I sold a parcel for some people to a guy in Glasgow called Fat Sam. When the money arrived, it was short but I was promised it would be made good, so I passed on what I had. The sellers came back to me with a second parcel and asked if I could do the same again.

Eric had the job of transport on both trips. I told him, 'They were a bit short on the first trip. That was my profit. Make sure you get what's owed and the full money for the second parcel.' This time when he came back he was £18,000 light. I paid out again, less the £2,000 I was owed, and told the people to hang on. After all I had not had a penny, they'd had plenty. Instead they screamed their heads off as if they had been fucked over. I would have given them less if I was buying for cash but I was only working the middle. I found out later that Mason had done a deal behind my back and had kept part of the £18,000.

It nearly started a war. People who knew me in Glasgow wanted to go and chop up Fat Sam but I said no, I wanted the pleasure of being there myself. He later got nicked and sent down for something else and as the years have gone on it is water under the bridge, but in Manchester it nearly caused bad blood. The sellers appreciated what I had done for them but they started creating, and people on both sides fell out with each other in a serious way. Fortunately it was eventually resolved and everybody became pals again, but for a time it was pretty nasty.

As if things could not get any worse, Les Simms rang and said he wanted to see me at his hotel. I went over and he said a cop had told him that the Board of Trade were investigating me, had taken a statement off Jack Trickett and were about to charge me over transactions dating back to the early 1980s. That was all I needed.

The next day a guy named John Stones was shot and all hell let loose again.

'GANGLAND SHOOTING IN city street,' declared the *Manchester Evenings News* front page of 11 August 1987. Two days later, under the headline 'Mystery of Jimmy the Weed', it said:

A club-owner wanted for questioning about a Manchester gangland shooting has vanished from the city. Police are trying to trace Jimmy 'The Weed' Donnelly, a ticket dealer and owner of the Cotton Club in Piccadilly. Mr Donnelly, known simply in city club circles as 'The Weed', was one of a number of people mentioned during the Sampson inquiries into ex-police chief John Stalker.

Serious Crime Squad police searched Mr Donnelly's home at Middleton for two hours. They used a metal detector. Today his wife Rita said: 'I don't know where Jimmy is. I think he is working on the Continent.'

The story went on to say that thirty-five-year-old John Stones had been shot outside a pub in the Bradford area of the city. The bullet went straight through his leg and he needed emergency surgery. Detectives were 'talking to' members of the QSG and had already interviewed 'men being suspected of organised crime'.

So where was I? Preparing to disappear to Spain again, was the answer. The bare facts are that there had been a dispute over some money owed on a deal. John Stones got shot and my name was dropped into the frame. In truth I respected John, a good villain who I have known for years. Unfortunately the cops had me down as the main suspect. The newspapers implied I disappeared because of the shooting but it was time for me to go anyway.

I sorted out a snide passport and, knowing the police would be watching the airports, I had a friendly make-up artist from Granada TV dye my hair and stick on a false moustache. I was walking through a car park, feeling pretty pleased with my disguise, when I saw one of the old faces, Harry 'the Savage' Hilton, walking towards us.

'Hello, Jimmy, how are you?' he said. 'What are you doing in all that gear?'

I had no choice but to tell him. He pissed himself laughing. So much for my disguise. Harry had a villa in Marbella and for years afterwards would tell the story to our pals in Spain. I bumped into him again one day in Gibraltar with his wife.

'Change of face, Jimmy?' he asked.

The thing that concerned me most was that I had to leave Rita. Even though she was sick with cancer she was still working at our Cotton Club. It kept her going. She would lend out money behind my back and tell the punters, 'Don't tell Jimmy, he will put interest on, so make sure you pay it back to me.'

I made it to Spain, despite my dodgy disguise, and had not been there long when Davie Moore came to me with a proposition.

'I have a printing business,' he said. 'My brother is running it but they are not working it properly and I have not had a penny out of it. Would you be prepared to run it for me?'

He had spent £120,000 on setting it up but had yet to see a single peseta in return. I knew printing could be big business out there, with all the bars, restaurants, property firms and time-share agencies needing printed material, so I went to have a look. I was impressed. I told Dave I would take it on and pay him a wage every week. I had a guy who did the setting up and printing on two machines and a girl who generated all the artwork on computer.

I did what I did best: went out and hustled every day getting work. I would walk into a bar, show some jobs we had done and get orders for business cards, flyers to advertise the bar, menus, and posters. I was soon bringing in 20,000 pesetas a day on my own. I would take the jobs back to the printer by late afternoon and we would stay late into the evening, printing the day's orders, black and white first, colour second. All jobs were completed in twenty-four hours. I was soon earning a nice £70 a day, which went a long way out there at that time, and was giving Dave's wife £100 a week. He was happy. I rented three cars off Maurice O'Connor, gave some young female reps one car between two of them, and we really started taking money. We had to get the printer on night work to cope.

Davie Moore, Ronnie Knight and I became partners in a cabaret show scheduled for New Year's Eve in Fuengirola. I worked for weeks to put it together and brought the Clive Allen Sound from the Cotton Club and Jonathan Young to compere. I also booked Angie Gold, a great singer who had a number one hit in Japan with the dance anthem 'Eat You Up'. I flew them over but was still stuck for a top of the bill when Angie mentioned Mick Miller, of *The Comedians* fame. Mick had done a few gigs for me in Manchester, so I rang him. He was a bit reluctant because he could get big money for a New Year's Eve, but I told him who else was on the bill and in the end he agreed. He would fly out in the morning and fly back the next day. The show was on.

It was a sell-out. The whole Costa del Crime turned out: Freddie Foreman, Ronnie Everett, John Mason, Cliff Saxe, Tommy Brennan, Eric Mason, Ronnie Knight and many others. We had a great night, until the countdown to midnight, when suddenly cameras started flashing. The British and Spanish paparazzi had somehow infiltrated the event and were running around everywhere. We grabbed them and threw them out but it spoiled things. One headline in the papers the following Sunday was something like 'Costa Gangsters Stick Two Fingers Up To The English Law'. They had a photo of me at the bar and called me Freddie Foreman!

The day after the show, I took Mick Miller to the airport and handed him an envelope with £1,000 in it, his wages plus air fare. He checked in and I walked him to the gate, where we shook hands. Then he stuck the envelope in my shirt and was gone. When I opened it, all the money was still there. He had worked for free and paid his own fare as well. It was a nice gesture: he knew I was on my toes. Mick would do a few more gigs for me over the years. My heads still hurts at the recollection of one boozy night with him and fellow comedian Roy 'Chubby' Brown, when we finished up at Mick's house because he had built a new bar and wanted to christen it. I don't recall getting home.

I put on another show in Spain with Ivor Davis from *The Comedians*, my house band from the Cotton Club and Jonathan Young, who later joined the Bachelors as lead singer. On the surface it must have seemed to everyone that I was fine, and I always kept up a front, but all the while I was conscious that Rita's health was deteriorating back in England. She and I had been a great team. I set up the clubs and brought in the custom, she ran them and looked after the punters, and it worked. She was also a fighter, and hated the law for what she had seen them do to me. Our son Dominic was jailed for five years in 1988 for trying to rob a security van, so she had both of us away from home. Typical of her, one of the last times we spoke on the phone she said, 'Don't come back Jimmy, don't give those bastards a chance to set you up.'

My wife died on 22 February 1988. I could not come back to be with her at the end. The police had warrants out for me and I did not want them arresting me at her bedside while she was so ill. My heart was broken. The love of my life was gone.

The number of people who lined the streets on the day of the funeral showed me the respect my lovely wife had. Over 1,000 people turned out, flying in from all over the world. All along the funeral route, police were at the traffic lights, stopping traffic to let the cortege through. I was told the Old Bill were also filming from a roof across from the service and had undercovers planted in the crowd. The reception was at one of my ex-pubs, the Egerton Arms. There was a strong rumour that I had come back and was in disguise, and the also newspapers were there in force looking for me. I had thought of it, but what if the Old Bill tried to arrest me? There would have been a riot and I could not have had that. I was in a church in Mijas with my mother at exactly the same time. We had a special mass after explaining our circumstances to the local priest.

Rita and I travelled first class through life. A typical Ancoats girl, she loved the big house we had bought at Alkrington in the mid-eighties, set in an acre of land. She had expensive tastes and would think nothing of spending £800 on a dress or £200 on shoes. I never said a word. She worked hard and never complained if I disappeared off to London or New York or Las Vegas. We were married for twenty-six years. She had washed blood off me, burned clothes, scrubbed my nails, stood bail and visited me in prison. She was a part of me and I still miss her today.

I CONTINUED TO run the printers in Spain. Then, once the dust had settled, I sneaked home for a few days to sort out my affairs and do some business. I drove with Wally McNelly and Denis Crolla to Worsley for a meeting with Tom Robinson, who ran the Talk of the North club. Unbeknown to me, Wally had hired the car using the licence of Terry Jeffreys, a notorious armed robber. The police somehow found out and must have tracked the car, thinking it was going to be used on a blag. Instead they found me.

As we left the meet, armed officers appeared from everywhere, surrounding the car and pointing guns at our heads. 'There is a warrant for your arrest,' one of them told me. They found £6,000 in the car, but had to let Wally and Denis go as they had done nothing wrong. Wally said the cash was his and so they gave it to him. I couldn't get out quick enough: you could not trust Wally with six grand! They put me before Salford magistrates on a holding charge of jumping bail on a motoring offence, but really they wanted to question me over the John Stones shooting. As it happened, they interviewed Stones in Strangeways and asked if I had shot him. He just said, 'As far as I know it wasn't him.' They took me back to Longsight nick, asked a few questions, got nothing and when they accepted they had no case, they let me go.

I went back to Spain, only to find the balloon had gone up. The Guardia Civil had raided Davie Moore's villa and Davie had fled. He was eventually arrested in Portugal on drugs charges, where I think he got a not guilty, then went to America. I heard that he left millions in banks, along with his villa, cars, boats and the print shop. The police put locks on everything, so that was the end of the printing business.

There was nothing for it but to head back to the UK. I bought back the Brown Bull for £35,000, revamped it and started doing good business again. The Cotton Club was still successful. My Irish connections were also still strong; while in Dublin I was offered some of the Beit paintings, a priceless collection famously stolen from a manor house by Martin Cahill and his gang in 1986. I passed. I had some experience with stolen paintings and knew it was very difficult to sell them. Most are nicked to order. Gold you can melt down; paintings have to be kept in perfect condition, and obviously cannot go on display. You have to find the man that wants to keep them in the cellar, and he is not going to advertise himself.

Cahill was a fuck-you man: he hated the authorities and took the paintings, whch included works by Goya, Rubens, Gainsborough and Vermeer, partly to stick up two fingers to the state. If he had given them to the IRA he probably could have got something for them but he turned his nose up at that and offered them sinstead to their Loyalist enemies, the UVF, which was not a clever thing to do in the end. The IRA shot him dead.

I knew his number two better, a guy called Noel. He rang me one day and said he had bought a pub in the Haymarket in Dublin.

'I know you're pals with Paddy Reilly,' he said. 'Can you get him to open the pub and sing?'

Paddy, who sang 'The Fields of Athenry', was at the height of his fame as a balladeer and was in great demand.

'Fuck me, Noel, I'm in Manchester. He lives near you in Naas. Can you not get him?'

'No.'

So I rang Paddy and asked him. He said he would do it but only if I was there and for me to pay him direct. I agreed.

I went over with Wally McNelly. The pub was packed with every major villain in the city. When poor Paddy arrived and saw all the faces, he turned white.

'Fucking hell, Jimmy, all the Dublin mafia are here,' he whispered.

He calmed down after a few whiskeys and it turned out to be a good night. Noel was delighted that Paddy had turned out and from then on I had excellent contacts in Dublin.

They heard about Wally's safe-breaking days and that he could handle gelignite, so next we were asked to arrange a few insurance jobs and burn down a few places over in Ireland. My pal Mo O'Connor had also moved to Dublin from Spain and I went to stay with him for a short while. Wally and I got up to all sorts over there. We moved down to Wexford, blew up one building and set fire to another. The wages were good, but when we were asked to nut a guy in a place called Ross, we left it out and had a few weeks with our friends in Tramore instead.

In the UK, things were not going so well. For a while I had been having trouble with the Ward firm. Dave Ward was an ex-boxer from Middleton, on the edge of north Manchester, who was becoming a big noise in security and door work. He would come to see me and I gave him a lot of advice. Had he listened, he would have made a fortune, but he was paranoid. Instead he started making waves all over town, hurting people. He and Eric Mason had come into my Cotton Club when I was in Spain. They were looking to move in. Rita was there and said to Mason, 'Now Eric, if you think because Jimmy's away this is easy meat, forget it.' They got no change out of her. No one was taking over my bars and clubs. I never worked with Mason again, although I saw him for years afterwards.

Eventually I fell out with Dave Ward over this and that. I expected some sort of reprisal, so I asked Wally McNelly to stay at my house, as I had a feeling they would take a pop at me there. I had a shotgun, Wally had a .38. As the hours stretched out, Wally went to the toilet, taking his shooter with him. Suddenly a car pulled up outside and the dining room windows went through with a crash. Wally jumped off the toilet, pulling up his trousers, and accidentally shot himself in the foot. I ran to the door and let off a blast at the car, which sped away. Wally was lucky, the bullet had just ripped open his big toe. Things like that could only happen to him.

I never found out who attacked the house. Dave Ward rang me and told me it was nothing to do with him. He later went down for a long stretch for beating and torturing two guys in a pub on his manor. He made a mess of them and left them on the moors, where they nearly died of hypothermia. One of them never fully recovered and later committed suicide. The other one gave evidence against Ward and he went down for twelve years.

Finall, in the midst of all this, came the move I had half been expecting for at least three years: the police came in my place with search warrants. They said they were looking for drugs, as they were convinced I was a major trafficker, but when they stripped the place down, they nothing. Instead, they arrested me on a warrant from the Board of Trade. I was charged with trading while an undischarged bankrupt, and with the theft of £5,000 relating to the Hagler-Hearns fight tickets back in 1985. To me, this was all related to the Stalker Affair: they were determined to get one of us to prove that all the money spent investigating us had not been wasted.

I opted to split the cases into two separate trials, which I was allowed to do. It was only now that I found out the full details of my former partner Jack Trickett's actions against me. I had heard on the grapevine that he had made a statement, and now it came to light. He said that when he found out I was selling Hagler-Hearns tickets as well as him, he sent his back. The implication was that I was of dubious character. It made me look like guilty man. Give him his due, Jack did later come to court to explain that he had meant to say there was not enough business for the two of us, not that I was an undesirable or involved in anything crooked, but the fact was he had already given his signed statement to the Board of Trade, and signed every page.

Why did he do it? Jack was Jack: his bottle fell out. He had taken my share of the boxing and given me the elbow, and did not want me anywhere near. In fact, I had returned my tickets and money to the box office. They later admitted this in court, so the judge stopped the trial and cleared me.

The case for trading as an undischarged bankrupt revolved partly around a receipt I had signed for a cheque made out to my wife. The brewery had given us a loan of several thousand pounds on the understanding that we would sell their beer in our pubs. I had signed for the loan cheque and the Board of Trade claimed that this proved I was running the business, even though as a bankrupt I was not allowed to. The evidence they cited went back as far as 1982, but they had not charged me until now. They estimated I had earned £1 million in legitimate dealings alone and wanted their pound of flesh.

I managed to get four of the five trading charges dropped. They said if I at least admitted one, I would get a non-custodial sentence, which I thought I had better do, as they also had a per-verting the course of justice charge dangling over me. Having been in custody four months, I decided to deal. I still believe if I had fought the case all the way I would have won, but I agreed to plead to one count, the rest to be left on file, and received a suspended sentence. In all fairness some of us should be serving life for what we have done over the years, so I couldn't com-plain.

I went back for sentence and the judge fined me £1,000. I told him I could not pay straight away as I was out of work.

'But you said this morning that you were working,' he said.

'Yes, but I was pleading not guilty this morning,' I said. 'Now that I have pleaded guilty, I have lost my job!'

The judge hit the roof and said I had deceived the court, but there was nothing he could do. I was free, and the long-running investigation into my business affairs was finally over.

It put the lid on my love affair with boxing. With my wife dead, one son in the nick doing a five-stretch and the other living out in Spain, I was at a loose end, and decided to disappear for a while on my own. I flew to New York to see friends, then to Los Angeles and Vegas, then on to Hawaii, New Zealand and Bali. I finished up in Phuket, Thailand, where I met a beautiful girl who ran a bar in Karon Beach. I hired a car and used to run her to the main town to get her beer and spirits from the cash and carry. She had a little calor gas grill at the back of the bar and used to cook for me all types of seafood. I fell in love with the place and the people. It was back to basics. For all the money and possessions that have gone through my hands, I am just as happy travelling light.

I was very sad to leave; there was no aggro there. But I had to get back to my clubs and bars and my family. I returned to Manchester in January 1990.

14

A FAMILY AFFAIR

THE RAVE SCENE blew in the biggest change in British clubland in a generation. Nothing could have been further from
the dance halls of my youth than hordes of young people in
jeans, trainers and bright tee-shirts, waving their arms around and
blowing whistles, out of their heads on ecstasy. For a new generation, the warehouse parties and raves also offered the chance to
make serious money. My sons were on it from the beginning, and
I helped Tony stage the first mass outdoor rave in the Manchester
area, at Stand Lees Farm, near Rochdale.

The owner of the farm, Steve Dale, was the cousin of Tony's
wife. We put a deal to him and it went from there. Then my
brother Arthur's lads, Anthony and Christopher, came in halfway
through and added the final touches. With Wally McNelly and his
wife helping out, we erected a marquee that could hold 500
people, put in a bar and supplied the beer. There was a large scaffolding stage for the bands and DJs and we hired a London firm
for £80,000 to do security, so you can see how much money there
was. It was one big weekend event and I would imagine we had
80,000 people there. We called it Joy.

It was crazy. We sold out of booze in the first twelve hours.
Luckily a pal of mine who had a cash-and-carry had loaded a
wagon in his warehouse with more and was on his way within the

hour. He offloaded, went back and loaded again with all his booze that was running out of date, cheap spirits and wine. With no shops nearby, we ended up in ther final hours selling cigs for £2 each and a nip of wine or spirits for £5. There were lot of problems, and the security were not on the ball, but it was not their fault, they could not cover the acres of unfenced open land. Nevertheless, it was the start of bigger things for the Donnelly family. Anthony and Chris went on to form the now international Gio-Goi clothing brand, inspired by the rave cutlure. It was recently valued at £50 million. Many starts wear their gear, the likes of Pete Doherty and the Gallagher brothers.

My own sons were involved in running Parliament nightclub, one of the best-known early acid house venues in Manchester. They knew all the Hacienda crowd, and Shaun Ryder, Bez and the rest of the Happy Mondays became great pals. We later promoted the Mondays at the G-Mex Centre on a Friday night and sold out, so they did the Saturday night too. I think we paid the band £40,000 and the G-Mex about £80,000 to rent the place.

Others quickly saw the potential of the rave scene. One day, I got a phone call off a pal called Paul Hogan.

'Jimmy, your lads have done a rave, haven't they? How would you like to do one at my place, Bowlers, in Trafford Park?'

Bowlers was a massive indoor bowls arena that could hold thousands. I went to see Paul with my Tony and we agreed to stage a rave and that, after expenses, we would split fifty-fifty. We would do all the advertising and print the tickets but without a venue on them, so the police would not know where it was, the usual thing in those days. Paul applied for an all-night licence, which they gave him. Everything was going well, until Paul rang and told me the police had been to see him. They said that if he had anything to do with me or the Donnelly family, they would close him down. Therefore the rave was off and he would send me my expenses.

So we walked away – then Paul went ahead and did it without us. He had picked our brains, got all our knowledge, all the bands, all the security, then ripped us off. We had let hundreds of people know about it, too. He had brought in a whizzkid manager on the quiet and they took fortunes on the night. They went on to run a rave every Saturday for a couple of years. My sons wanted to take revenge but Hogan, a Dubliner, was a straight man. He had a massive insurance company as well, but he liked to be around the chaps. We left him over. He retired a couple of years ago to the Algarve and dropped dead, some say with a little help. Who knows?

My lads did a few more raves, one in a former church on Stockport Road. We broke into the building and set up inside, boarding over the windows. We had the booze stashed in a room that went through to an outbuilding at the back, and could move the altar to cover up the passageway, so that when they police arrived, they couldn't find any beer. We told them people had brought their own. We finished up selling pints of tap water from the toilets.

Of course, I was still doing my own things too. By pure chance, I took a lady friend out for a drink. It was a couple of years since Rita had died and this woman was from my manor and knew the script. She introduced me to a relative of hers in the bar and he asked if he could come to see me the next day.

When he turned up, he said he worked for a construction engineer based in Hong Kong and that they had a proposition for me. Would I meet his boss? I said yes but if it was a set-up he would end up in the river. He swore it was genuine. So we met.

First, I asked them both to go into the gents and said I was going to strip search them. They didn't baulk.

'No problem, Jim. You have to be safe.'

They had passed the first test, so we sat down to talk.

'I've got this family of Chinese,' said the boss. 'They want to come to England. They're very rich but they've got no chance of getting passports. Can you help?'

'It's possible,' I said. 'But it'll be expensive. How much do you think they can pay?'

I could not believe what he said next.

'Well, they have told me they will pay thirty-five grand up front, and another forty grand when the first one has passed through. So seventy-five thousand, if that is okay. After that there are another seven members of the family. And they will pay seventy-five thousand each.'

'Fucking hell,' I said. 'Do you know how much that is?'

'Yes,' said my man. 'It's six hundred thousand. But Jimmy, that is not the end. There are twenty-six of them altogether. If they all come in, it adds up to two million pounds.'

He produced an A4 envelope and emptied it onto the table. He had photos, dates of birth, everything you needed to produce decent forged passports. I had a look through everything and then told him I would be in touch.

I got busy. My first call was to a pal who knew about these sorts of deals. He said he would talk to his dad, who lived in London. I was careful not to mention how much money was on the table. After a short while, he came back to me.

'No problem, Jim. It will take a couple of weeks. But it'll cost you five grand. We can even do you a visa as well with the first one.'

'Okay, we are on,' I said, 'and there is another two grand in it for you.'

I got in touch with the builder and told him it was on. Sure enough, at the next meet they gave me £35,000.

Two weeks later, I got a call: 'The thing is there,' *thing* being passport. I went to pick it up and it was perfect. It was not even a forgery: my pal told me that they would just stick dodgy applications in the middle of a bunch that were handled by agencies on commission, and leave it to them. Better still, my pal's dad had an 'in' with the agency.

I paid him off with the extra two large and gave him the other seven photos and particulars. The builder was over the moon when he got his goods. The first Chinaman came to England via Singapore and passed through immigration with flying colours. I was in clover. I received my remaining forty grand and then another £75,000 upfront for the next one.

Some things are too good to be true. The shit hit the fan through a close friend who was on the firm. He called for a coffee at the house of the girl who had first put me onto her relative.

'I've got to meet Jimmy,' he told her. 'I have got something for him.'

'Oh, he will be happy,' she replied. 'He has got a massive deal on.'

My pal read the signs. When he met me, he said, 'There has been a change of plan. The people in London want ten large each.'

I should not have fallen for it but I did.

'Okay,' I said, 'that's seventy large and fourteen for you. It's a deal.'

A few days later he rang me.

'I have to see you, Jim. Another one has arrived.'

When I went on the meet, I could tell by his face that something was wrong.

'Jimmy,' he said, 'you had better put me in proper. There is more to this than you are telling me. I am getting the passports and you are getting a fucking fortune.'

258

Fuck it, I thought, I might as well come clean. He nearly fainted when I told him the truth.

He asked why the punters had not come to him in the first place. We did get a lot of money but now greed had come in. The builder eventually did a disappearing act. I tried to find him, as he owed a lot. What I only heard later was that the Chinaman had given him £250,000, thinking everything was okay. The work we did was perfect and everything was working out but the builder could not resist clearing off with the readies. It was getting messy, so I pulled out and left my pal to chase things up. I told him to keep what he got when he found the builder. I had had a good earn, so why not get out when you are in front?

Most of the QSG were still close but everyone had made money and was very fussy about what they did. Jim Swords was big in the property game, as were Vinnie and Louis. Their land and other holdings must be worth millions today. Jimmy's other great passion was racehorses and he owned some good ones, including a runner in the Gold Cup at Cheltenham. The same horse was running in Yorkshire with Peter Scudamore on and was in front by a whole fence coming up to the last. Scudamore had only to ease it over but it fell and later had to be put down. Jimmy went berserk and chased Scudamore across the paddock calling him a cunt.

We had some wonderful times together. His late wife, Lynn, was a special person with a great sense of fun. She loved hearing tales from our past. When we were out for a meal, she used to say, 'Tell me that story again about you and Jimmy in the nick,' or, 'Tell me about the shoes.' Jimmy and I had been in the Lewis's store once for him to buy some shoes to go to Majorca with Lynn. His feet were different sizes and he was too tight to buy two pairs, so he removed a size seven from one box and a size eight from another and paid for them as if they were a matching pair. 'Don't you dare tell anyone,' he ordered. Of course I told everyone. I used to drive him mad retelling the story to Lynn, who loved it. They were good days. But the big nights out were getting fewer; now we were happy with a coffee at the corner café, rather than a banquet and a booze-up.

Unfortunately I also came across the odd liberty-taker as I got older, people who would not have looked me in the eye when the QSG were in their heyday. One loser even tried to frighten me by invoking the UDA fron Belfast. I had closed the doors of the Brown Bull for the night when I heard the letterbox flap. I went to have a look and there was an envelope lying on the floor. It was addressed to me with no stamp on it so it had been delivered by hand. I opened the door and looked up the street. A Ford car was pulling out across the road.

I had a feeling about the letter and I was right. When I opened it there was a page from the *Irish Press* newspaper with a story about loyalist paramilitaries threatening retaliation if the IRA killed any workers at the Shorts aircraft factory in Belfast. None of this had anything to do with me, but scrawled across the page was a note written in black felt pen. It said, 'Keep your son Tony under control. If not we will. Tell him to stop now. If not it will be you and him.'

I was shaking with temper. Some arsehole with no bottle was threatening me and my son, pretending to have terrorist connections, and I did not know who it was. Then it hit me. Tony had had a tear-up with a guy in a club in Levenshulme, an Irish area of Manchester. It could be him. There was not a lot I could do, I would just have to watch myself and warn Tony to do the same.

I had all but forgotten about it when, a few weeks later, I walked into Les Simms's pub, the Commercial, and a voice said, 'Here's Jimmy now.'

Billy Dodds, George Derbyshire and his wife were talking to a bloke.

'This guy's looking for you,' said Billy Dodds.

With that, the guy walked over to me.

'Are you Jimmy the Weed?' he asked, in an Irish accent.

'Yes, that's me. What can I do for you?'

It suddenly occurred to me: this was the guy.

'Just hold on a minute will you,' I said, 'I've left my car open.'

I nipped out and sure enough, there was a Ford parked outside, the same one I had seen outside my hotel. I went back in and he was leaning on the bar.

'What's your problem?' I asked.

He told me that my son beat up his son, so he had come to see me.

'You're the cunt that pushed a letter through the door threatening me with the IRA, aren't you?'

'No,' he said, 'it was the UDA.'

I hit him on the chin. His head went back and hit a pillar and burst open. I battered fuck out of him. He was on the deck. I walked into the kitchen, grabbed a steak knife and went back to do him properly. Billy Dodds had got him on his feet. I ran at him again but he was in a bad state so I just pushed the knife under his chin and told him he was lucky but if I saw him again he would get a bit more, and if he was going around using the name of the UDA he was in plenty of trouble, as I would pass it on to my Irish connections. With that he was off. There was blood all over the place and I did not know if anybody had phoned for an ambulance.

I never heard another word from that date but it just shows you what happens when some barmpot thinks you are past it.

Another time, I was in my pal Denis Crolla's hotel in

Blackpool. Among the drinkers in the bar were two brothers from Glasgow who used to sell Denis booze they bought by kiting cheques. They were normally not bad lads but on this night they were having a go at Denis over putting too much money on top of a parcel I had given Denis to sell for me.

I was catching a snooze in the lounge next door to the bar when I felt a kick. I woke up and one of them was standing over me.

'How much have you charged Denis for that parcel?' he said.

I told him it was fuck all to do with him.

He said we were taking the piss. I told him to ask Denis as it was nothing to do with me. With that he pulled out a blade and said he was going to cut Denis.

I stood up. He was tall but not well made. I hit him on the chin and he went down like a sack of spuds. I then went into the bar where his brother was. I did not give him a chance. I gave him a few right hooks and that was that.

The first brother, who by now had got himself up, came into the bar still cheeky, so I gave him another crack. Both of them were now laid out. What I did not know was that they had booked into Denis's hotel, so with a bit of help from people in the bar we had to get them to their room. The next morning I came back at breakfast time. There were the brothers, both with black eyes. I went over to them but before I could speak they stood up and both said they were sorry. That was it, we became pals.

WHEN I HIT fifty years old, I decided it was time for a change. I sold the Brown Bull for the second time, accepting an offer of £160,000, and also got £75,000 off Jim Swords for a flat in Puerto Banus that I had taken for a debt. I closed the Cotton Club, the last of my clubs in Manchester, and bought a penthouse flat in

Blackpool, overlooking the Irish Sea. I had always liked Blackpool. My pal Denis Crolla had been there since the scrapyard days, running the Tres Bon Hotel in South Shore with his wife, Mary. Another old pal, Bob Spanner, had been there for years, while Rudi Mancini owned the biggest independent hotel in town, the Queens, close to where I lived in South Shore. I loved Rudi to bits, and would often have coffee and a piece of toast with him in the mornings. He was renowned for playing the piano accordion and organ and he and his wife Pat were great hoteliers – she later wrote her life story and called it *Queen of Blackpool*, which was right.

I now ran my business life from the Fylde coast. It was only fifty minutes' drive to Manchester, less time than it takes to cross London, and I was just a phone call away from a deal. I still had my big house on the edge of Manchester. I obtained planning permission to build another house on the acre of land and sold that plot for £100,000. I then put the main house up for sale. It had no mortgage on it and was valued at £250,000. Putting my money to work, I opened a cash-and-carry in Blackpool selling frozen foods. I also opened two massage parlours, Babes and Baby Doll. Whatever the masseuse did in the private cubicle was not my responsibility. The police came in the odd time but I had no problems.

I continued to travel a lot. I was still a regular to Dublin and other parts of Ireland and also went back and forth to Spain, where my sons had been left money and property in their mother's name. My brother John turned up there too, in unfortunate circumstances. John had made a lot of money in the eighties property boom. His house was worth millions: it was described during a court case as 'one of the most expensive houses in south Manchester' and his neighbours included the Edwards family, who owned Manchester United. The house was how John got into trouble. He had worked for himself all his life and eventually owned a factory that employed a lot of people making steel pallet packing and shelving. After years of hard work, it went bust in the mid-eighties and John signed on the dole. He then borrowed a large sum for the bank – neglecting to tell them he was now unemployed – and spent it upgrading his house, which was huge. He saw it as a future investment and put a new roof on it and made the eleven bedrooms en suite. Ultimately he was arrested and he and his wife were charged with working while drawing dole, claiming £42,000 housing benefit and with dishonestly obtaining a home loan.

At a pre-trial hearing in 1991, the judge told him to expect a long prison sentence. You read the papers today and the most people get for that kind of thing is six months, but he was a Donnelly, so he was going to get slammed. John felt he had no option but to go on his toes. Had he gone to jail, he would not have been able to pay back the loan and the bank would have repossessed his house. His wife turned up for the trial and pleaded guilty. They gave her three months – and then gave John *four years* in his absence. The sentence was unprecedented.

However, he managed to save his house. He and I started to import cars to Spain, selling them through newspaper adverts, and he was able to maintain the mortgage payments. After a couple of years, he returned home to face the music and served his sentence, most of it in Walton Prison in Liverpool. He then carried on upgrading his house. It had eleven bedrooms, four bathrooms, two lounges, a dining room, kitchen and a granny flat, all set in four acres in a prime area of Alderley Edge, where all the stars and footballers live. A couple of years ago, he sold the main house and part of the land for £2.5 million. The other half of the land, with a five-bedroomed house, he sold for over £1.5 million. Not bad for an ex-borstal boy.

My son Dominic also turned up in Spain. He had finished his five-year term for an attempted security van raid, and in June 1991 was on a night out with a friend, Mike Pollitt, in the Express Club in Manchester. A few other pals of Dominic's were in there but unfortunately some of them had a beef with each other. Words were directed at Mike and a row started. One of them left and came back tooled up, a fight broke out and Mike was stabbed. He died on the spot. I could not believe it; they were all pals. Dominic was caught in the middle, as he would not give evidence for or against his friends, so he had it away to Spain. There were plenty of other witnesses, and two guys were charged, convicted and jailed for life. Years later, on appeal, both had their convictions overturned, though tragically one of them had already committed suicide while in prison. By then, Dominic had returned to England and new evidence was presented that Mike Pollitt had been seen pointing a gun at the two accused. Somebody told Dominic years later that they had picked up the gun and put it down a grid in the street.

I noticed Spain changing while I was out there. Many of the old London villains had fled or been arrested after they reinstated extradition with the UK. Dangerous gangsters were arriving daily from Russia and the Eastern Bloc after the fall of Communism, many of them with KGB links. At the same time, the Moroccans and Colombians, the kings of the drugs trade, were getting stronger. It was starkly brought home to me the day I had several Uzis pointed at my head. I had gone for lunch at the villa of Neil Robertson. I first met Neil in 1983, when he arrived in Spain from London with £1 million from a VAT swindle. He later got fucked out of it by a fellow who went on to have Neil and his pals nicked for kidnapping. Neil went on to do what he did: over in Spain you could have nothing one day and a million quid the next, and I don't mean legitimately. Through various deals, he ended up owing some Colombians £75,000.

I was sitting at dinner table with Neil, his wife, their two sons and his brother when four men armed with Uzi submachine pistols and wearing baseball hats pulled down over their eyes came crashing through the door. I nearly choked on my roast potatoes.

'Get on the floor,' one of them shouted.

I thought they were going to let us all have it.

'Where is the money?' another one demanded.

I thought fast.

'Hold up, hold up,' I shouted. 'I have just come here to see Neil. I owe him money. One more week and he will have it.'

They fell for it. I guess I saved his life, and probably mine too, though it was touch and go. I have no doubt they were prepared to whack us all. Instead they finished up staying for twenty minutes and having a can of beer each. I believe it was later sorted.

Neil was a good guy. He was another who had helped me when I was on my toes and he later spent time in Manchester with me. He was not a tough man but was brave at his work. Sadly it cost him his life. In 1997, he fell to his death from the window of a tower block in London. I went to his funeral and firms from all sides of London were there, all saying he was murdered. I even heard a story that he had been tied to a chair. The police said he had jumped and the investigation fizzled out. I knew Neil owed money all around and had got himself in a state, but not enough to jump off a roof. He always earned and paid it back and he never had anyone over, in fact it was the other way, people knocked him for money.

At one stage he asked me to mind a lot of cash for him. He did not get in touch for two years but when he did, his money was there waiting. That is trust for you, and that is how I found Neil and most of the Cockneys.

In Spain, you now saw different gangs all running around trying to sell drugs. One mate of mine had a great business serving wholesale customers ten kilos of cannabis at a time, like a sweet-shop. There was not much else to do to make money. It was very hard to earn legitimately in Spain. To make a business work you had to have a Spanish partner, and they could never be trusted. Freddie Foreman couldn't even make his country club work. Then there was the difficulty of dealing with the expats: how could you chase up someone for a £15 bill? All sorts of problems came from money. You might give credit to someone and not get paid, or if a parcel was lost on its way to England, or France, or Germany, you had to prove it was lost to the people who supplied it. Everybody was running up debts.

And where the international villains went, the police followed. I was in the restaurant of a guy called Manolo, who married a Manchester girl, when he came over.

'Jimmy, you won't believe it but we have got a hundred and forty policemen in here.'

'What for?'

'They are from all parts of Europe and they are swapping notes. They have got thousands of car numbers and the names of the owners and have spent a month walking around the bars taking numbers of British plates and phoning it through to England so they know who is in Spain.'

There were officers from Germany, France, Holland, the UK and elsewehere, all passing on notes about suspects depending on who they had been seen with. Then they started nicking people. I already knew the cops had me down as a drug dealer because of my contacts and the amount of time I spent in Spain. It seemed like a good time to go.

I flew to Frankfurt, Germany, where someone had put me onto a deal to buy 20,000 cloned Sky TV cards. There was a massive market for them in England. I only got in at the end of it, after other people had made fortunes, but there was still a wage in it. I was buying the cards for £3 each for them and selling them for £10. They even worked in Spain, where you were not supposed to be able to get Sky. I stayed in Frankfurt for a good while and my girlfriend flew over at weekends.

With things going well, I bought a beautiful house in upmarket Lytham St Annes and for the first time relaxed. Even the Old Bill seemed to have gone quiet on me. I commuted into Manchester most days, still working with Denis Crolla and Wally McNelly, doing deals all over the country. We were so close we were like brothers. firm within a firm. I spent most of my leisure time drinking with Denis. He had a cracking thing going. He was getting the savings chits that were used to save for your TV licence. He could buy £1,000-worth for £200 and sell them for £500. We had a good run at that for about a year and probably did ten grand a week. For all of my long friendship with the QSG, I did most of my criminal work with others. If I could handle something on my own, I would, taking one or two of my close friends to do whatever was necessary.

For instance, in a friend's pub I was approached by a woman who had a problem with an ex-boyfriend. He was squatting in her house and had the keys to her apartment in Marbella. She had split with him and met another guy, but her ex would not leave. She even offered to put a deposit on a new flat for her ex to get rid of him, but he kept telling her to fuck off. He must have been after her money from the start. She offered me ten grand to talk him round. Wally and I caught up with him in Manchester. I told him to give me the house keys and pack his bags, and gave him a smack with a rubber cosh to let him know we meant business. We also got the keys back to the Marbella apartment after he got a second visit. That was an easy few quid.

I took on a lot more dangerous things that cannot be put in this book. I don't deny I have spent my life with violence. I was never a blatant blagger, I used my brains, but I have always been highly dangerous. I never gave a fuck for anybody. If they hurt me in any way, even by insult, they had better be on full alert for the rest of their lives. I never forget.

I would let no man take a liberty. In 1992, a young man called Stephen Yates had been shot dead in Wythenshawe. He was a nice lad who palled about with my nephews. It was a weird affair. A man was charged with the murder but was later acquitted. There were all sorts of threats from both sides going about but they came to nothing. A few years later, a pal of mine who lived in Wythenshawe died suddenly. Peter 'Pedro' Nolan was a good grafter and family man who worked for Jim Swords. A lot of the firm turned out for his funeral and afterwards we went to a place where food was laid on. I was having a drink with my pals Tex Taylor and Tony Guest when this guy barged over and insulted Tex. Tex told him to go away and reminded him he was at a funeral. He walked off to his own pals but came back a bit later. This time he asked if I was Jimmy the Weed. Then he started to insult me.

I told him to fuck off and that I would see him on another day. He offered to go outside with me but I still turned him down, it was not the time or place. With that, he again walked back to his pals.

'This has gone too far,' I said to Tex. 'I am going to stop this shit.'

I walked over to the feller, hit him a right-hander and then set about him. I would not let up until Tex and Tony dragged me off. His blood was everywhere: he had a large gash above his eye and was in a terrible mess. Some people took him outside.

The barman just said to me, 'Go back and have your drink. I have been watching him all day trying it on with people.'

Somebody came back in the bar and said he had been put in a car and was on his way to hospital. He was claiming that I had hit him with a pint pot but I had not: I was wearing a diamond ring and had hit him so many times it must have cut him up. It was only when I got back to the bar and straightened myself out that Tex told me who he was. He was allegedly involved with shooting my young pal Stephen Yates. Now I felt a lot happier, though I was still sick about the trouble at my friend's funeral. Word got about that I knew this guy but I did not, he knew me and my family and thought I was easy meat. I was about fifty-seven at the time but he got a shock.

There were a few rumblings about him having a go back. Six months later, Pedro's lovely wife Marie died, another shock. The same guy was at the funeral service again there but this time nothing was said.

Another wannabe hardman was not so lucky. Frank Cassell was a Jock who lived in Manchester. He was a first-class bully. I came across him in the leafy suburb of Didsbury. He had been doing a lot of damage to people and even tested me a couple of times. When I bumped into him in the street, he acted friendly and stuck out his hand. I ignored it.

'You are making a few waves, Frank,' I said. 'What's it all about.'

He mumbled somehitng and moved on.

About a month later, I got a phone call from a pal of mine

called Don. He was not a villain but he used to drink in my pubs.

'Jimmy, can you come and see me?'

I drove over to his house. He was a in a terrible state: he had a slash wound across his face from his ear to his mouth.

'Fuck me, Don, what happened.'

He had been at a party at a house. Frank Cassell was also there, being a nuisance. In the early hours, Don fell asleep in a chair. He woke with an awful pain in his cheek. Cassell was standing over him with a carpet cutter. Don had to be taken to hospital to be stitched up. Now he begged me to help him get even.

I told him that with a dog like Cassell, you would have to bury him.

'Just help me,' said Don. He just wanted the guy to get a taste of his own medicine.

I told him I would think about it, and I did. Soon afterwards, Cassell turned up in Spain, not far from where I lived, telling people he was a friend of mine. I went to look at the area where he was staying and get a feel for the layout. One day, Cassell was found dead. He had apparently fallen down some stone steps near a bar. All I can say is, he did go down some steps but it was more likely he was thrown down. Somebody had beaten me to it.

When I rang Don, he was over the moon. Nobody will miss Cassell. He was an animal.

EVENTUALLY MY REPUTATION caught up with me even in Blackpool. I had put down a £7,000 deposit to buy a nightclub there called Sticks, a rough but busy place that had potential. However, when Gilly Grundy went in for the licence, the authorities said, 'We know you are working for Jimmy the Weed, and we want him out of Blackpool.' The local police were convinced I was still a major criminal and basically gave me my marching orders.

I returned to Manchester and did a deal to buy the Brown Bull Hotel for the third time, giving my refrigeration shop and two massage parlours in part-exchange. As the Bull's licensee, I put up a guy who had run three pubs before, so there could be no objection. However, I had reckoned without my old foes in Greater Manchester Police, who now jumped up and made a fuss. 'This man is working for one of the biggest drug importers and dealers in the north-west of England,' they told the licensing magistrates. Unsurprisingly, my man was turned down, so I had to do something else with the building, which had twenty-four years left on the lease. I decided to turn it into a hostel.

I had previously done a few deals with a guy called Peter Smith, from Edinburgh, and when I decided to convert the Bull he said he would buy the furniture for a pub he had in Musselburgh. I arranged to meet him in Les Simms' Commercial Hotel. Peter turned up with his son and a pal. I put a briefcase down on the bar and sat down to talk. After about five minutes, we had done the deal and he left. What we didn't know was that he was under police observation and had been followed from Edinburgh. He went on some other meets, then headed back to Scotland and was arrested as he crossed the border. The pal with him had got on a train with ten kilos of cannabis. All three were charged and a warrant was put out for me.

I laid low for a while, then sneaked back to the Fylde coast. I still saw Eric Mason socially, and met him for lunch. Afterwards we spent a couple of hours in a bookmakers. Eric had some tips and we won a few quid. Then he said he had to go, as he was on his way to London to pick up some money. An hour later, I was driving home to Lytham St Annes when I was tugged in my car by the police on the pretence of a breathalyser. Instead I was taken all the way to Edinburgh, charged with dealing drugs and remanded to Saughton Prison for a week. I appeared in court and was bailed but they took my passport. They claimed I had been in on the deal for the smoke and that they saw me pass over a floppy leather briefcase at the meet. In the end Peter Smith was found guilty, as was his pal; his son was cleared. I was never tried: they kept me on bail for two years, then informed me there was no case to answer. I have never had a conviction for drugs.

Eric Mason says complimentary things about me in his book, *The Brutal Truth*, but the real truth is I never won a prize with him. Almost every deal we had went wrong or left a sour taste. He brought a creditor to find me in Spain. I was told he had been in on the scam to screw me with Fat Sam in Glasgow. Then there was a deal in which he claimed not to have been paid by a Scouser called Barratt, who admittedly was known for having people over. When I caught up with Barratt, he swore that he had paid Mason.

A pal of mine in Spain was nicked for something. After two years in custody he was found not guilty, but by then he had lost everything to legal costs, including his magnificent villa. He swore Eric had set him up.

Eric landed me in it on another occasion when he asked me to meet for lunch in Harrogate. I arrived to find him there with a guy.

'Jimmy,' he said, trying to tip me the wink, 'I want you to confirm that gear was supposed to be okay. It turned out to be shit and my friend here has got the needle. We can change it, can't we, and put the thing right? He has paid top dollar.'

I could feel the anger rising in me. Whatever he had done was nothing to do with me, but I covered for him anyway.

'Yes,' I said to the guy, 'I will get it sorted for you.'

'That's okay, Jimmy,' said the guy. 'I have heard of you. You are a man of your word. Thanks for coming over.'

After he had finished his drink and left, I pulled Eric.

'What the fuck are you doing putting me in it? And with that shit?'

'You were a bit late,' he said. 'I was going to fill you in first but I had no time. I knew you woud see what was going on.'

Eric had been with me when a pal said he had a parcel of cannabis that he was going to dump because it was complete shit. Eric had taken some off him for nothing, and must have sold it on as good. You could get £2,400 a kilo for it. Eric told me he had sold this guy ten kilos.

I told him he was bang out of order for putting me in it, and that he had better put it right or I would tell the guy the truth.

So when I was nicked after being in the bookie's with Eric, I decided enough was enough. I was going to kill him.

I knew the pefect place. Styal Woods is an isolated spot in the Cheshire countryside. It is just south of Manchester Airport, and planes land and take off every few seconds, drowning out any noise. It was an area I knew well, as we went there as kids to swim in the River Bollin.

I arranged to meet Eric in a pub out that way. I took a semi-automatic in my pocket, and my plan was to drive him afterwards to a secluded parking area, and do the deed. I did not expect to see anyone who knew me, but as luck would have it, a guy walked in who knew us both as we were having a drink at the bar.

'Come on, Eric,' I said, 'I'll take you for a meal.'

We went to another place called the Ship, next to the woods. Again we were at the bar when a retired copper who had nicked me and Jim Swords years earlier recognised me.

'Hello Jimmy?' he said. 'How are you? What brings you out here?'

Shit. I told Eric we had to move again. He started to get edgy.

'What's all the secrecy about?' he asked.

'I've got a deal on,' I said. 'But we can't been seen together after this. You'll understand when it goes down.'

I knew I had blown my chance. Two people had seen me with him, so I had to drop it. He made it home in one piece, and never knew how close he came to getting nutted. I simply left him off my guest list after that.

I hate saying it because we were once so close, and as a man he would die with you in a fight, but all the faces and firms he befriended say the same thing: there was a stench about Eric at the end. Not long afterwards, he brought an undercover cop into a big cannabis deal with some of the chaps in Spain, and they ended up with long sentences. Eric somehow got the shortest term and ended up in an open prison. Maybe he had one fight too many with the authorities, though you can never prove anything.

HAVING OBTAINED THE freehold of the Brown Bull from the brewery for a hundred grand, I set to work converting it into a hostel. It was licensed to sleep thirty-eight people and I charged £110 each a week. Staff wages and expenses only cost me a grand a week, which left £3,000 a week profit. Not bad. From there, I went on buying and selling properties in the UK and Spain.

I got a message that my mate Dave Moore was in Portugal in the nick. Dave had bought a Spanish apartment off me and given me a large deposit for it before he had disappeared from Spain with the police on his heels. After a few years, he had not returned and no-one had heard from him. The apartment was still empty and the fees for the community had mounted up. By Spanish law, they can garnishee the flat and sell it if it has remained vacant for a certain period. I rang the lawyer who had done the deal when I bought the place. He told me that the deeds were with him, having taken years to arrive from Madrid. I went to see him, paid his bill and he gave me the deeds. I later sold the apartment again. I have not seen Dave since, but after nearly twenty years I don't think he will ask for his money back, he was too much of a man and was very good to me when I was on the run.

After a good run with the Brown Bull as a hostel, the council decided to reduce weekly payments to £69 a week per person. They were paying immigrants over £300 a week. I only had people with a British passport and on welfare staying at the hostel. So we decided to sell. We sold the hostel plus my big house in Lytham for £760,000 in a deal that Jim Swords negotiated for us with some of his pals. I decided to have a holiday and went on a cruise for a month on the QE II. I found for the first time in thirty-five years I had no business interests, so I spent the next year travelling. I was on a Caribbean cruise in November 1994 when I received a phone call to say Mick Brown of the QSG had sadly died. It was said to be in his sleep, from a mixture of cocaine and alcohol. Mick always did play hard.

I came back, found a nice place in Didsbury, south Manchester, to lay my head, and thought about what to do next.

15

THE YOUNG QSG

MY SONS NOW had their own firm and were doing well. They had for years been involved in the ticket job and in making and selling programmes for the European tours of pop and rock superstars like Madonna, Michael Jackson and Bruce Springsteen. They had their own team of workers and would also supply other grafters working the gigs. It went mega. One of their best earns was the night Jean Michel Jarre played an outdoor concert in Royal Victoria Dock, London, which the Prince and Princess of Wales were due to attend. My sons checked the weather report, which forecast heavy rain and high winds, and bought 30,000 bin liners. It was incredible: on the night, they flogged the liners as waterproofs for £5 each and sold out in two hours. The next day, Princess Diana and Prince Charles were pictured in the papers with bin liners over their clothes.

My Dominic always knew his own mind. As a kid he was obsessed with locks and padlocks and would spend hours trying to open them without a key. I once bought him a small safe for Christmas and deliberately refused to tell him the combination. He spent weeks trying to open it and finally did. When his mother and I bought the Kensington pub, a friend of mine with a fruit machine business put in a pool table and two bandits. He came back two weeks later to empty them but there was no money inside.

'Fuck me, Jimmy,' he said, 'I think somebody has got a copy set of keys and taken the money.'

'But how could they get away with it in the pub?'

He said it was easy when a pub was packed. He changed the locks and went off to his next call, but I knew what had really happened. A week later, we got a call from Dominic's school: he had turned up driving a Rolls-Royce and was buying all the kids ice cream. I looked out of the window and sure enough my Rolls was gone. He was only thirteen. I knew then he was never going to get a straight job.

By the time he was nineteen, he had planned his first security van robbery. That became his life. No jeweller's or wage van was safe when he was plotting, but as a consequence he was in and out of the nick as a young man. When he finally got five years, he decided against the 'pavement' and put his money to work for him with his brother Tony. They had plenty left by their mother in properties in Spain and Ireland, and had a crew of Ancoats kids with them.

Tony, my eldest, was a good boxer and a fearless streetfighter. He would take on anyone, as he proved one night when he came up against Dessie Noonan, one of the most feared names in Manchester. Dessie was on the door of a club called Konspiracy, where he passed some remark to Tony while he was in the company of Paul Massey from Salford and some other heavy-weights.

Tony just said to Noonan, 'Fuck you, get outside.'

Now Tony is only five foot six, while Noonan was well over six foot, at least five stone heavier and the most dangerous doorman in Manchester. That meant nothing to Tony. A crowd formed a ring outside Konspiracy and they went at it. It was a good fight until it was stopped. Tony was hurt but his reputation soared.

I ran into Dessie a few times over the years. I found him a nice guy. He always bought me a drink and asked about the lads. It has to be said that the Noonans were a major firm. All the brothers had a letter D in their first names: Dessie, Damien, Dominic, Derek and a few more. They were only toddlers when the QSG were in their prime but in the nineties they made a big name. White Tony was allegedly shot over money Dessie taxed from him. He was no fool himself, a good moneygetter who was said to have murdered a guy in Moss Side by shooting him in the head. Acquitted along with Dessie was a feller called Paul Flannery, another lunatic. They terrorised clubs like the Hacienda and ended up controlling a lot of doors. Dessie Noonan was later stabbed to death, while his brother Damien, who had been the head doorman at the Hacienda club, was killed on holiday in a motorbike accident. Dominic was the subject of a 2007 TV documentary called *A Very British Gangster*.

By the nineties, most of our club owner friends had passed on, although I still had my Cotton Club. Big companies moved into Manchester, opening massive venues, and drugs were on sale in every one of those places. It was different to the clubs that we went to and looked after. Trouble at clubs was often gang-related and my sons had a few rows along the way. Their friend Paul Massey got twelve years for stabbing a man outside a club while participating in a TV documentary. Paul is now out of the nick and taking things easy. His was the most prolific of all the new firms, with cult status in Salford. I have always said he could have been the main man in Manchester. Paul could organise and he was game and tough, but like the QSG time is catching up with him. He sits back a bit now and keeps a low profile.

Another good firm are the Mullen family. Like me, they are of Irish extraction. The brothers, Mark, John and Anthony, are again very close to my sons. They have bars, restaurants and a security business and always used to call in my bars when they had time. Another good guy is Patrick Ward, a member of another big family. I had problems with Dave, the main man, for a while. Dave is doing okay and I see him now and again, a very tough man.

Manchester is always changing but most of the new firms, even the Moss Side gangs, are respectful to us older members of the QSG. If I go into a bar where one or two of them are having a drink, it is all, 'Mister Donnelly, how are you? Can we buy you a drink?'

IN MAY 1995, the Quality Street Gang was back in the headlines for the first time in years when Kevin Taylor's case for malicious prosecution against Greater Manchester Police finally began. Kevin was suing for millions of pounds in damages, claiming that the damage to his reputation caused by the lengthy probe into his links with John Stalker had destroyed his property empire. The hearing, at Liverpool Crown Court, promised to finally reveal some of the secrets of the Stalker Affair.

One of the first things to emerge was the extent of the trawl for information made by the police's so-called Drugs Intelligence Unit. The DIU had compiled files on 5,000 names, equivalent to the adult male population of a small town. They ranged from the football manager Malcolm Allison to the Sinn Fein leader Gerry Adams to the barrister George Carman. No explanation was given in court for the appearance of many of these names in the files nor what connections they were supposed to have had to Kevin or the QSG. By now there was no longer any pretence that the DIU was about drugs: it was clear it had existed to find links between us,

Kevin Taylor and John Stalker. One DIU report listed thirteen names connected to the QSG, with numbers one to eight described as the 'inner sanctum'. Mark Klapish and Mick Brown were alleged to have run guns for the IRA. The same report claimed the QSG was 'allowed to flourish' because of connections with Manchester police officers. The one thing lacking from this fanciful document was, as ever, any evidence.

One especially ridiculous claim was reported in the *Manchester Evening News*:

> A crime syndicate boss put a £50,000 contract out on the life of a top police undercover officer, it was alleged in court today.
>
> James Monaghan, alias Jimmy Swords, who was claimed to be a leader of Manchester's Quality Street gang, was said to be behind the assassination plot.
>
> The £50,000 contract was originally offered on the lives of two supergrasses called Pilot and Scott, and then extended to Det Sgt Henry Exton.
>
> The regional crime squad's top undercover infiltrator was said to have cultivated Pilot, who gave him information about organized crime.

The story referred to the two leaders of the Crazy Face Gang, who had turned supergrass against the rest of their crew in the early eighties, and the detective who had interviewed them. In truth, neither Jim Swords nor any of us had any reason to put out a hit on Pilot and Scott, let alone a copper. They did not work with us and knew little about us: I think the only mention of us in their statements was some claim about an arson job that was bullshit anyway.

John Stalker was called as a witness and took the stand for

more than a week. He was scathing about the origins of the investigation, describing the tittle-tattle that started it as 'dross' and the informant David Burton as 'Walter Mitty'. He read out details from one intelligence dossier that claimed that the football director and scrap metal magnate Freddie Pye was a 'banker' for the QSG, yet Chief Constable James Anderton himself had been a guest of Pye's at a dinner at Maine Road football ground while Stalker was being investigated. Stalker's point was that if he was investigated for knowing Kevin Taylor, why had his boss not been investigated for knowing Freddie Pye? Not that Freddie had anything to do with the QSG anyway, although we all knew him. Stalker told the court he was sceptical that there even was such a thing as the Quality Street Gang, and a senior drugs squad officer backed him up.

The police defence quickly unravelled. One month into the hearing, and more than ten years after it all began, Kevin agreed to accept an out-of-court settlement for an undisclosed sum, later reported to be over £2 million. He had wanted to take the case all the way to get the full truth out, but was forced to settle or his legal aid would have been cut off. Disgracefully, the police claimed their decision to settle was simply to avoid huge costs and was not an admission that they had done anything wrong. In total, the case cost £10.5 million in damages and legal costs.

Kevin came to see me a week later and gave me ten grand. I had helped him out over the years while he awaited his hearing, paying his utility bills and suchlike. The stress on him had been enormous but he had kept going, a great man and a great pal. The only thing I have to put right is that at his trial and in his book he said I was an uninvited person at the house party at which I was photographed with Stalker's wife. Why then did I supply drinking glasses? But I understand why he said it.

To this day it is still not clear what went on in the Stalker Affair. There was, however, an ironic postscript to the saga about ten years later. I was by then living in a luxury three-bedroom apartment in central Manchester, and was in one evening with a pal when we heard a knock. A guy was at the door. His face looked familiar.

'I am sorry to trouble you,' he said, 'but I live in the flat below and there is water coming through the ceiling.'

I invited him in, went into my kitchen to check the plumbing and sure enough the washing machine was leaking, so I cut off the water. As I turned back to this fellow, it struck me who he was.

'You're Mike Todd, the Chief Constable, aren't you?'

'Yes,' he said, 'and you're Jimmy the Weed.'

We stood there staring at each other.

'Fuck me,' I said, breaking the silence, 'one of us will have to move now.'

'Well, it's not going to be me,' he said

In the event, he chatted for a short while before returning to his flat.

A few weeks later, he stopped me in the car park.

'Jimmy, I have had my car broken into and a briefcase stolen,' he said. 'Can you try to get it back for me?'

So after all that, after thousands of man-hours and millions of pounds spent investigating Kevin Taylor, John Stalker and the QSG, after prosecutions, ruined careers and massive payouts, newspaper investigations and television documentaries, here was the new Chief Constable of Greater Manchester not only living as my neighbour but also asking the notorious Jimmy the Weed to get his stolen briefcase back. You could not make it up.

Todd later killed himself when he walked onto Mount Snowdon while lightly clothed and froze to death. The tabloids revealed that he was a serial adulterer who had conducted a string of affairs. I received a visit from the Special Branch after his death and told them what little I knew. I also asked how a Chief Constable could move into flats where a serious villain was living. Didn't they have any security checks?

They did not give me an answer.

I CARRIED ON behind the scenes throughout the nineties, advising my family. I also got an offer from the trainer Billy Graham to get back into boxing, and for a while was sorely tempted. I had an interest in a premises in Salford that I was turning into a gym with a pal, Perry Hughes, who went on to manage Russell 'The Voice' Watson. Billy asked if he could use it as a camp for his team. He had three champions at the time, including Ensley Bingham and Carl Thompson, and several top prospects.

'Jimmy, why don't you get back into boxing?' he asked. 'You were the only proper person around and everybody trusted you. You manage us and I will train.'

What a chance. I could have really gone on, especially as he had Ricky Hatton waiting in the wings. Instead I turned him down. I was being investigated again at the time and did not want to bring any criminal taint into boxing. I was also still bitter at so-called pals who let me down for their own ends.

A word about Ricky Hatton. I have known him for years and followed his career all the way. People know he has a great personality but he has to watch out for himself now his boxing career has ended. He will have a lot of time on his hands. He has been through the mill with tabloid stories drink and suchlike, but will be the better and wiser for it. He just needs to keep himself busy with new projects. His promotions seem to be doing well but when you have spent a lifetime in the gym, time can weigh heavily.

He needs to find a charity to support, maybe run a few marathons. There are lots of things to aim for. Why not 'Sir' Ricky Hatton? Odds on you could do it, pal.

With money from the sale of my house and the hostel, I instead moved into the furniture business. I found a 22,000-square-foot warehouse in central Manchester and bought £600,000-worth of stock: three piece suites, dining room furniture, everything you would find in a good store. I was back in business.

Then disaster struck. In June 1996, a huge IRA bomb blew up the centre of Manchester. It was the biggest-ever peacetime blast on the mainland, and damaged hundreds of buildings. Even the streets were carpeted in brick-dust and shattered glass. The blast funneled down the old-fashioned chimneys in my warehouse and sent soot and rubble everywhere. I never got a penny for the damage, as I wasn't insured: I didn't see the point, as the building was impregnable, but I had not counted on the IRA. I salvaged what I could, sold off the remaining stock in a three-day auction, then opened a carpet warehouse instead, which was quite successful. Then I split up from my girlfriend, decided to close the doors of the carpet store, called it a day and went back to Spain, wheeling and dealing.

The police, unfortunately, still had the Donnelly family in their sights. In February 1996, my brother Arthur was sent down for selling £10,000-worth of Turkish heroin to an undercover cop at his scrapyard behind Piccadilly Station. They set up a sting operation on him and unfortunately he fell for it. First this undercover offered him booze for sale. Then he asked if Arthur could get any drugs. At around the same time, a new acquaintance of Arthur's offered him some heroin for sale. Arthur put the two of them together, got arrested and the mysterious acquaintance then vanished. Arthur was told he was looking at fifteen years, so he pleaded and they still gave him eight years. We felt it was entrapment but that was not how the court saw it.

By 1998, I had had enough. My sons were doing well, so I decided to step back and only get involved in the odd deal. All my old pals were pretty much the same. We were all nearing the sixty mark and while we still met most days, the late nights were fewer. New firms were springing up. We had no problem with them. I had a complete break and just chilled out in the sun. The pub game was still in my blood, however, and I could not resist acquiring an old Ancoats boozer called the Bank of England, on the corner of Pollard Street. I ran it for about a year and even lived above it for a while. It was near the canalside and still had brick stables in the cellar for the donkeys and shire horses that once pulled the barges.

Some people found its name confusing. I took a phone call one day and the caller asked me if I could give him the current price of gold. I told him it was a pub, not the real Bank of England. He said, 'It doesn't say that in the Yellow Pages.' When I looked, it was true: it was listed under 'Banks', with the correct address and the phone number. I asked one of the barmaids about it and she told me that they were always getting calls like that. My mind starting going ten to the dozen: there had to be an angle here.

'In future,' I told the staff, 'when you answer the phone do not say, "The Bank of England pub," just say, "Bank of England." Then put the calls through to me, or take a message and callback number if I am not there.'

People were constantly phoning to ask the value of krugerrands and other gold coins. My plan was to say that we did not give valuations over the phone, but people could send their coins in. I ran a test and asked one person to put their coins in the post, special delivery, which they did. I duly sent them back, but I knew I was on to a move. People wanted to change money and all sorts of things. My idea was to have the telephone number and address diverted to somewhere in the town. I could see a good earner here, but because of a problem I had with a gang of travellers, I put it on the back-burner and it never came to anything.

The gypsies kicked off when I called 'time' one night in the pub. They started with the verbal, demanding more drinks, so I walked from behind the bar with a hammer wrapped in a towel and hit the nearest one. It went off good style and they did not win. I got them out, locked up and phoned my sons, who came over. We tooled up and awaited their return. It must have been five o'clock in the morning when the windows came in. We ran to the doors. I had a two-shot Derringer-type of gun and let both barrels go. The gypsies were gone in seconds.

The next day, I phoned Paddy Doherty, the local 'king' of the travellers and a bareknuckle champion. Paddy is a great pal of mine, and he and his family all used my bars. He was in Birmingham but drove straight back to see me with his dad. I told him the story.

'Leave it to me,' he said, and that was the end of it. I never saw or heard from that group of travellers again.

Paddy and I have been close for twenty-five years and still have a drink together. I sought his help on another occasion when a friend from London, a very big name, rang to say his pal had had trouble with some travellers in London and one was going to give evidence against him in court. I got him to ring Paddy and it was sorted in twenty-four hours. Paddy is a bit of a legend, and starred in the television documentary series *My Big Fat Gypsy Wedding* as well as winning *Celebrity Big Brother*.

The police raided the Bank of England a couple of times after that. Then one night, a guy was stabbed in a fight. He was on the pavement outside when the ambulance arrived, in a bad way, but the pub was closed and the lights were off. I was upstairs with my Tony in the dark. The police burst in and searched the place, looking for a knife. They didn't find one but they did seize a couple of boxes of bootleg shirts. The next day, they were back. 'If you sign away the rights to the shirts,' one of them said, 'we won't charge you.' I had little choice but to sign. I also knew it was time to go again.

We had more bad luck when my lads got involved in a music festival being staged in Devon and Cornwall to celebrate the solar eclipse of August 1999. It was meant to be a mini Glastonbury and tens of thousands were expected to attend. The main event, called Total Eclipse, was promoted by the famous Harvey Goldsmith and there were four other festivals nearby. My lads rented a clubhouse and a half-mile stretch of beach for four days and called their event Eclipse 99. They paid eighty grand for the rights and had the Happy Mondays topping the bill, with 808 State backing and DJs like Paul Oakenfold and Danny Rampling. They rented sites to sell food and drinks and a campsite with mobile toilets and washing facilities for forty grand. Everything looked good: tickets were selling even at £135 a pop and people were renting pitches. Then the local council and police got involved. They put it about that a lot of the roads would be closed and said thousands of visitors would cause grid-lock and chaos. The weather forecast was gloomy. Even the Government's chief medical officer got in on the act, saying people should stay at home and witness the eclipse on TV to avoid damaging their eyes.

It was a fiasco: they were turning people back from the motor-way. Even Tesco had eight lorry containers of water stuck on the roadside unable to get through. One campsite licensed to take 7,000 people had only 100 campers. Another business bought all the local landing rights for private aircraft and helicopters but ended up with no flights at all. Our show went on to just 2,000 people. The bands and DJs cost £180,000, security guards £70,000. In all, we lost the best part of £600,000. Certain people had invested with my sons, so we had to sell some assets to pay them off. It was not just them: it ultimately led to the collapse of Harvey Goldsmith's business, and this was a man who had promoted everyone from Luciano Pavarotti to the Rolling Stones.

The main excitement came when I was woken at 6.30 a.m. by the sound of two helicopters hovering over the site. From twenty feet up, men in black started abseiling out of them: they were armed police. They sealed off the camp and the only road to the beach. It turned out they were looking for a pal of mine from London who was suspected of involvement in a robbery in Manchester. We were lucky because we were just outside the cordon. My pal wished me good luck and was off.

The reason for the raid was a spectacular job some years earlier, in July 1995. A Securicor van carrying £10 million in cash and cheques, the weekend takings from stores across Manchester, was hit outside the Midland Bank clearing centre in Salford. The gang conned the driver of the van that they had his colleague hostage and would shoot him if they were not let into his locked, bulletproof vehicle. They then drove the van behind Salford fire station, blindfolded and gagged the driver, tied him to railings and transferred over £6 million in bags, before switching vans and escaping. It was one of Britain's biggest ever robberies. A £500,000 reward was later offered for the gang's capture and police followed leads in Holland, Israel, Poland, Russia and Spain. They said a team of professional criminals drawn from different parts of the country was believed to be responsible and that 'the QSG' were involved. After a four-year investigation, twelve people were arrested, including my pal Jimmy Hayes, who was then in his mid-fifties. The charge against him was later dropped, and the crime remains unsolved.

There were many stories about at this time that the QSG were finished and had gone into retirement. That was not entirely the case. My sons had chosen the same lifestyle as me and built up a firm, about forty-handed, that had the respect of all the other firms. They had mates like Chris Onley, who did two eight-year stretches back-to-back, Harry Critchley, the Power family, Billy Wyre, a very loyal pal who was always there to help out, Dom's best pal, Mike Pollitt, who was murdered, Anthony Maylett, another very tough kid, and his cousin Steve. However, the children of most of my QSG mates were dead straight. Jimmy Swords' son was all business and went to private school. Vinnie Schiavo had two sons but tragically lost one on a night out, while Louis' kids do not get involved in anything shady. Joe Leach had two sons. One of them, David, shot a guy. He got ten years and was later sectioned and put in a mental hospital, where he has sadly been in and out for years. His other son does not get involved. Mick Brown had no offspring. So really there were only my sons to take over the mantle.

Since 2000, I have effectively been retired but, though the legs may have gone, the heart is still there – and the brain. I am always there to help my sons when they need it. The Donnelly name can be a hindrance to them but they never resent it and I am proud of them both. My brother Arthur's lads have also done fabulously well with their clothing company.

I spent some time in South Africa looking at the wine business and advised my sons when they formed a company to import wine from there. It was set up nice and legal, with licences in place, and the first deal was for 1,700 cases, all paid for, the duty and VAT paid too. We were told the date of arrival at Southampton docks and booked and paid for a haulier to our warehouse in Manchester. Then the wine failed to arrive. We were informed it had gone to Liverpool docks by mistake. Two days later, we were told it had gone back to Southampton. Then we were told it had been inadvertently loaded as an empty container and was on its way to Hamburg in Germany. Then it could not be offloaded as it was on the bottom of a stack. It finished up in Brazil.

What a load of crap. Customs and Excise had it all the time, convinced that there was more than wine in it. After six months it finally 'arrived' at Tilbury docks. We tried to claim compensation from Lloyd's, the insurers, saying that after six months at sea the wine could have been affected, but they had some samples tested and said it was fine. In the meantime we had been forced to reorder in South Africa and the reorder arrived before the original order. All in all we were put out of business, having paid up front for the wine and the duty and with idle staff and an empty warehouse. Customers who were lined up to buy were let down and bought elsewhere, so the powers-that-be ruined a legitimate venture costing tens of thousands of pounds.

Everything changes. The café-bars have taken over the old pub culture in Manchester and even act as nightclubs. I am sure you can still have a great time, but everyone is a stranger now; to me there is no closeness of people. My sons follow the old style but mix it with the new. I am glad to say that after I retired they have gone into straight business. With all the new technology the Old Bill have at their disposal, and the greater powers, crime is a mug's game. You only have to lend a friend a grand and you can be charged with money laundering. So that is it for the Donnelly family. Sixty years of crime has come to a stop. I look at my grandsons who have all had private schooling and see a different life for them.

16

HARD MEN AND CHARACTERS

I HAVE KNOWN many hard men, but I have always said Jim Swords was the best street fighter in Manchester. I stand by that. In fact I doubt there was a gangster, villain or hard man in the country who could have taken him in his prime. Long after his boxing career was over, there was talk of JS fighting the infamous Roy 'Pretty Boy' Shaw in an unlicensed bout. It never happened, but I know who my money would have been on. Shaw and the other most famous unlicensed fighter, Lennie McLean, were very tough cookies but neither of them could have beaten Jimmy on the cobbles. There is a difference between a man who can have a fight and a man who will kill you rather than lose. A third type is the armed robber who couldn't put his hands up in a street fight but has the bollocks to go out with a gun and face what comes. My great pal Cliff Saxe had plenty of bottle but was no fighter, though he did chase that lunatic reporter Roger Cook. To me, JS was the ultimate fighting machine.

Neither of the Kray twins could have beaten Jimmy either. In fact I think Fred Foreman, Alfie Gerrard and their crew were more dangerous than the Krays, who in truth never attacked any other big London firm. Their feud with the Richardsons was over-hyped. And why they killed Jack the Hat in the hamfisted way they did is beyond belief. Why did they not set him up nice?

They would still have got the glory. It was the same with Ronnie Kray's shooting of George Cornell; maybe he was too much to fight man-to-man.

I have read books and watched TV programmes and people like Tony and Chris Lambrianou, who served a lot of porridge because of what the Krays did, were sick at the way things happened. They could have been out of it if the Krays had been thinking right and done their work in the right way. It did not make sense to act like cowboys. Over the years, many firms I have spoken to all say the same: had the Krays done things differently they could have gone on for years. And that is why the QSG lasted for over forty years under Jimmy Swords, and all became wealthy men.

One of my reasons for writing this book was to remember the Manchester men of my era whose stories have never been told. There were many other hard men, and some great characters, in my day. Ancoats in particular was a breeding ground for fighters, and Archie and Norman Maylett were two brothers who took no shit off anybody. They were a bit younger than me and Jimmy, and as we started doing other things and having more interests outside the area, these were the up-and-coming lads from the local council houses. Norman I think had the edge on Archie, but I could fill pages with the fights they both had. Norman's sons, John and Anthony, are like their dad, and Archie's son, Steve, a full-time boxing coach with some good prospects, is of the same mould. They are great guys, very respectful and good pals with my sons.

Alfie Wright was another regular at the Green Dragon pub in Ancoats who was best avoided in a punch-up. Alfie was our age and knew us all but did his own thing. Nobody messed with him. He made plenty of money out of breeding, racing and selling pigeons. Ancoats had many other good names who kept to themselves. Bobby Power could fight. His sons, Bob, Steve and Karl, are like him. Karl has been with my sons since he was a kid. He made a name for himself by donning disguises to appear uninvited at major sporting events, most famously when he walked onto the pitch before Manchester United's Champion League final against Bayern Munich dressed in Eric Cantona's kit and lined up with the team. He also beat Michael Schumacher onto the winner's podium at the British Grand Prix in 2002 and had a knock-up on Centre Court at Wimbledon before a Tim Henman match. There are lots of personalities like that in Ancoats, a special place. They say you will always come back, and after all my big houses in lovely areas, I have, as I now live back there, in a cosy flat that suits me to the ground.

Denis Donnelly, no relation, was another friend of mine from the early sixties who liked a scrap. He and his brothers, Brian, John, James and Terence, were a formidable lot. They worked tarmaccing motorways, and were not worried about anybody in their day.

When I was first married, I went out drinking with Denis most Saturday nights. For several weeks we went to a well-known pub, the Band on the Wall, and on each occasion we ended up having a row with drunks. Denis flattened them every time.

Then one night, a feller came to our table. He had a flat nose and looked a hard bastard.

'You're the one that knocked out my pal last week,' he said to Denis. 'Now try it on me.'

Denis looked at.

'This one's yours, Jimmy,' he said. 'I have done the work the last three weeks.'

I was in it, whether I liked it or not, so I stood up.

'Either fuck off or fight me,' I said.

As the guy turned to face me, I hit him with the best right-hand I have ever thrown. Down he went, out cold.

'Well, Jim,' said Denis, with a grin on his face, 'you have just knocked out a pro boxer. That was Andy Lambert. He had over thirty fights.'

'Thanks for telling me.'

I saw Andy a few times after that when he was sober, and he never mentioned it. I had some good times with Denis Donnelly and his wife, Margaret.

One of the most violent men in Manchester was Ray Vickers. I first met him in the late fifties, when he had just finished a ten-stretch for chopping up an American airman with a razor at a Portland Street coffee stall. The judge had described him as a 'very dangerous person', which was true. I was on my barrow with an older pal, Tommy Barlow, when this lone figure approached. He had a hangdog expression and eyes that bored into you.

'Can you do me a favour?' he asked, although it was more of an ultimatum than a question. 'I'm going into the Stork Club. Will you mind this for me?'

He pulled a meat cleaver sheathed in a leather pouch from under his coat.

'Okay,' I said, 'but I am only here until six o'clock.'

'No problem,' he said, 'I won't be that long.'

When he had gone, Tommy put me in the picture. He said Ray Vickers was a loner but was known to do work with the likes of Terry Jeffreys, an armed blagger who spent a lot of time in London, and Wally Downs, another notorious villain. Vickers was the muscle, and everyone feared him. He came back after an hour, picked up his cleaver, thanked me and left.

I would occasionally see him about after that. He was a lone wolf who went everywhere on foot: he would walk for miles, with a sword stick that he carried at all times – and used. His face alone put fear into people. He never smiled and had the eyes of a serial killer. People still shiver at the name of Ray Vickers.

A true legend from an earlier generation was Joe Bamford, better known as Jock McAvoy, the Rochdale Thunderbolt, one of the greatest middleweight boxers Britain ever produced. Joe was made of granite and had a punch like a wrecking ball. Polio crippled him in his old age and he walked with the aid of sticks, but it didn't stop him from getting into fights. The man never lived who could frighten Joe Bamford.

He used to visit Jim Swords' car pitch to talk about old times. I was there one day when his car pulled up. By this time he was in a wheelchair and he struggled to get out of the car and into it. A bloke in a car behind started shouting at him to hurry up. Jim Swords walked over and asked what the problem was.

'Tell him to move,' said the bloke, 'or I will move him and then move you.'

Jimmy instantly gave him a left hook and laid him out. Old Joe loved it. He liked nothing better than a good scrap.

Billy Blower and Frankie Martin were two more very tough boys, from Hulme. When I was sixteen I sometimes went in a little pub called the Standard, where nobody worried about your age. My brother and his pal Albert Gibbons had a problem in there, Billy and Frank offered their help and we all became pals. They went on to make quite a name for themselves in their younger days. They had a row with one guy and Billy set about him with a rib saw, cutting him up. They both got long sentences for that. They were like two peas in a pod, always together and very dangerous. Frank was a good joiner and a mad pigeon fancier. He is still about but I have not seen him for years. Billy is in the scrap metal game and I see him from time to time. Two good lads from the old days.

Another formidable pair were Barry Pendleton and Barry Pollard, two more close pals, who we called the Two Barries. They went everywhere together. Baz Pollard, from Salford, is a fitness fanatic and another rugged streetfighter. I have previously mentioned that he was in the cell next to me in Strangeways in 1984. A few months after his release, he told me he had met a girl and was getting married for the second time, and invited Rita and me to the wedding. I said he could use my Rolls-Royce on the day. In due course, I received an invite, and the day before the wedding I had the Rolls valeted and sent it round to his house.

The wedding was a grand affair, with the men in top hat and tails. After the service, the Rolls took Baz and his bride off, then came back to pick me up. I was getting in when I heard a voice. Three elderly ladies were sat in the back.

'What do you want?' one of them snapped.

Before I could explain, she said, 'Get out and get on the coach with the rest of the people. Who do you think you are?' It was Baz's mam. She did not know the score. We still laugh about it.

Not long after, I got a call from Baz to say he had a problem with a firm, there had been some trouble with his brother. A meet had been set up to sort it out but Baz did not trust this firm. I told him not to worry, I would get people there to hang about, just in case. Some of my family stayed in the background, armed to the teeth. The firm did not show so later we all had a drink. It was then we showed Baz the tools. He had done me favours in the past and a few of my pubs were in his part of the city and he always called in, so I was glad to be able to look out for a pal.

Barry Pendleton, or Baz Pen as he was known, came from Cheetham Hill, so he and Pollard were near neighbours. A fanatical United supporter, he would travel on my football coaches to

London for big games. He is also very respected to this day, while his brother Tommy is another pal of mine in the pub trade.

Jimmy Castile was another person you did not fuck with. I first came across his large frame – six feet two inches tall with shoulders to match – on the door of the Fiesta Club, a small joint with a disco, a blackjack table and a roulette wheel owned by George Derbyshire. We hit it off right away. In the daytime, Jimmy fitted false ceilings and partitions so we often talked about the construction business. He always had a cig in his mouth but he was fit and fast. I saw it go off one night with some guys in the club and Jimmy tore into them. He did three of them and they ran for their lives. I knew then I was right – he was special.

As the years rolled on, I saw him now and then. He went out with one of the croupiers at the club, then when they split up George Derbyshire started going out with her, eventually leaving his wife and marrying her. Jimmy then married George's wife! George took umbrage at this, though all the time he had been banging the staff. Jimmy still worked the door there and one night Sonny McDonagh came in with his brothers. They were a family of travellers and Sonny, a big man, was a bareknuckle fighter. George Derbyshire had wound him up to fight Jimmy Castile and he had come in looking for blood. It was after 2 a.m. so there were few people in, and the pair of them squared up on the dance floor. I have seen some fights but this one was a belter. It went on for an hour; they would stop, have a drink and a breather and start again, until it ended in deadlock. They shook hands on the night but their rivalry lasted for years.

Jimmy was a quiet man and never caused trouble. He had six kids he was bringing up on his own and would go straight home when the club closed. He only worked the weekends for extra money and was a straight goer, so not a lot of people knew him, but if he ever heard I was having a problem he would turn up at my club and just say, 'I called in to see that you're okay, Jimmy.' Steve Castile, his son, worked on the door at my Cotton Club for years. Sadly he had an accident in November 2010 and died, aged fifty-three. Your little pal feels for you, Jimbo.

Another tough character was Eddie Sullivan, a flower seller who travelled the local markets. His pal was a great friend of mine called Bobby Jones. Eddie's daughter married Ray Camilleri, one of the top Salford men, while Bobby finished up running a car park facing my JR Club in Chinatown. It was handy for my customers and Bobby made a good living. His sons were good friends of mine and I still see his eldest, Glynn. I read the paper the other day and saw that his grandson, who had escaped from Strangeways, had been nicked in Spain on a bank robbery. There are not many men like Bobby Jones about today. He never spoke ill of anybody, he just did his wheeling and dealing quietly. Glynn is just like his dad, a respected guy who keeps to himself.

Johnny Morrisey is known as 'the Nightmare' and was once called the most dangerous man in Europe. I first met him in his early twenties, when he was doing bits for my business consultant Tom Robinson. John was originally from Ardwick Green, where his Irish parents had a pub. He moved to Rochdale when he was sixteen and made a name for himself when he was charged with putting six soldiers in hospital with an axe in a bar fight. I had known him for a few years when I had a problem with some people. John came to see me and offered to sort it out his way, as I had to keep a low profile at the time. 'I will chop a finger off one of them and send it to you so you know it has been done,' he said. I refused his offer but it was good to know I had John on my side. He was ruthless.

John came out to Spain to see me and I introduced him to Ronnie Knight and a few more Londoners. He had a jewellers back in Manchester but was getting ready to close it down and emigrate. He had already run up thousands of pounds worth of credit. John rang me one day to trade some antique lampposts I had for gold. A few weeks later, he rang again and said, 'Jim, meet me, I want to give you the keys to the shop. There is still stuff arriving in the post, plus there is the contents, clocks, fixtures and fittings and a large new safe. Keep what you get. There is also an Audi four-by-four that is worth a few grand. Pick that up.' I drove to a service station on the M62 to meet John and he was ready for the off. He gave me and Denis Crolla the keys to the shop, told me where the Audi was and that the keys were on the driver's side wheel. I got a nice earner out of it. Gold and diamond samples were still being delivered daily and 'disappeared'. I sold the safe and contents just before the scream went up.

John went on to build a name as a hard man on the Costa del Sol and got into all sorts of scrapes, before moving to Kinsale, in Ireland, where he opened a magnificent restaurant. Then the Irish Criminal Assets Bureau went after him, so he had to leg it again, leaving behind hundreds of thousands of pounds in money and jewellery. He is still about in Spain. Newspapers over the years have had him involved in eleven murders, two of them in Holland. John is capable of it but I do not know if any of it is true. I have not seen him for a while but we keep in touch. As a person I have always found him very generous and easy to get on with.

Another dangerous bastard was Johnny Bamber, who I have known from the market days. He was always unlucky and spent the best part of his younger years 'away', in fact we met up in Strangeways in 1962 when I was on remand. I had not seen him for years until recently I met him at my brother Arthur's scrap-yard. Johnny is notorious for biting the throat out of a police dog. They had come to arrest him over a robbery, cornered him and loosed the dogs. Johnny fought one and killed it by ripping its throat. He now lives the quiet life in Wythenshawe.

TONY MILLBANKS IS the all-time villain. Game all his life, he has been involved in many kinds of criminality and spent years in the nick. His nickname is 'Mailbags', for obvious reasons. His last sentence was ten years with Jimmy Hayes and John Shearer, both Jocks who lived in Manchester. They attacked a jeweller, who turned on them with a knife and stabbed Tony in the neck, almost cutting his throat. He was nicked in hospital and later convicted using DNA evidence. Tony has seen it all in the prison system. He tells me he is now a straight member.

I first came across Scotch Jimmy Hayes over forty years ago, as a sixteen-year-old. He had moved to Manchester with his family and settled in Ardwick, a mile outside Piccadilly. He was in and out of jail and took up with my great pal Wally McNelly. They went on to attempt a bank robbery in Nottingham with Terry Duxbury and Albie McMahon from Liverpool, not knowing that Duxbury had rolled over and was to become Manchester's first supergrass. They were arrested in a hotel hours before the break-in with a set of keys. After a ten-year sentence, Jimmy went on to other big things and got more long sentences, including the ten years with John Shearer and Tony Millbanks. Jimmy was later charged with a £6.6 million security robbery in Manchester in the mid-nineties. Hardly anyone outside Manchester talks of the raid but it was one of the biggest in history. My ex-doorman Shay Power was convicted of involvement but it was a miscarriage of justice and he was cleared on appeal. Jimmy Hayes was held on remand for six months until the charges were dropped. In the end, no-one was convicted. I still see Jimmy a lot, he has been involved with a couple of bars over the past few years, one of the old school.

Wally McNelly never had a care in the world. He liked his drink and his spliff but he was a good worker and loyal to me and my sons. When the QSG was going strong, he and I worked closely together. We rarely had a dull moment.

One night in Spain, driving home up the winding road to the hillside village of Mijas, near Malaga, Wally stopped the car and said, 'I need a piss.' He got out and hopped over a little wall. I heard a scream, jumped out and looked over the wall: there was an eighty-foot drop. Wally, with unbelievable luck, had landed in a tree sticking out. We had to get the fire brigade to rescue him. Another time, arriving back at night, he thought he would take a swim. The pool area was lit up so Wally took a run and dived in. Not a drop of water. He was lucky to live.

We were having a drink in Manchester one day when he pointed to an office block facing the *Daily Mail* and said he had blown a safe there with Duxbury the grass and Stan Ritchie. Duxbury packed the safe with gelignite, then said, 'I think I will give this a bit more, we'll have only one shot at it, we're too near the main street.' They let it go and the safe jumped in the air. The door handle flew through the window like a bullet, went through the front windscreen of a newspaper van, burst through the back door and hit the shutters of the loading bay. The safe was on its side, mangled. Wally told me there was chaos, people running around, they thought they had been attacked from Mars. The three of them slipped away in the confusion. That was one they lost.

In the late eighties, Stan Ritchie came to see me in Spain. The old master had retired with his wife, Betty. His safe-blowing days were over, but he was struggling.

'Jimmy,' he said. 'I'm having it hard. I haven't got much money. Can you find me some work?'

I found a few little bits for him to do. I had been asked if I could find a driver for a London firm, so I put Stan forward and he got the work, though he was careful not to tell me what it was and I did not ask.

A month later, I was in a pub in Manchester when Stan came in. He said he had done a run from Spain to London with cannabis concealed in the doors of the car. Once in London, the people took away the car, removed the smoke, then gave the car back to him along with £5,000 wages. He was having a few days in Manchester and then going back to Spain.

A week later, I got a call from my pal in London.

'Have you seen Stan Ritchie about?' he asked. 'There's a problem. Something is wrong.'

It turned out that the crew who had taken the car had only emptied the front door panels, thinking all the puff was in them, but half of it had been in the back door panels. When they weighed it up they realised half was missing and suspected Stan had fucked them over. In fact poor old Stan had unwittingly driven all the way back to Spain and been swanning around the Costa del Sol in a car still half-packed with cannabis. We had some fun with him after that, asking if he could deliver 'half a parcel' and so on, but it showed how staunch he was. Stan carried on in that vein for a couple of years but eventually was nicked and got five years, at the age of seventy-two. He is dead now but is sorely missed, a true villain.

Wally McNelly also worked with Jimmy Dodds, another tough nut from the Openshaw area of east Manchester. Jimmy is over six feet tall, still trains at seventy-five years old and is as fit as a butcher's dog. He has done his share of porridge and has had some good tickles throughout his life. He always called in at my bars over the years and, though he would not suffer fools lightly, he was always well behaved and good company, and would stand by you if need be. He has been retired for years now, or so he tells me. He has a very good name in Manchester and has worked with some of the best in all sorts of things, always in the heavy department.

Jimmy told me about a few of his escapades over the years, one of which I can relate because he got caught. He planned to burgle a jeweller's on Oxford Road, entering a premises a couple of doors away that he had obtained keys for, then breaking through the connecting walls. He needed someone on the outside, as the job would take all night and he would be leaving the premises via the front door in daylight, so he had to make sure no-one was there to see him. He arranged for Wally McNelly to be outside the door at 7.30 a.m., before the workers arrived, to ensure the coast was clear. It could only happen to Wally: when he got there, a policeman was sheltering from the rain in that very doorway. Jimmy Dodds was waiting on the other side for three knocks for the all clear. It was like a scene from the Keystone Cops. After finishing a crafty cigarette, the policeman moved on just minutes before the staff were due to arrive. Wally banged on the door and a sweating Jimmy and company appeared and were off. They were later nicked for the job and got four years each.

Peter Cassin and Peter Casey were two of the best grafters and creepers in Manchester. They toured the world creeping jewellers', hotels, offices, anywhere they thought they could get a few quid. When they got a 'prize', the first thing they did was post it home so that if they got pulled by the police they had nothing on them. They always had an extra body who they passed the gear to and would not check into hotels with them. In minutes he would be gone to the next town, where they would meet to plan the next move and then split up again.

Creeping jewellery stores was a well known move to grafters all over England, but in those days there were not many at it. Some of the best teams were actually Australian. One of the Aussies was called Joe the Kid. He was a good worker but he made the mistake of keeping the tom with him when he checked into a hotel. The owner became suspicious and phoned the police. Joe the Kid was eventually deported, but the two Peters went on for years. They are well retired now and when I see them we have a good laugh about the funny things that happened, the lucky escapes when someone farts while you are creeping a shop and other escapades.

I first met John and Micky Sammon in the early seventies. Two kids of Irish traveller descent, they had squatted on some land near me and were selling cheap cars; old bangers really. They were only kids, about fourteen, but cheeky bastards. I asked them to move on but they put two fingers up to me. I had many run-ins with them but I had to admire them. Micky was the more dominant of the two. Over the years they got into all sorts of things and worked with a guy called Frank 'Bagger' Crawford, the king of the long-firm fraud. Their last big LF was worth about £4 million. It went to court and Crawford got six years. Micky went on the run and the judge gave him four years in his absence. He remained on the run for eight years. The police couldn't find him, but I used to see him all over the place. He moved to Blackpool and had a pound shop there. He even turned up at his brother's wedding in Manchester while on the run.

I bought a three-storey house off him in Longsight for forty grand. It caused a problem between us, as I told him if I had a good earn I would give him another five grand on top. Then I called Kevin Taylor, who I was doing a few deals with and who had been paid £2 million from his case against the police. I told

Kevin about the house deal and took him to see it. It was a big Victorian pile and worth a lot more than forty grand. Two weeks later, I sold it to a property dealer for £65,000, still cheap as it was worth up to £100,000. Kevin gave him a private mortgage and that was that. I got ten grand as my cut and left a drink in the pot for Micky, as promised, via a pal.

A couple of years later, he came in one of my bars drunk and started slagging me off and saying he was going to burn down the bar. I got in touch with him and asked what the fuck he thought he was doing. He got a bit aggressive on the phone so I told him to meet me in Manchester. I had had enough: he was going to get hurt bad. We set up a meet and I had two people standing by, one tooled up and ready to give it to Micky. When the time came, however, there was no Micky. I rang him and asked where he was. He said he was in Leeds. He then said, 'Jimmy, I have fucked up. I am sorry, I know what's waiting for me.'

I said, 'If you are sorry you had better say that to my partner as well.' So he apologised all round, even to the bar staff.

That was that, until I met him in Blackpool at Denis Crolla's funeral. We sat and had a chat and I told him I had given some readies to his pal, called Smithy. He never got the money, apparently, hence the bad blood. Anyway, we shook hands. He also carried my great pal Denis's coffin at the funeral even though he was still on the run.

Micky never stopped working and you could always earn with him and John, though sometimes the booze got in the way. After meeting him in Blackpool, he told me about some other properties he had and asked if I would be interested. A few weeks later, I picked up the newspaper and he was on the front page, named as the alleged main man in a firm nicked for bringing blank-firing guns into the country and converting them by the hundred in a machine shop in Ancoats. He was still at large but the rest of the mob went on trial and got big sentences. Micky was eventually caught at a travellers' camp. I had by then spoken to him on the phone a few times and when I asked about the guns he told me it was all shit. He had been offered them, like other people, but did not want to know. I believed him but he was found guilty and got thirty years.

I have known the brothers for forty years and they were LF men, not into heavy stuff. Micky lost an appeal against conviction and against sentence but I wish him luck. I see his sons often at my brother's yard. I wish you well Micky, you deserve a break.

Many older folk will remember Tommy Parry, the 'Gentle Giant', who never had a bad word to say about anybody. Tommy was a Salford man, and when I met him, in my early twenties. he had a night club and a couple of pubs in the area. His club did good trade and I used to call in for an hour a few times a week. He had the wrestler Giant Haystacks on the door and later Ronnie Camilleri. Like most clubs in those days, it had a blackjack table, brag and poker games going on. There was very little trouble and Tommy was a good host. He would always buy me a drink. Tommy was not a villain or a tough guy, he was a genuine, easy-going man and would chat to everyone. Later on he put George Derbyshire in to run the club. It was the worst thing he could have done. George started letting all the dregs in and it got a bad name.

Tommy's son Raymond is just like his dad and has palled about with the firm for forty years. Even now, he still turns up every Friday for an evening out, but there are not many left for the late nights. Raymond has done well for himself and we often chat about his dad.

The Chuwen brothers were among Manchester's best known faces. They were Jewish wheeler-dealers, into everything, and were pally with all the old school names. Maurice, or Mo, the oldest, was a bit flash and was one of us, he could talk. His brother Jackie was the same. A third brother was quieter and very wealthy: he owned properties all over Manchester and even had a limestone quarry.

Maurice saw service in the Second World War. He had boxed when he was young so they put him in the RAF as a PT instructor, teaching how to parachute, while Jackie was at Anzio and the D-Day landings. After the war, Mo worked markets around the country. He told me a story about how he was in London working on Petticoat Lane and trying to get someone to put money into a little venture, making and selling ironing board covers. He told some people over a drink in a pub and one of them was Ronnie Knight, who liked the idea and they went into partnership.

Mo also worked what was called the run-out, a mock auction where you gathered a crowd of punters around a stall and offered an expensive item, then added a watch, which you would sell very cheaply. Next you would sell a bag. No-one knew what was in it. Then you would ask the crowd to put up their hands if they wanted to buy a bag. Lots of people put up their hands. They were quickly served, their money taken, but when they got outside they found only cheap trinkets in their bags. If they came back they would find no-one to complain to, hence it was called the run-out.

One day I was in Ronnie Earl's pub in Chinatown when Mo walked in and came straight over.

'Jimmy! How are you? I am glad I have seen you. I have a horse running tomorrow and it is a cert.'

He ordered a bottle of champagne and started telling me he was in the money-lending business and if I ever got stuck, to come to see him, he could get me a loan. I went on to send a lot of punters to

Mo's loan business. He did not care about their backgrounds. 'If Jimmy has sent you, it's okay,' he would say. He would take a name, address and date of birth and that was it. 'I will fill in the rest,' he would say. I was getting a nice drink out of it. A couple of years later, I rang him. He said the loan firm had gone out of business and a firm he worked with was suing him for a lot of money that appeared to be missing from the books. That was Mo.

He was also in the motor trade, as well as owning racehorses. By the seventies, the Chuwens were wealthy men. When I had a charity night in my clubs they were always there, bidding or just donating. They were very big spenders and great Manchester men.

Frank 'the Yank' Dalami was a New York Italian who came to Manchester during the Second World War. He deserted from the armed forces and stayed on the run for years, supported by the New York mafia family to which he belonged. One of his most prized possessions was a gold pocket watch inscribed, 'To Frank, from your friend Dutch Schultz'. I met him with Mo Chuwen when I was twenty; he was working the markets and had some of the best pitches in Liverpool, Manchester and Leeds, selling shirts. Frank met and married a Salford girl and had two sons, John and Tony. John was a lunatic gambler, running his father's business in the day and splurging in the casinos at night. A prolific card and backgammon player, he started running about with the firm. He was good company and always had money, but as the years went on we started to hear things, nothing too bad but that he was sticking the firm's name up when caught cheating at cards in private spielers.

On a trip to Las Vegas, it came to the notice of the PR people at the Sands Hotel that a professional card player, John Dalami, was staying with eight pals. The casinos love a high roller, so the group were upgraded to bungalows around the pool area. It was now that John started showing his true colours. He entered a backgammon competition with money borrowed from Vinnie Schiavo, who was one of the group. He got to the final, as did the movie star Omar Sharif, an inveterate gambler. Sharif won, while Dalami came second and got about $20,000. He decided to go to New York to see relatives and kept the money, saying he had been invited to a big game and could use it to win even more. Vinnie even lent him his gold watch and a diamond ring so he would look the part. The next time Dalami was spotted, he was skint. He had done the money, sold the watch, the ring and his family's market stalls and fucked off. When we eventually caught up with him, his family came to his rescue, paying the money he owed plus a fine. He still got a good kicking.

That was when the dog turned. Dalami started palling about with all sorts of toerags, pulling strokes. Peter Leach, my brother-in-law, felt sorry for him and helped him out, as he had nowhere to live and had done all the family money. It was the worst move Peter ever made: Dalami ran off with his wife. He then got nicked with cocaine and told them Peter had some buried in his garden. They kept Dalami in special custody in a private part of Bootle Street police station. Pete got out of it in the end but Dalami had now been confirmed as a grass. Old Frank must have turned in his grave: the New York mafioso having his own son labelled a grass.

These men, and many more, have I known in my seven decades. I took them all as I found them. It is not for me to judge another. Whatever others may say about them, they were part of my life, and the fabric of my city, and they all made a lasting impression. To steal from an old Irish folk song, they were the men you don't meet every day.

EPILOGUE

WISDOM IS ONE of the few compensations of old age. Otherwise it's a pain in the arse. Your health suffers, Your senses fail. Even a nice cognac loses its savour. But the worst thing is the number of funerals you find yourself at.

Many of the old gang mentioned on these pages have passed away. It is a shame that no-one went around with a tape recorder before they died and collected their memories. You would have some stories there.

Honey Boy Zimba was one of the first to go, the old wrestler finally taking the count in 1991. As I have already told, Mick Brown died in 1994, when I was away on a cruise.

Denis Crolla left us several years ago, just a couple of days after returning from a holiday with me in Spain, while Wally McNelly died in 2006, aged seventy-seven. The three of us shared many good times, and many secrets.

Rudi Mancini died in 1998, while his widow, Pat, survived him for another thirteen years. I have been told their hotel in Blackpool is valued at over £10 million; not bad for the Ancoats-born son of an Italian immigrant.

Kevin Taylor died in 2001, seven weeks after major heart surgery. Even after all his troubles, he had managed to buy a new house and set up his two daughters in business. 'His life was not defined by the events of the eighties,' said his wife, Beryl. 'It was awful but he was not bitter.'

Frank Pearson, better known as Foo Foo Lammar, died in 2003, at the age of sixty-five. He rose from a poor background – his dad was a rag and bone man – to run a string of clubs, bars and restaurants. He amassed a fortune of more than £5 million and raised even more than that for charities. Frank was a one-off.

Tommy Burke passed away in April 2009, at the age of eighty-one. I travelled the world with Tommy and he is sadly missed. Mark Klapish continued his criminal career for much of his life – he even swindled British Telecom in what was called an 'ingenious' chatline phone fraud. He has also been dead now for a number of years.

Joe Plant, who had the famous Chez Joey club and later opened the Bierkeller, is another one that has left us. Alan Kay, the Man Who Broke the Bank at Monte Carlo, has gone and is missed by the old boys. Hard man Mick Tierney died of cancer in his early sixties; I was fortunate enough to spend many hours with him before he went.

Denis Maher from the Market Mob remained a close pal, calling to see me in my bars over the years, but sadly he passed away a couple of years ago. Jim Hancock, who I fought in Wythenshawe and then remained pals with for the next fifty years, sadly died in 2008.

Jimmy 'the Brains' Coulter fell for a stripper and ended up committing suicide over her. Wally Downs, another legend of the Mancunian underworld, is also dead. Ronnie Earl suffered a heart attack at a bus stop at the age of sixty-one. Nat Basso died in 2001 at the age of eighty-four.

Les Simms settled in a small hotel in the late eighties and

remained mine host until he died in 2009, aged seventy-nine. In many ways he was the godfather, and we'll never see his like again.

Dougie Flood passed away a couple of years ago. He became one of the biggest club owners in the north of England and left a declared fortune of £14 million. His two sons and a daughter then fought a highly-publicised legal battle over his will.

Denos Kitromilides died in 2004 at the age of seventy-nine after a long battle against cancer and emphysema. The king of the Greek club owners will never be forgotten in Manchester.

John Shearer sadly passed away and was buried in September 2010. He was only fifty-nine. There was a massive turnout for him and I met a lot of old friends there, including big Robbie McCann, who I once got out of the country when he was wanted for murder. I have lost another good pal and a great worker.

The singer Karl Denver is another who has departed, and the number of celebrities who turned up at the funeral was testament to his talent and his personality. Late on in his career, Karl was drinking too much and had lost all his money. He borrowed off me and left his Fender guitar as security. It was his pride and joy. I must have had it for six years. Then, not long before he died, he came to see me. He had kicked the booze.

'I have got something for you,' I told him.

I went upstairs, brought down his guitar and gave it to him. He never thought he would see it again. I never mentioned the money, it was enough reward to see his face. He did one more gig for me, playing his Fender.

Rab Carruthers, the Scottish ganglord, died in 2004. He had served a couple of long sentences for drugs and had become too fond of the substances himself. His name still gives some folk the terrors.

Others who are gone but not forgotten include Ronnie Baker, Peter Nick, George Derbyshire, Albert Rossi, the Chuwen brothers, Ronnie Camilleri, Gilly Grundy, Bobby Ball, Peter Tut-Tut and, most recently, Tiny Brown, good men all.

There are still a few of us about though. Les Simms' old mate Dougie Welsby looks well in his mid-eighties. Another of the greats, Sid Otty, is going strong in his nineties, while old Curly Lowe still meets up with all the jewel dealers once a week and is as sharp as ever.

I kept in touch with Angelo Dundee, a lovely man. The last time we spoke, he told me he was doing a bit on the film *Cinderella Man* with Russell Crowe. Will any boxing trainer ever surpass his achievements? I doubt it.

My old pal Brendan Withers lives in Cyprus. Polish Janis is seventy and still drives a taxi, smokes big cigars and has a drink in the Press Club after work. Bob 'the Jeweller' Spanner has been in Blackpool for three decades. He still works in the jewel trade and visits Manchester twice a week to do deals.

I have not spoken to Eric Mason since some good pals of mine from London got nicked with him and finished up with big sentences. Eric had an undercover Old Bill in tow and put them all in it. He swore that he did not know but he got the least sentence and was out in the minimum time. You can never prove anything but he should have known better. I believe he still lives in Blackpool.

I phoned Kenny Connors of the Crazy Face Gang recently. He was not well and having a hard time, so I told him about a documentary programme about the Manchester underworld that was being made for the National Geographic channel and that there was a few bob if he wanted to do an interview. He hated Scott and Pilot for getting him the ten years, so he did it.

Another character who did not care for anybody was Johnny nunders. I saw him recently and he is still working the markets at the age of eighty-four. He has been up to everything in his life and is indestructible.

AND WHAT OF the remaining Quality Street Gang?

Jimmy Shaw is serving fifteen years for conspiring to import and supply cocaine, an occupational hazard for those who chose to move into that game.

Paki Pete was another who got nicked for drugs, bringing Class As into England from Pakistan in the late eighties. The courier put him in it and he got ten years, but he escaped and fled to Pakistan. He stayed there for a while but, having lived in Manchester for most of his life, he got pissed off and came back, faced his bird and got another two years for escaping. He came to see me recently and told me he had opened a takeaway near Piccadilly Station with his sons, who are good lads. Pete is in poor health, so get well pal.

Mick 'the Golly' Friend will be about seventy and with his hair dyed black looks like Colonel Gaddafi. I heard his latest business was closed down by the tax man.

Jimmy Riley went into scaffolding, then bought non-ferrous metals from all over the world and invested heavily in property. He sold his scrap business for millions and now lives in Marbella, but travels back and forth to Manchester and still sees the boys.

Jack Trickett sold his Acton Court Hotel in 2005 but the new owners ran into financial difficulties and it was demolished in 2010, a landmark building that took many memories with it. I did not speak to Jack for a decade. I still love him and his family and still see him at the odd event, but he hurt me and I have told the truth.

Ricky Gore was always his own man. He would disappear for weeks at a time and never tell you where he had been. In the first Iraq war he was in the desert behind enemy lines, buried in the sand for weeks, and in 1991 he was awarded the MBE for his actions. Today he is a multi-millionaire, with a security firm in Abu Dhabi. He says he is in oil exploration but to my knowledge he guards a lot of Middle Eastern royalty. He is still a handsome fellow, strong and fit. We only see each other once in a while, as he lives in the Middle East, but we will always be close. I loaned him a few thousand quid in the early eighties, and when he gets pissed he tells the story to my sons, 'He was the only man who helped me when I had no money.' Well, you couldn't go to JS for money: the rates were too high!

Joe Leach married the daughter of a multi-millionaire. Always a wild card, Joe is still a prolific gambler and lives the good life.

Joe Swords still looks good. Joe is an excellent businessman and retains interests in leading restaurants. He is laid back but always on the ball. He was my silent partner for years and never said a word when we had a divvy up, he trusted me and how could you beat that?

Vinnie Schiavo, my other partner, was exactly the same. He and Louis still go to their mother Joan's every night for their evening meal: she is ninety-three and still lives in Ancoats, a lovely woman. Her boys have done well for themselves.

Jimmy Swords lives in an exclusive Cheshire village in a lovely house with a swimming pool. He also has a magnificent pile on the Costa del Sol and another place on Lake Como. My pal never stopped training and still has a six-pack even as he nears seventy years old, though he recently had some health problems.

As I always say, Jimmy was hard in his dealings but fair. You could owe him money but your word was your bond. His Joe was

,ame; he put a lot into my schemes in the seventies and eight-
, and had a very good return for his money. He never once asked
to check the books. That was the trust we had.

Their mother, Flo, was once talking to a neighbour who said,
'Jimmy the Weed works for your Jimmy, doesn't he?' Flo put her
straight. 'No,' she said. 'Jimmy Donnelly works for himself. He is
my son's friend and partner.' And that is how we have been since
we first met all those years ago.

In my view, JS and the firm, who worked so hard in business,
deserve every penny they have. I look at things today, politicians
getting nicked for fiddling their mortgage expenses and running
off with each other's wives, bankers robbing whole countries
blind, and think, what an example. We came from nothing and
made ourselves something. We might have been rough and ready
but we never preyed on our own. We could have made a fortune if
we had gone into, say, the protection racket, but we did not, we
helped club owners and small businessmen and that paid divi-
dends in the respect we got. So if a club owner wanted a new car,
he would come to us, and also send his pals and his family. I have
seen many firms over the years try to go at the taxing job and they
never lasted. There have always been plenty of fish to fry and
that's why JS and many of my friends prospered.

That's what we were all about. We were multi-faceted. We did
things together but also on our own and never got too deep about
what others did on the side. I would never ask details. There might
be the odd remark, 'There's a few grand here to put into something Jimmy, if you need it,' and you knew something had gone
down. You didn't need to know what.

I have been asked the question, how far would I go if somebody
took a liberty with me? Well, the answer is that I have already
been there. I am here and they are not. But for chance, it could

have been a few more. Now the shop is closed for good. I am relaxed in knowing I always stood my round and people were happy to have me in their corner. I am still bitter with some who took advantage of my friendship, and they know who they are.

Today we may be old men but it still does not pay to cross us. Only last year, I was in a bar when a big feller I slightly knew got on my nerves, going on with himself. I told him to cool it but he said, 'Fuck you.' I walked into the kitchen, picked up a carving knife and went back to the bar. The guy must have seen the knife I had behind my back. He screamed 'Noooo!' and ran for his life. He knew, and I knew, he was going to get hurt.

The gypsy fighter Paddy Doherty had just walked in and saw what happened.

'Fuck me, Jimmy,' he said, 'are you still at it at your age? I have warned that man before not to upset you.'

Still, I don't suppose I can get into too much trouble these days. I am now in my seventy-first year. I spend a lot of time in Thailand, and have met some nice, kind people, in particular a special woman called Orawan Phakdee Aksorn – Nancy for short. She is not like most of the girls in the bars there: she owns three bars and a hair and beauty salon and is a very smart business-woman.

I cannot finish without mentioning my family. John worked for me in the early days but went on his own in 1969 and made millions. Arthur worked for me for twenty years, running my contracting and scrap businesses. In fact all his life he worked the yards, putting in fifteen hours a day, seven days a week. He was by my side in many a deal and never gave a fuck for anybody but me. We were like twins, with only sixteen months between us.

Arthur's daughter, Tracy, worked for me in my hotel when she was sixteen. She is a very special girl. Rita and I never had a daughter, so Tracy always received special treatment from us. And her brothers, my nephews, formed the Gio-Goi clothing company, which is worth a fortune today.

Rita's family also worked me for me in my bars, including her sisters, Pauline, Beryl and Angela, and our niece Adele. They were all grafters and kept their eyes open for me. My own four sisters are also all still going strong. All in all, I have to thank my family a lot for their support over the years.

When I'm home, I live in a flat on my own in a lovely area of Ancoats. I no longer feel the need for big houses. I get a kick out of giving advice and helping younger pals and the sons of pals. And though we have all followed our different paths, I still talk or meet with some of the QSG a couple of times a week. The banter and the camaraderie are still there, and it only takes a place, or a name, or a look, to spark another memory.

I took a phone call from Dublin recently; it was Phyllis Lynott.

'Do you remember when you did a streak for charity at my hotel?' she asked. I had forgotten.

'You looked well, Jimmy,' she laughed.

Good days.